Praise for

Speech to Print: Language Essentials for Teachers, Second Edition

"Moats has again provided the field with the most in-depth and comprehensive scientific analysis of the linguistic and orthographic complexities that beginning readers and spellers must master. . . . This book is simply the most brilliant and informative example of how effective instructional practices are informed by converging scientific evidence."

—**G. Reid Lyon, Ph.D.**
Distinguished Professor and Chairman
Department of Education Policy and Leadership
Annette Caldwell Simmons School of
Education and Human Development
Southern Methodist University, Dallas, Texas

"An essential book. . . . Dr. Moats has done an outstanding job of integrating research and application from the field of literacy. Required reading for teachers as well as for those who prepare them in the colleges of education."

—**R. Malatesha Joshi, Ph.D.**
Associate Dean for Graduate Program Development
Professor of Literacy Education, ESL, and
Educational Psychology, Texas A&M University
Editor, *Reading and Writing: An Interdisciplinary Journal*

"Includes all a teacher needs to know about the English language in order to teach reading and writing . . . a must-read for all teachers."

—**Marcia K. Henry, Ph.D.**
Author, *Unlocking Literacy: Effective*
Decoding and Spelling Instruction
Former President, The International Dyslexia Association
Professor Emerita, San Jose State University

"The second edition expands and strengthens this invaluable resource. The content is truly essential for educators and specialists responsible for helping students succeed at learning to read."

—**Susan Brady, Ph.D.**
University of Rhode Island and
Haskins Laboratories

"[*Speech to Print*] is always front and center on my reference list. I look forward to recommending this revised edition. If every educator mastered the content of this volume, I am sure that our instruction and intervention efforts would be much improved."

—**C. Melanie Schuele, Ph.D.**
Vanderbilt University

Speech to Print

Write a reading response to para-phrasing.

Speech to Print

Language Essentials for Teachers

2nd EDITION

by

Louisa Cook Moats, Ed.D.

·P·A·U·L·H·
BROOKES
PUBLISHING Co®

Baltimore • London • Sydney

Paul H. Brookes Publishing Co.
Post Office Box 10624
Baltimore, Maryland 21285-0624
USA

www.brookespublishing.com

"Paul H. Brookes Publishing Co." is a registered trademark of
Paul H. Brookes Publishing Co., Inc.

Manufactured in the United States of America by
Sheridan Books, Inc., Chelsea, Michigan.

The individuals described in this book are composites or real people whose situations are masked
and are based on the author's experiences. In all instances, names and identifying details have been
changed to protect confidentiality.

A companion *Speech to Print* workbook is also available from Paul H. Brookes Publishing Co.
(1-800-638-3775; 1-410-337-9580). For more information on the *Speech to Print* materials, go to
www.brookespublishing.com

Library of Congress Cataloging-in-Publication Data

Moats, Louisa Cook.
    Speech to print : language essentials for teachers / by Louisa Cook Moats.—2nd ed.
        p.   cm.
    Includes bibliographical references and index.
    ISBN-13: 978-1-59857-050-2 (pbk.)
    ISBN-10: 1-59857-050-1 (pbk.)
    1. Language arts (Elementary)   2. Language arts teachers—Training of.   I. Title.
    LB1576.M56 2010
    372.6—dc22   2010015291

British Library Cataloguing in Publication data are available from the British Library.

2019   2018   2017   2016   2015

10   9   8   7   6   5   4   3

Contents

About the Author

Louisa Cook Moats, Ed.D., President, Moats Associates Consulting, Inc., Post Office Box 3941, Hailey, Idaho 83333

Dr. Moats has been a teacher, psychologist, researcher, graduate school faculty member, consultant, and author of many influential scientific journal articles, books, and policy papers on the topics of reading, spelling, language, and teacher preparation. She earned her bachelor of arts degree from Wellesley College, her master's degree at Peabody College of Vanderbilt University, and her doctorate in reading and human development from the Harvard Graduate School of Education. She began her professional career as a neuropsychology technician, teacher of students with learning disabilities, curriculum director in a residential school, and education specialist in a hospital learning clinic.

After completing her doctorate, she spent 15 years in private practice as a licensed psychologist in Vermont, specializing in evaluation and consultation with individuals of all ages who experienced learning problems in reading and language. Subsequently, she was employed as the visiting scholar in the Sacramento County Office of Education, where she helped obtain a $1 million grant to write teacher training materials for California's reading initiative.

Dr. Moats spent the next 4 years as site director of the National Institute of Child Health and Human Development (NICHD) Early Interventions Project in Washington, D.C. This longitudinal, large-scale project was conducted through the University of Texas, Houston, under the direction of Barbara Foorman. It investigated the causes and remedies for reading failure in high-poverty urban schools.

Dr. Moats's other publications include, in addition to many journal articles, *Spelling: Development, Disability, and Instruction* (York Press/PRO-ED, 1995); *Straight Talk About Reading: How Parents Can Make a Difference During the Early Years* (with Susan Hall; Contemporary Books, 1999); *Parenting a Struggling Reader: A Guide to Diagnosing and Finding Help for Your Child's Reading Difficulties* (with Susan Hall; Broadway, 2002); *Basic Facts About Dyslexia and Other Reading Problems* (with Karen Dakin; International Dyslexia Association, 2007), and the series *Language Essentials for Teachers of Reading and Spelling* (Sopris West, 2003–present). She is well known for authoring the American Federation of Teachers' (1999) "Teaching Reading Is Rocket Science: What Expert Teachers of Reading Should Know and Be Able to Do" and remains focused primarily on improvement of teacher preparation, certification, and professional development.

Acknowledgments

In the decade since the first edition of this book, I have received helpful suggestions and feedback from many teachers and students. Some who stand out are my colleague Bruce Rosow, who has taught umpteen courses with this book through Simmons College, who read and improved the draft manuscript, and who will contribute his humor and creativity to the forthcoming edition of the *Speech to Print Workbook;* Mike Minsky of the Greenwood Institute, who contributed the sample lesson plans to this book; Sandy Barrie Blackley at the University of North Carolina, who shared her course material and requested expansions of many chapters in this new edition; and to anonymous reviewers who submitted critiques to Brookes Publishing. I am grateful to Alice Furry, who directed the Reading Lions Center in Sacramento, for reinforcing my belief that all teachers should know and apply the material in this book—not just the specialists. Numerous colleagues associated with the Board and Branches of the International Dyslexia Association have reminded me of the value and necessity of teaching language explicitly to all students, but especially to those students who do not intuit how language works and who need our help. The American Federation of Teachers has also done its part to inform the teaching profession about the importance of knowing and teaching language structure, and I appreciate their encouragement and publication of articles related to these topics. The trainers of LETRS (Language Essentials for Teachers of Reading and Spelling) remind me constantly that I am not alone in this mission; thank you for your collegiality and for all that you have taught me.

As with the first edition, I must acknowledge how lucky I was to be taught by Professors Carol Chomsky, Catherine Snow, Helen Popp, and Jeanne Chall at Harvard, who opened my eyes to language structure and language processing in the context of literacy.

Finally, I would not have been able to accomplish this work without the constant love, patience, and support of my husband, Steve Mitchell.

*To all teachers who inform and excite
their students about the power of language*

Why Study Language?

By the end of this chapter, you will understand:

- How language, reading, and writing are connected
- Why learning to read and write is challenging for many students
- How reading and spelling develop
- The research evidence supporting differentiated instruction
- Principles of effective reading, spelling, and writing instruction

The Missing Foundation in Teacher Education

Linguists, speech-language pathologists (SLPs), actors, singers, and anthropologists are expected to study the forms and functions of language, but teachers often are not held to that same expectation. Many teacher education programs give short shrift to the particulars of language structure and how children learn it.[1] Nevertheless, explicit teaching of oral and written language remains the core principle of effective instruction for both novice and struggling readers.[2] For those who must be taught how to read and write and who do not learn naturally or easily, good teaching of necessity requires awareness of language structure and how students acquire literacy.[3]

Even if teachers are exposed to language concepts, they may have little or no support in applying this disciplinary knowledge base to instruction. Textbooks on reading and literacy methods or typical reading instruction courses often exclude the particulars of language structure.[4] In fact, most commonly used textbooks have been found to impart misinformation about speech and print, especially about phonology and the nature of English orthography.[5] Moreover, typical courses for reading teachers may cover none or only some of the critical components of effective teaching.[6]

This book addresses these traditional gaps in teacher preparation for reading and language instruction. It approaches language as the foundation for reading and literacy education. Its aim is to make language concepts accessible for teachers of reading and writing so that they can use instructional programs with confidence and flexibility. It is detailed enough that teachers can find answers to their questions about children's reading, speaking, and writing behavior, but it avoids overloading the reader with information about other languages or the more technical aspects of linguistics.

The teacher who understands language and how children are using it is more likely than others to impart clear, accurate, and organized information about sounds, words, sentences, and discourse. He or she should be able to respond to student errors with helpful corrections and feedback and aim instructional activities to a purpose. Expert teaching of reading and writing is only possible when the teacher knows not just the meanings conveyed by language, but how language itself works.

Language and Literacy

Literacy is an achievement that rests on language competence at all levels, from the elemental sounds to the most overarching structures of text.[7] There is a high correlation between students' overall language abilities and their reading achievement.[8] Even recognizing printed nonsense words rests on elemental language processing. To help the teacher deliver successful instruction, this book delves into the nature of the lower level building blocks that drive printed word recognition and production, including sounds, syllables, letters, and morphemes. It also addresses aspects of language important for comprehension, including phrases, sentences, and word meanings. Table 1.1 summarizes the major systems of language and their relevance for reading and writing.

Table 1.1. Language systems and their relevance to literacy

Language system	Relevance to reading and writing
Orthography: the written system of spelling patterns and correspondences between speech and print	The spelling system represents phoneme–grapheme correspondences, syllable patterns, and meaningful parts of words (morphemes); it must be decoded for reading and encoded for writing.
Phonetics: the articulation and perception of speech sounds	Descriptions of and comparisons of speech sounds enable the teaching of phoneme awareness and word pronunciation. These in turn enable printed word recognition and spelling.
Phonology: the system of rules governing the sequencing and distribution of speech sounds in words	Sounds are combined according to rules and patterns; knowledge of these patterns facilitates word recognition, spelling, and vocabulary.
Morphology: the smallest meaningful parts from which words are created	Compounds, prefixes, suffixes, roots, and combining forms are examples of morphemes important for vocabulary, word recognition, and spelling.
Syntax: the rule system that governs how words are combined into phrases, clauses, and sentences	Interpreting syntax is essential for reading comprehension; producing grammatical syntax is essential for written expression. Punctuation marks syntactic structures.
Semantics: the aspect of language that concerns the meanings of words, phrases, and sentences and the relationships among word meanings	Semantic processing is recognizing, constructing, storing, and retrieving meaning represented by language.
Discourse: the organizational conventions of connected text	Paragraph structure, dialogue, narrative form, expository forms, and other text organizations enable reading comprehension and written expression.
Pragmatics: how language is used in social contexts; rules of social discourse	Audience awareness in writing and author awareness in reading are pragmatic skills.

Not only is literacy dependent on language processing, but the language demands of reading and writing also differ from those of spoken language. Print is a visual, symbolic medium that must be recoded or translated by the reader or transcribed by the writer. The visual print system (orthography) is alphabetic: Its graphemes correspond to phonemes—the abstract but discrete building blocks from which words are created. A proficient reader rapidly and accurately connects print patterns to phonological information stored in the brain—the smallest speech segments—and then makes sense of words that have been identified.[9] As words are named and identified, sentences are deciphered; the reader gains access to meanings in the context of discourse, constructing a mental model of the information.[10] The words in written text tend to be more unusual than words used in speaking, and the sentences of written text tend to be longer, more embedded, more formally constructed, and more challenging to decipher than those of speech.[11] Mountains of evidence on the nature of proficient reading converge on an unavoidable truth: Language itself should be an important focus during reading and writing instruction, along with the facts, themes, and concepts conveyed by text.

Children bring knowledge of spoken language to the printed page and the tasks of reading and writing. They must learn the written symbols that represent speech and develop the ability to apply that knowledge to deciphering print. Knowing the difference between *sacks* and *sax*, *past* and *passed*, or *their* and *there* or knowing that *antique* is pronounced "anteek" requires language awareness at several levels. Students without awareness of language systems will be less able to sound out a new word when they encounter it, spell correctly, interpret punctuation and sentence meaning, and learn new vocabulary words from reading them in context. One of the most important jobs of any teacher of reading and writing is to direct students' attention to the details in printed words so that they can readily access the meanings that print represents.

The Development and Complexity of Language

Generative language is an achievement unique to human beings. Human language is creative because its systems allow us to invent new messages without limit. Unlike the signing systems of some highly evolved animals, such as wolves or whales, human language enables us to produce many messages that have never been spoken before. Speakers of a language share an understanding of the rule systems that govern the production of sounds, words, and sentences and when to use them. Speakers of English, for example, know that the sequence *Understanding basic is to language teaching reading* is not an allowable sentence, but *Understanding language is basic to teaching reading* is permitted. Speakers of English know that the names *Nkruma* and *Zhezhnik* are not English because sound sequences in those words do not occur in the English language sound system.

People around the world have invented languages for talking with one another. More than 4,000 languages exist on the Earth today,[12] but many are disappearing quickly as Western civilization encroaches on developing societies. All of these human languages share properties known as *universals*. From a finite set of speech sounds (phonemes), speakers of an oral language say and understand thousands of words. Words are composed of meaningful units (morphemes) that often can be recombined to make new words. Words themselves have meaning; the study of word, phrase, and sentence meanings is called *semantics*. Words belong to grammatical categories and are spoken in an order determined by underlying rules of syntax or sentence structure. Every speaker of a human language shares with every other speaker of that language the capacity to produce and comprehend an infinite number of sentences whose structures share basic properties. *Pragmatics* is the rule system that tells speakers how to use language for social communication. Some human societies have devised systems of written symbols (orthographies) to represent the sounds, syllables, and morphemes of spoken language.

The invention of tools for reading and writing sets humans apart from all other creatures. In evolutionary terms, reading and writing are recent accomplishments. Humans did not invent writing until the Chinese and Mediterranean peoples used meaningful written signs for concepts and words between 5,000 and 10,000 years ago. *Alphabets,* systems that use symbols for individual speech sounds, were invented little more than 5,000 years ago. It is understandable, then, that learning to read is not as natural or biologically "wired in" as are speaking and listening,[13] and reading must be taught directly to most children over several years through formal education. Our brains are not as fully evolved for processing written language as they are for processing spoken language, and, therefore, learning to read and write are more challenging for most of us than learning to speak.

Languages are constantly changing as the need for new expressions arises and as old expressions become obsolete. Every year the speakers of a language such as English generate several thousand new words and word uses to add to their language systems. The age of electronics, for example, has spawned terms such as *blog*, *text* (verb), *webcast*, and *tweet*. Committees that are created by some governments to preserve language purity, prevent change, or establish a standard are bucking a natural human tendency—to generate new language forms and uses within an established system.

No language is superior to any other in terms of the complexity of the rule systems that it embodies. English, however, has one of the most complex alphabetic orthographies, is spoken and written as a first or second language throughout the world, has the largest vocabulary,[14] and has become the language of international commerce. Nevertheless, English has many variants—including some "dialects" that are really different language systems—that present a significant challenge for teachers of reading and writing.

Reading Is Difficult for Many People

Few would deny that teaching children to read, write, spell, listen, and speak is among the foremost responsibilities of educators. Without well-developed reading skills, children cannot participate fully in classroom learning. They are at much greater risk for school failure and lifelong problems with employment, social adjustment, and personal autonomy. Literate cultures expect literacy of everyone, even so-called low-skilled workers who must read labels, directions, lists, forms, and records. Although a fairly large number of individuals in our society have always had difficulty learning to read, it is no longer acceptable to ignore them, give them failing grades, or banish them to the ranks of lower status jobs. The cost to society is too great. In addition, there are many children who would learn to read and write much better if they were taught to understand the systems of their own language (sounds, spellings, meaningful networks, sentences, text organization) in addition to reading textbooks and literature.

When children are taught well and, consequently, begin to read in kindergarten or first grade, they are likely to reap benefits throughout their schooling.[15] Those who read successfully from the start are more likely to enjoy reading, develop their knowledge of words and language patterns, and attain knowledge of the world by reading. Failure to read well, in contrast, undermines vocabulary growth, knowledge acquisition, verbal facility, and writing skill. Once behind in reading, few children catch up to grade level[16] unless they receive intensive, individualized, costly, and expert instruction.[17] Teaching everyone to read well, however, is a goal that has eluded us in the past.

About 20% of elementary students are very poor readers; at least another 20% do not read fluently enough to enjoy or to engage in independent reading.[18] Thus, it should not be surprising that on the 2006 National Assessment of Educational Progress (NAEP) about 38% of all fourth-grade students in the United States scored at a level "below basic." According to the National Adult Literacy Survey,[19] 14% of American adults are unable to perform functional reading tasks such as reading medicine labels or train schedules. Another 29% are at "basic" levels, below "intermediate," and do not read and write well enough to perform the literacy requirements of a typical job. The rate of functional illiteracy in Washington, D.C., is the highest in the nation at 37%.[20] Individuals who are poor readers are much more likely than literate people to drop out of school; end up in jail; or struggle to find and keep meaningful, satisfying work.[21]

For children who live in poverty or are from ethnic minorities and attend urban schools, the incidence of reading failure is astronomical and completely unacceptable for a literate society. African American students, Hispanic students, students whose native language is not English, and those from impoverished homes fall behind and stay behind in far greater proportion than their Caucasian, middle-class counterparts. The rate of reading failure in these groups is 60%–70%.[22] This figure alone explains much about the poor academic achievement of some minority students and why they are underrepresented in professions that depend on higher education.

One's family background and cultural context, however, do not guarantee literacy. Students of all backgrounds and intellectual talents may experience difficulty with language and reading that erodes their overall academic achievement. In 1996, California initiated a series of laws to reform reading education after 49% of children of college-educated parents in that state scored "below basic" on the NAEP. One third of fourth-grade students who are poor readers nationwide are from college-educated families who presumably encourage literacy in the home.

These statistics show that exposure to books and motivation to read, although vital to becoming a good reader, are not enough for many students to learn to read. Biological factors interact with environmental conditions to determine how easily students will learn. Even if their parents read to them at home or they are surrounded with good literature, a sizable proportion of our students need to be taught how to read. Many students must be taught how spoken and written language work so that they have the tools to decipher and generate the written word. The good news is that most students can learn to read at acceptable levels when teaching is skillful, explicit, and informed and intervention begins early.[23]

A Research Consensus About Language and Reading

The findings of scientific research in the field of reading[24] have had a major impact on federal, state, and local policies pertaining to teacher preparation and reading instruction. Teacher preparation and teaching itself was driven more by fads and philosophies than by facts[25] prior to the publication of the National Academy of Sciences' *Preventing Reading Difficulties in Young Children*[26] and the *Report of the National Reading Panel*,[27] two influential consensus documents. This should not be surprising because the methods of psychological experimentation necessary to unravel the mystery of reading were not developed until the mid-1970s, and there is always a long delay between developments in academic research disciplines and their incorporation into teaching practice. The tools and concepts of modern cognitive and linguistic science have been applied to understanding reading only since the mid-1970s.[28] As with other fields of scientific investigation, many studies in related disciplines were needed before consensus findings could be accepted and disseminated. Research-based insights into language, reading, and writing have only recently driven changes in funding mechanisms and policies affecting teacher preparation and professional development. Several other realities explain why we have been slow to understand how reading is accomplished and how best to teach it.

Language Processing, Including Reading, Is Largely Unconscious

Processing language, especially at the level of sounds, syllables, and words, is automatic—that is, fast and unconscious.[29] If we are good readers, then processing print has also become automatic. We are not aware of how we are actually reading as we are doing it, and we are not aware of the mental events that allow reading to happen. *Automaticity* is the word for the ability to execute tasks without conscious attention. It is a characteristic of skilled performance of any kind, such as playing an instrument, playing an athletic game, or operating a machine. The mental processes of good and poor readers are neither self-evident nor easy to grasp because they occur below the level of consciousness by design. *Introspection*—that is, viewing one's own mental activity—is misleading for understanding the mind of the skilled reader because the print–speech associations that occur during reading are too rapid and automatic to be perceived.

For example, do you think that you skip over words when you read and somehow extract the meaning of the print without seeing what is really there? That idea was prevalent in the early 1970s, when instructional methods that promote guessing at words on the basis of context were promoted.[30] In fact, laboratory experiments that track eye movements during reading, using different stimuli and many kinds of subjects, have shown that skilled reading is print driven.[31] That is, we process almost every letter of every word when we scan print, even though we fixate or focus our eyes primarily on the content (meaning-bearing) words as we scan a line. Those who read well process the details in the printed words accurately; those who read poorly do not process the details of the print and tend to skip over words they are unsure of because they cannot decode them. As many studies using eye movement technology have shown,[32] that tendency to skip over words is not a result of any vision problem in most cases but a result of a problem matching the print to sound completely, accurately, and efficiently. Those

review for fluency

who accomplish letterwise text scanning with relative ease and fluency have a better chance of comprehending well. Those who comprehend poorly often lose meaning because they cannot read the words accurately.

Primary processes that drive reading include our ability to associate print units (letters, letter combinations, letter sequences, words, and punctuation marks) with linguistic units (phonemes, onsets, rimes, syllables, morphemes, words, and phrases; see Figure 1.1). Linguistic units, including speech sounds, are neither auditory nor visual; they are abstract, mental phenomena and can be understood even by people who are hard of hearing. Because our attention is on meaning, we are not aware of the code translation process by which meaning is conveyed. Nor should we be—unless we must teach someone the same process deliberately, step by step. When we are faced with a class of children who are learning how to read symbols that represent speech sounds and word parts, we may suddenly need to analyze language at the level required for explaining and teaching it. Similarly, we may not know how a paragraph is organized or how a story is put together until we teach writing to students who do not know how to organize their thoughts. Thus, to understand printed language well enough to teach it explicitly requires conscious study of its systems and forms, both spoken and written.

Language Structure Is Not Self-Evident

Even well-educated adults often do not know exactly what goes into speaking, understanding words, using phonics, spelling, interpreting sentences, or organizing a composition, even though they use these language structures every day. On direct measures of language knowledge at the "lower" levels

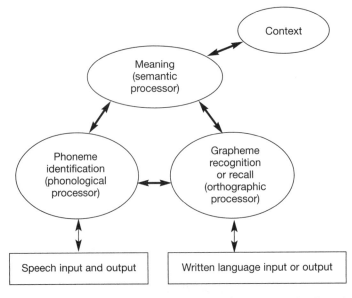

Figure 1.1. A simplified model of the processing components of word recognition and spelling. (*Source:* Rayner et al., 2001.)

(sounds, word parts, spelling), most adults show cursory or incomplete mastery at best.[33] For example, even experienced teachers may not clearly understand the concept that a letter combination (*ch, wh, sh, th, ng*) can represent one unique speech sound. Many identify these units by rote but are unable to differentiate conceptually between these spelling units (digraphs) and two letters that stand for two distinct sounds (consonant blends such as *cl, st, pr*) or silent letter spellings that retain the sound of one spelled consonant (*kn-, wr-, -mb*). Very few adults, unless they are studying and teaching the material, can explain why we double the consonant letters in words such as *misspell, dinner,* and *accommodate* or why there is a "silent *e*" on the end of the word *love*. A deeper, explicit level of knowledge may not be necessary for teachers to read the words, but it will be necessary to explain pronunciation and spelling, where the words came from, and how spelling is related to meaning.

In addition, the relationships among the basic skills of reading and reading comprehension are not obvious or self-evident. When children read poorly in the middle and upper grades, we may assume that the problem is one of comprehension. We may not realize that difficulties with word recognition, accuracy, speed, reading fluency, and comprehension strategies all contribute to poor reading in older students and that word recognition and fluency problems must be explicitly addressed in instruction.[34] Students who cannot read words well usually demonstrate weaknesses in *phonological processing*—the ability to identify, manipulate, produce, and remember speech sounds—but educators might not perceive this weakness without the special training that begins with language study.

Good Readers Intuit Language Structure

Some children learn language concepts and their application easily, in spite of incidental teaching, and with few examples. Just as some children seem to be born with insight into how the number system works, others just figure out how the system of print represents speech. They are "wired" for print processing. Figure 1.2 shows the writing of Hannah on her fourth birthday; she had already intuited a great deal about how sounds are spelled.

Hannah's understanding of sound–symbol correspondence was precocious; for example, she knew that letter combinations *th* and *ng* were used to represent sounds. She clearly had a good sense of the sounds that make up words because she was able to use letters that spell them. A more typical preschooler would have written a few letters or marks that bore no relationship to the sounds in speech. Awareness of speech sounds, or phoneme awareness, is an aspect of a fundamental linguistic competence known as *phonological processing.* Children who learn to read well are sensitive to linguistic structure at the level of speech sounds, parts of words, meaningful parts of words, sentences, and text. They can recognize repetitious patterns in print and connect letter patterns with sounds, syllables, and meaningful word parts quickly, accurately, and unconsciously. Effective teaching of reading presents these concepts in an order in which children can learn them and reinforces appreciation of the whole system in which these elements are arranged.

Figure 1.2.   Hannah's birthday note.

Poor Readers' Problems Begin with Phonology—A Hidden Processing Capability

The language skills that most reliably distinguish groups of good and poor readers are specific to the phonological, or speech sound, processing system. These skills include awareness of linguistic building blocks of words (consonants, vowels, onsets, rimes, syllables, grammatical endings, meaningful parts, and the spelling units that represent them) and fluency in recognition and recall of the spelling patterns that make up words. Problems with these underlying linguistic skills may be hidden from view unless the educator knows how to look for them. Students may present themselves as slow, avoidant, or unable to understand, when the real obstacle lies within the foundational networks of the language processing system.

Students who have the most trouble comprehending written language also do poorly on print-related tasks that have little to do with verbal reasoning; moreover, children who comprehend well when they read also do well at tasks such as reading words taken out of context, sounding out nonsense words, and spelling nonsense words.[35] Thus, skilled reading presents a paradox: Students who can most easily make sense of text are also those who can most easily read nonsense.[36] Decoding print, in turn, is dependent on the ability to map speech sounds to print, and herein lies the rub for typical poor readers.

What about IQ score and its relationship with reading? Intelligence and verbal reasoning ability do not predict reading success in the beginning stages as well as decoding skills do.[37] One major study found that 80% of the variance in reading comprehension at the first-grade level is accounted for by how well students sound out words and recognize words out of context.[38] The relationship between decoding and comprehension changes as students move into the middle grades, after they have learned how to read words. Comprehension strategies and knowledge of word meanings become more of a factor in reading success as students move into more advanced stages of literacy.[39] When appropriate, the emphasis of instruction will shift to reading itself and using interpretive strategies central to comprehension: summarizing, questioning, and monitoring one's own understanding. *DRA has this at end of 2nd grade*

How Reading and Spelling Develop

Again, longitudinal research indicates that most students who read well in high school learned early to sound out words and read new words with ease. That is, they gained the insight that letters in our writing system more or less represent phonemes and used this knowledge to map written words to spoken language. Early reading follows a predictable course regardless of the reader's speed of reading acquisition. The learner progresses from global to analytic processing, from approximate to specific linking of sound with symbols, and from context-driven to print-driven reading as proficiency is acquired. Learning to spell and read words is not a rote process of memorizing letter strings of increasing length. Figure 1.3 shows the typical progression of word recognition and spelling development in the early phases.[40]

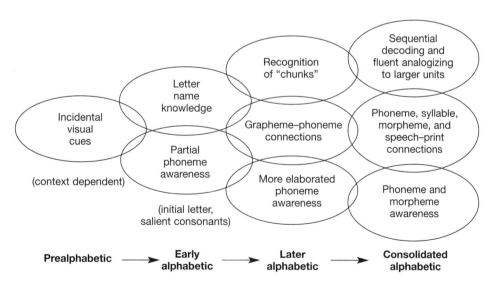

Figure 1.3. Schematic representation of reading and spelling development. (*Sources:* Ehri, 1994; Ehri & Snowling, 2004.)

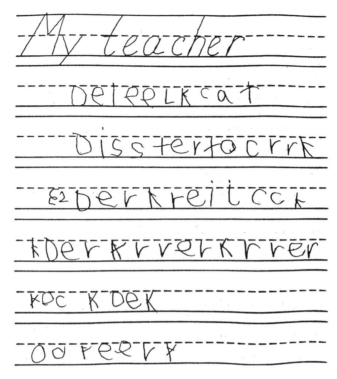

Figure 1.4. Example of prealphabetic writing.

Prealphabetic Reading and Writing

In the first phase of reading and spelling development, the **logographic, pre-reading,** or **prealphabetic** phase, children do not understand that letters represent the sounds in words, although they do know that print represents spoken messages. Up through age 4 or so, children may remember words such as family names and signs by configuration or general visual appearance and may be highly reliant on the context in which words occur to recognize them. They have no strategy other than rote memory of visual patterns or recognizing a word in its physical or meaning context to read it. Their spelling of words is often a string of familiar letters in random order, perhaps with a few idiosyncratic symbols or numerals thrown in the mix. They do not yet know the *alphabetic principle,* that is, the basic concept that letters represent segments of their own speech. An example of prealphabetic writing appears in Figure 1.4.

Early Alphabetic Reading and Writing

Next, there is a qualitative shift of approach in both reading and spelling when children discover a critical fact: Letters correspond to the sounds that make up spoken words (the alphabetic principle). From their growing awareness of speech sounds and knowledge of letter forms, children begin to spell and read by sounding out parts of words, often a few consonants

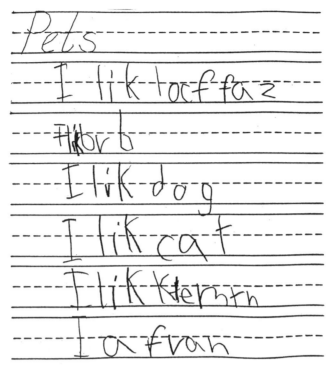

Figure 1.5. Early alphabetic writing. Child's rereading of own writing: "I like elephants, I like birds, I like cats, I like kittens, I a friend."

that are salient in speech (as in KR for *car* and HP for *happy*). At this point, they may attempt to "read" words by guessing from the initial consonant and the context, and they may spell by writing a few consonants but leaving out the vowel or the internal, less distinct speech sounds. They are beginning to demonstrate awareness of phonemes and the use of the alphabet to represent them. This shift of awareness occurs typically at kindergarten age or about age 5–5½. Figure 1.5 shows one child's early alphabetic writing.

[handwritten margin note: initial consonants and context Missing vowels]

Later Alphabetic Reading and Writing

Skill at sounding out words and spelling them phonetically unfolds gradually as children are able to identify all of the speech sounds in a word to which letters must be matched. As more elaborated phoneme awareness is acquired, children learn quickly how print patterns represent speech. At this stage, children render detailed phonetic spellings of unknown words and try to sound out words if the strategy is encouraged. They are usually rather slow and disfluent as they start to sound out words because so much conscious attention is needed to match symbols to sounds in sequence. Automatic recognition of whole words occurs when words that have been decoded are encountered often enough. One of the important findings of Ehri's research[41] is that automatic recognition of whole words is dependent on and facilitated by knowledge of phoneme–grapheme correspondences

[handwritten margin notes: Gradual development; slow disfluent; automaticity from repetition]

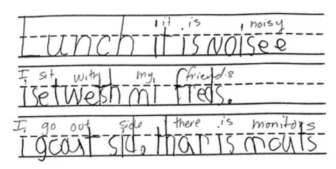

Figure 1.6.   Later alphabetic writing with teacher's notes from student's rereading.

memory

Exposure & reading practice

(phonics). Young readers are most likely to form memories of words that they have examined in sufficient detail, that they can read or spell accurately, and that they read and write often.

Exposure to text and reading practice are critical in moving the process of spelling development along quickly. If children in this phase are asked to identify nonsense words that look the most like real words, then they often show surprising awareness of the letter sequences and orthographic patterns that characterize English spelling, even though they may not associate all of those sequences with speech sounds. For example, they may know that *-ck* is used at the ends of words but not at the beginnings, that letters can be doubled at the ends of words or within words but not at the beginnings, that only certain letters are doubled, and that syllables typically contain a vowel letter.[42] *Orthographic knowledge,* which is knowledge of the spelling system itself, develops when the student has internalized awareness of the sounds to which the letters in words correspond. A sample of later alphabetic writing appears in Figure 1.6.

Learning the Spelling System— The Orthographic or Consolidated Phase

Children must learn a whole system of correspondence between sounds and their symbols to spell one-syllable words. Long vowel spellings, the use of silent *e*, vowels followed by *r*, and the conditions for spelling certain consonants certain ways at the ends of words, such as *-dge/-ge* and *-tch/-ch*, are learned as patterns, wherein many sounds are spelled with more than one letter. Children who are progressing typically then build up associations to syllables, word parts, and meaningful parts of words such as the ending *-ing,* which in turn allows rapid recognition of whole words after a few exposures to them. They learn about the relationships among sound, spelling, and meaning in phases; for example, they learn gradually that *-ed* means the past tense but is pronounced three different ways: /t/ as in *raked,* /d/ as in *played,* and /əd/ as in *painted.* Children use an analogy strategy to recognize unfamiliar words as soon as their lexical knowledge permits. That is, they will identify an unfamiliar word by mentally comparing it with a known

Comparing

word that has the same pattern or configuration, such as comparing the /g/ pronunciation of *gh-* in *ghetto, ghoul,* and *Ghana* with the more familiar *ghost.* Instruction that calls attention to sound–symbol correspondence and patterns in print hastens the learning process considerably.

Effective teaching, which is responsive to students' developmental levels, requires the explanation of both spoken and written language. The content of any lesson should depend on what students already know and should move them through the system of language organization. Teaching children about sounds is appropriate at the very early stages; an emphasis on meaningful parts, or morphology, is appropriate when the foundation is secure. Direct instruction about the alphabetic code should be integrated with instruction on word and text meaning.

Skillful Teaching Prevents Most Reading Problems

Most reading problems can be greatly ameliorated through appropriate instruction.[43] According to the convergent findings of numerous studies,[44] classroom instruction that builds phoneme awareness, phonic decoding skills, text reading fluency, vocabulary, and various aspects of comprehension is the best antidote for reading difficulty. Although parents, communities, and volunteer tutorial programs do influence how well and how soon students read, informed classroom instruction that begins to teach critical language and reading skills in kindergarten and that is sustained throughout school ensures success for all but a few students with moderate or severe learning disabilities.[45] Reading scientists now estimate that 95% of first-grade students can be taught to read at a level constrained only by their reasoning and listening comprehension abilities.[46] It is clear as well that students in high-risk populations need not fail at the rate they do.[47] Students who live in poverty can be as successful as their more advantaged peers when placed in schools with strong leaders, valid programs, and well-prepared and well-supported teachers. Teachers who incorporate critical language skills into direct, systematic, sequenced lessons can reach most children. Reading programs that are well designed and well implemented are the best guard against reading failure.

Teaching Reading Is Complex and Challenging

The case has often been made that teaching reading and writing requires considerable expertise.[48] Nevertheless, many teachers are licensed with only one survey course on reading methods and little background in reading psychology or language structure, leaving them without the understanding and tools that enable instruction. Some special education teachers are not required to take any course in reading instruction or reading psychology, even though the large majority of their student caseload will have specific reading disabilities.

Research evidence continues to show, however, that teachers who are most effective with struggling readers have both content knowledge and practical skill and are more inclined to use direct, systematic, explicit, structured language methods for those who do not learn easily.[49] In addition, a documented relationship exists between what teachers know and what they are willing to learn and willing to do. Teachers who know more about the written code of English are more favorably inclined to teach phonics and spelling to students.[50] The students of knowledgeable teachers are more likely to progress than students of teachers who score low on a knowledge survey.[51] Teachers who accept and support the necessity for teaching language explicitly are also more receptive to the professional development offered by classroom reading coaches and are more likely to have successful students.[52]

direct systematic explicit

Teachers must be prepared to choose the practices and programs that work best with specific kinds of students. Some approaches are more effective than others with well-defined groups of children.[53] The best teachers differentiate their instruction. For example, some students are fairly strong in decoding skills but are relatively lacking in language comprehension and vocabulary; others, usually the majority of struggling readers, need to focus on learning to read the words and reading with sufficient fluency to support comprehension. The teacher who directly strengthens students' areas of weakness (e.g., phonological awareness, decoding, vocabulary, reading fluency, language comprehension) is most likely to help students improve.

What does an effective teacher actually do? Hundreds of small decisions guide the teacher's actions hour to hour. In the course of any day, the teacher must continually pique children's interest in reading through incentive programs and discussions in which students respond to many kinds of texts, including stories, informational pieces, and poetry. The teacher must also organize the class so that he or she can instruct groups of students according to their abilities and needs. For those who need basic reading or writing skills, teaching must be direct, systematic, cumulative, and explicit to get the best results. To accommodate children's variability, the teacher must assess children and know how they are progressing. He or she must interpret errors, give corrective feedback, select examples for concepts, explain new ideas several ways, and connect many component skills with meaningful reading and writing experiences. Without a doubt, teaching reading and language is a job for a quick-minded, informed, committed, flexible, and knowledgeable professional.

Principles of Effective Teaching of Reading, Spelling, and Writing

Effective teachers of reading and writing draw on many resources. They raise students' ability to interpret and generate sound-spellings, syllables, morphemes, phrases, sentences, paragraphs, and various genres of text.

They also balance skill instruction with daily writing and reading that is purposeful and engaging, no matter what the skill level of the learner. Children in middle and upper grades who have poor reading skills can be brought up to grade level with appropriate instruction, although the time and effort involved are considerably greater than that required to teach younger children.[54] Analyses of dozens of research studies[55] have consistently supported these findings:

- Direct teaching of phonological skills, sound–symbol correspondence (phonics), fluent word recognition and text reading, vocabulary, text comprehension, and literature appreciation is necessary from when children begin school until they become proficient readers and writers.

- Phoneme awareness instruction, when linked to systematic decoding and spelling instruction, is a key to preventing reading failure in children who come to school without these prerequisite skills.

- It is better to teach the code system of written English systematically and explicitly than it is to teach it randomly, indirectly, or incidentally. The units for instruction (sound, syllable, morpheme, word) should vary according to students' reading and spelling skill.

- The most effective programs include daily exposure to a variety of texts and incentives for children to read independently and with others. Practices that build reading fluency include short practice drills in component skills, repeated readings of text, alternate reading with a partner, simultaneous oral reading of easy material, and daily independent reading.

- Vocabulary is best taught with a variety of complementary methods designed to explore the relationships among words and the relationships among word structure, origin, and meaning. Close reading of text for topic-specific content is the most important activity for building comprehension.

- Key comprehension strategies include summarizing, clarifying, questioning, and visualizing; these should be modeled explicitly by the teacher and practiced overtly if students are not comprehending well or if they approach reading comprehension passively.

- Effective teachers encourage frequent prose writing to enable deeper understanding of what is read.

To master all of these teaching principles and apply them well takes most of us a long time. At least we can proceed with the confidence that there is a solid body of evidence about what works, for whom, and why. It is beneficial to teach children about language structure. Teaching students about language can be engaging, active, and enjoyable. Knowing about phonemes, syllables, morphemes, and the spelling system enables children to read words accurately and quickly. Knowing how language works enables children to learn words, interpret sentences, and write fluently. If we teach children this content, then it means that we, the educators, must know it well. Just as a physician must study anatomy to understand physical functioning, we must know the linguistic frameworks for literacy instruction.

The major systems of language, with the exception of pragmatics and discourse, are treated in this book. Within- and end-of-chapter exercises are included in this book and in the accompanying *Speech to Print* workbook. Among the appendixes is an answer key and a glossary of terms highlighted in bold in the text. Deeper discussion of pragmatics, discourse structure, social uses of language, and language acquisition is left for other writers to tackle.

The surveys of language knowledge at the end of this chapter can be used by the reader for self-assessment or as a pretest in a course of study.

Endnotes

1. Joshi, Binks, Hougen, et al., 2009; Walsh, Glaser, & Dunne-Wilcox, 2006.
2. Aaron, Joshi, & Quatroche, 2008; Berninger & Wolf, 2009; Birsh, 2005; Fletcher, Lyon, Fuchs, & Barnes, 2007.
3. Brady & Moats, 1997; Moats, 1999; Moats & Lyon, 1996; Snow, Griffin, & Burns, 2005.
4. Joshi, Binks, Graham, et al., 2009; Joshi, Binks, Hougen, et al., 2009.
5. Joshi, Binks, Graham, et al., 2009; Spencer, Schuele, Guillot, & Lee, 2008.
6. Walsh et al., 2006.
7. Adams, 1990; Catts & Kamhi, 2005; Liberman, Shankweiler, & Liberman, 1989.
8. Mehta, Foorman, Branum-Martin, & Taylor, 2005.
9. Ashby, Sanders, & Kingston, 2009.
10. Cain & Oakhill, 2007; Perfetti, 1999.
11. Cunningham & Stanovich, 1998.
12. Fromkin, Rodman, & Hyams, 2003.
13. Liberman et al., 1989; Wolf, 2007.
14. The *Oxford English Dictionary* lists more than 650,000 words in English.
15. Cunningham & Stanovich, 1991, 1998.
16. Francis, Shaywitz, Stuebing, Shaywitz, & Fletcher, 1996; Good, Simmons, & Kameenui, 2001; Shaywitz, 2003.
17. Mathes et al., 2005; Torgesen, 2005.
18. Good et al., 2001.
19. National Adult Literacy Survey, 2003.
20. National Center for Education Statistics, 2006.
21. Sweet, 2004.
22. National Center for Education Statistics, 2006.
23. Blachman, Schatschneider, Fletcher, & Clonan, 2003; Mathes et al., 2005; Torgesen, 2002, 2005.
24. See, for example, Rayner, Foorman, Perfetti, Pesetsky, & Seidenberg, 2001.
25. Bos, Mather, Dickson, Podhajski, & Chard, 2001.
26. Snow, Burns, & Griffin, 1998.
27. National Institute of Child Health and Human Development, 2000.
28. Adams, 1990; Fletcher et al., 2007; Rayner et al., 2001.
29. Ashby et al., 2009; Rayner et al., 2001.
30. Adams, 1998.
31. Ashby et al., 2009; Rayner et al., 2001.
32. Rayner, 1998.
33. Brady et al., 2009; Cunningham, Perry, Stanovich, & Stanovich, 2004; McCutchen, Harry, et al., 2002; Moats, 1994, 1995; Moats & Foorman, 2003; Spear-Swerling & Brucker, 2003; Spencer et al., 2008.
34. Catone & Brady, 2005.
35. Fletcher et al., 2007; Good et al., 2001.
36. Rayner et al., 2001.
37. Fletcher et al., 1994; Shankweiler et al., 1999.
38. Shankweiler et al., 1999.

39. Vellutino, Tunmer, Jaccard, & Chen, 2007.
40. Based on the work of Ehri, 2002; Ehri & McCormick, 1998; Ehri & Snowling, 2004.
41. Ehri & Snowling, 2004.
42. Treiman, 1993.
43. Haager, Heimbichner, Dhar, Moulton, & McMillan, 2008.
44. Fletcher et al., 2007; Foorman, Francis, Fletcher, Schatschneider, & Mehta, 1998; Foorman & Moats, 2004; National Institute of Child Health and Human Development, 2000.
45. McCutchen, Abbott, et al., 2002; McCutchen, Green, Abbott, & Sanders, 2009.
46. Hatcher, Hulme, & Snowling, 2004; Mathes et al., 2005.
47. Moats & Foorman, 2008.
48. Berninger & Wolf, 2009; Moats, 1999; Snow et al., 2005.
49. Piasta, Connor, Fishman, & Morrison, 2009.
50. Cunningham, Zibulsky, Stanovich, & Stanovich, 2009.
51. Foorman & Moats, 2004; Kroese, Mather, & Sammons, 2006; McCutchen, Abbott, et al., 2002; McCutchen et al., 2009; Piasta et al., 2009.
52. Brady et al., 2009.
53. Aaron et al., 2008; Connor, Morrison, & Katch, 2004.
54. Torgesen et al., 2001.
55. See, for example, National Institute of Child Health and Human Development, 2000; Snow et al., 1998.

Brief Survey of Language Knowledge

Phoneme Counting

Count the number of speech sounds or phonemes that you perceive in each of the following spoken words. Remember, the number of speech sounds may not be equivalent to the number of letters. For example, the word *spoke* has four phonemes: /s/, /p/, /ō/, and /k/. Write the number of phonemes in the blank to the right of each word.

thrill __4__   ring __3__   shook __3__

does __3__   fix __3(4)__ "y" says cks __2__   wrinkle __5__

sawed __3__   quack __3__   know __2__

Syllable Counting

Count the number of syllables that you perceive in each of the following words. For example, the word *higher* has two syllables, the word *threat* has one, and the word *physician* has three.

cats __1__   capital __3__   shirt __1__

spoil __2__   decidedly __4__   banana __3__

recreational __5__   lawyer __2__   walked __1__

Phoneme Matching

Read the first word in each line and note the sound that is represented by the underlined letter or letter cluster. Then, select the word or words on the line that contain the same sound. Underline the words you select.

1. **pu**sh   although   sugar✓   duty   pump
2. **weigh**   pie   height   raid✓   friend
3. **doe**s   miss   nose✓   votes   rice
4. **in**tend   this   whistle   baked✓   batch
5. **ri**ng   sink✓   handle   signal   pinpoint

Recognition of Sound–Symbol Correspondence

Find in the following words the letters and letter combinations that correspond to each speech sound in the word. For example, the word *stress* has five phonemes, each of which is represented by a letter or letter group: s / t / r / e / ss. Now try these:

b|e|s t   f|r|e|s h   s|c|r|a|t c h
t|h|o u g h   l|a u|g h|e d   m|i|d d|l e
c h|i|r|p   q u|a i|n|t

Definitions and Concepts

Write a definition or explanation of the following:

1. Vowel sound (vowel phoneme)
   need in a syllable
   ✱open sound nucleus of syllable

2. Consonant digraph
   2 letters - one sound

3. Prefix
   (morpheme)
   meaning addeded before root word to change the meaning of the root word "dis" means not "re" do again ←

4. Inflectional (grammatical) morpheme *(sound meaning - group of letters)*
   changes the number (plural)   tense (past, present future)
   degree   ✱but does not change meaning of root.

5. Why is phoneme awareness important? *awareness of linguistic building blocks and fluency in recognition and recall*

6. How is decoding skill related to reading fluency and comprehension?
   automaticity takes focus off decoding so one can focus on comprehension.
   lack of fluency can break down comprehension

Comprehensive Survey of Language Knowledge

1. From the list below, find an example of each of the following (answer will be a word or part of a word):

   Inflected verb _Slowed_

   Compound noun _sandpaper_

   Bound root _credit   psych_

   Derivational suffix _~ible   -ful_

   Greek combining form _neuropsychology_

   peaches   incredible   slowed   although   shameful   doughnut
   bicycle   neuropsychology   sandpaper   vanish

2. For each word on the left, determine the number of syllables and the number of morphemes:

	Syllable	Morphemes
bookworm	2	2
unicorn	3	2
elephant	3	3
believed	2	3
incredible	4	3
finger	2	2
hogs	1	2
telegram	3	2

3. A closed syllable is one that _short vowel one or more consonants_

   An open syllable is one that _long vowel- open e one vowel letter ends the syllable_

4. How many speech sounds are in the following words?

   sigh _2_   thrown _3_   scratch _____

   ice _2_   sung _3_   poison _____

   mix _4_   shrink _____   know _____
   cks

5. What is the third speech sound in each of the following words?

joyful /f/   should x/d/   talk /k/

tinker k ng   rouge j /zh/   shower r/w/

square /w/   start /ar/

protect /o/   patchwork /ch/

6. Underline the schwa vowels:

telephone   addenda   along   precious   imposition   unless

7. Underline the consonant blends:

knight   climb   wreck   napkin   squished   springy   first

8. Underline the consonant digraphs:

spherical   church   numb   shrink   thought   whether

9. When is *ck* used in spelling?

at the end of words

10. What letters signal that a *c* is pronounced /s/?

i   e

11. List all of the ways you know to spell "long *o*."

o_e   ough   oa   ow   oe
rose   though   boat   row   toe

12. List all of the ways you know to spell the consonant sound /f/.

f   ough   ph   ff
fun   tough   telephone   ruff

13. When adding a suffix to a word ending with silent *e*, what is the spelling rule?

drop and add ing, ed, er (vowel)
leave for s   (consonant)

14. How can you recognize an English word that came from Greek?

myth, science, math
ph - /f/   y - ī or ĭ   ch - /k/

Phonetics
The Sounds in Speech

By the end of this chapter, you will understand:

- Why the identification of phonemes is difficult
- How to transcribe speech sounds using a phonetic alphabet
- Consonant speech segments and how they are grouped
- Vowel speech segments and how they differ
- Articulation of speech sounds in the mouth

Why Start with Speech Sounds?

Phonetics is the study of the production and perception of speech sounds that occur in each language and in all languages. It is a topic within the broader topic of **phonology**, which is discussed in Chapter 3. Speech sounds (phonemes) are the basic building blocks of words, the smallest units that make one word different from another. Perception of, memory for, and the ability to think about phonemes play a central role in learning to speak, read, and spell.

Why should we focus on phonemes? First, phonemes determine the identity of words. The spoken words *built, belt,* and *bolt* all differ by one phoneme—the **vowel** sound—and mean different things. Conversely, we know that the vowels in those words are phonemes because their presence signals different word meanings. The spoken words *sake, shake,* and *lake* all differ by one phoneme—the initial **consonant.** Those consonants are phonemes because they distinguish word meanings. *Tenet* and *tenant, perfect* and *prefect, syllable* and *syllabus* differ only slightly in sound but considerably in meaning. Spoken word recognition, pronunciation, and interpretation depend, in part, on accurately processing phonemes.

The second reason why phonemes are important is that alphabetic writing systems, such as English, more or less represent language at the phoneme level. Much more will be said about English orthography in Chapter 4, but without awareness of the speech sounds that letters represent, one cannot match letters to sounds and read unfamiliar words. The alphabet is a useless tool for someone who does not understand "what them letters is for," as a student once remarked.

Third, one of the most robust findings of modern reading research is that proficient reading is strongly associated with the ability to identify, remember, and sequence phonemes.[1] Good readers associate the sound segments of language with the letters in written words. The National Reading Panel[2] found more than 50 studies verifying that explicitly teaching phonemes was one critical component of effective reading and spelling instruction. Teachers, therefore, should know the speech sound system, why it is important, and how to teach it.

Becoming Metalinguistic

Few of us can list the consonant and vowel sounds of the language we speak. Strangely, although people who know a language are constantly using its sounds, most are not consciously aware of the inventory of consonants and vowels. Thus, a linguist cannot simply ask the speakers of any language to tell him or her the sounds in that system. Speech sounds are seldom spoken in isolation and certainly are not directly taught to toddlers learning to talk. In linguistics, a phoneme list for any language must be deduced from analysis of many spoken words.

To list and learn the inventory of phonemes in any language is an exercise of **metalinguistic** skill. *Metalinguistic* thinking involves thinking about and reflecting on the structure, form, and use of language. *Meta* is a Greek word part meaning "beyond" or "higher." Metalinguistic or conscious

phoneme awareness (handwritten margin note)

knowledge of the structures of language is usually developed through formal study and reflection. Recognizing the separate sounds (phonemes) within whole words is a kind of metalinguistic skill called **phoneme awareness.** Many adults and children need considerable practice before they are proficient at this kind of language analysis.

Being literate, in a peculiar way, is an obstacle to thinking about the speech sounds in spoken words. Printed forms often do not reveal exactly what the sounds may be in a given word. For example, the word *butte* has an extra /y/ sound that is not in *boot*. To detect sounds, we cannot rely too heavily on what we know about spelling. We must learn to pay close attention to what our mouths are doing and forget what we know about print—at least temporarily. Exercise 2.1 illustrates why phoneme awareness may be challenging.

Counting Phonemes

It is easy to demonstrate that many speakers of English have trouble identifying the discrete segments in words that constitute the inventory of speech sounds or phonemes. Try counting the number of speech sounds in familiar words and identifying the specific sounds within those words. This task will be easier if you try not to think about how the words are spelled.

 Exercise 2.1

Count the number of phonemes in the following words:

ice _2_	choose _3_	mix _4_	soothe _3_
sigh _2_	sing _2_	pitched _4_	her _2_
day _2_	thorn _3_	straight _5_	boy _2_
aide _2_	quake _3_	measure _5_	shout _3_

Compare notes with someone else who did Exercise 2.1. Did you make the same judgments? In what way(s) did you disagree? What would cause a group of educated people to disagree about the number, sequence, or identity of individual segments within English words? What causes the ambiguity of phoneme identity?

Why Phonemes Are Elusive

Sound order number feature (handwritten margin note)

What are the sounds of English? How many are there? Very few of us can answer these questions because we learned the sounds from exposure to them in naturally articulated words, and we usually produce the sounds without conscious attention to their number, order, or other features. The speech sound inventory, even in our native language, is not something we are likely to have been taught prior to taking a class in language structure. The human brain is designed to attend to the meaning of the message between speakers, not to the specific sounds in words, so our knowledge of phonetics tends to be tacit or implicit rather than overt and formal.

Although speakers of English may not be able to list all of the sounds of the language, they recognize when words do and do not conform to English phonology. For example, most people recognize that the French *tu*, the Swahili *Ngoro*, the Russian *tovarishch*, and the Japanese *tsutsumu* are not English because these words have sounds or sound sequences that are not heard in English. Speakers are also capable of inventing new words or nonwords that follow the speech sound constraints of their own language, such as *yemble*, although they might not be able to explain why *yemble* conforms to English word-formation rules and why *ylebm* does not.

Even linguists do not agree on the inventory of sounds in English and other languages. Estimates of the number of speech sounds or phonemes in English range from 40 to 52.[3] Every reference consulted for this chapter used a different phonetic description of English and offered a somewhat different inventory of sounds.[4] Only the inherent ambiguity of phoneme identity can account for such disparities.

To become aware of the speech sounds in our own language, we must bring to consciousness that which is largely unconscious and impose divisions on spoken words that exist as wholes. Phonemes are segments in a stream of speech that flows continuously without pauses or acoustic breaks. Words are not spoken as a sequence of separate segments, even though those segments can be identified. Rather, individual sounds or phonemes overlap in speech or are **coarticulated** in the unbroken speech stream.

An effect of coarticulation is that sounds within words are slightly changed by the sounds that come before and after them. Look in a mirror. Say the words *see* and *so,* and as you anticipate the vowel that follows /s/ in each word, feel the different mouth position for /s/ that begins each word. Say the words *tap* and *trap* and notice how different the mouth feels and looks when it shapes the sound we think of as /t/ in the beginning of both words. Now try *cheese* and *choose.* In each case, the initial consonant sound is influenced by what comes after it. Our brains know what is coming next in a word and make adjustments in articulating individual segments so that the sequence of speech is one coordinated gesture of articulation—a word.

Phoneme segments in isolation do not sound as they do when they are embedded in words. Even if we were to isolate the individual sounds in *stop* (/s/ /t/ /a/ /p/), we would not be saying them the same way when they are combined. The segment /p/ alone is not exactly the same as the /p/ in *picture, spider,* or *stoop.* The sounds we identify as /p/ are spoken in different words and by different speakers in slightly different ways. Our brains, however, overcome these subtle differences and lump the slight *phonetic variations* together in one category. Our brains tell us that the phoneme /p/ exists in all those words. Because the spoken form of any given sound varies according to the word it is in or the person who is speaking it, recognizing phonemes in words depends on a phenomenon called *categorical perception.* We perceive a category of sound when we learn to recognize a phoneme.

As we study the consonant and vowel sounds of English, keep in mind that sounds in isolation are abstract phonemes that exist in our minds but do not exist in exactly the same form when they are combined in spoken words. Our capacity to recognize phonemes in speech and to produce them is a marvelous—and unique—human language adaptation.

Speech Sound Identification

If counting speech sounds, as in Exercise 2.1, is neither simple nor straightforward for adults, then why should it be easy for children who are just learning to read and write? Again, several factors conspire to prevent children from developing the insight that the words *ice, sigh,* and *me* all are made of two speech sounds even though we use a different number of letters to spell each of them. Children have not spoken the sounds in isolation and have not had to break words into their component phonemes; for them, the sounds exist only in combination with others, and awareness of the segments is not necessary for everyday verbal communication. Many children who enter kindergarten know letter names but do not know that those letters are used to represent the segments of their own speech. Many first- and second-grade students, and even some older students who are poor readers or spellers, also have not acquired this essential insight. In virtually every classroom, some children will not understand this fundamental fact. The teacher may need to provide explicit phoneme awareness instruction for children before instruction in letter–sound association for reading and spelling can be effective. Phoneme awareness is the linchpin for early reading success.

The most basic building blocks of a language are the sets of consonants and vowels that make up the speech sound inventory. The terms *consonants* and *vowels* are used in this book to refer to segments of speech, not to the letters that represent them. Every language has a set of consonants and vowels; English has more than most. It is interesting to note, however, that linguists usually differ to some degree in their description of consonants and vowels, offering varying opinions about the segments and the features that describe them. The descriptions in this book may not be the same as the phonetic classifications made by other authors. Again, ambiguity appears to be a characteristic of phonetic description because the sounds must be "recovered" from running speech. The inventory of consonants and vowels that follows is based on the classification of the linguists Fromkin, Rodman, and Hyams.[5]

The task of classifying sounds is complicated by the fact that no two speakers of a language form their sounds exactly the same way and by the fact that regional dialects cause audible differences in sound production. One of the remarkable characteristics of the speech-processing module in the brain is that speakers can understand one another in spite of regional and individual differences in speech production. We can extract from the speech of others the acoustic signals that determine what the utterance means even though we all do not talk the same way. To describe what goes on when we talk, however, we must have a standard classification system for consonants and vowels. If you are unsure of exactly what is and is not a speech sound, then Exercise 2.2 is going to be a bit challenging.

Exercise 2.2

Identify the third phoneme in the following words:

choose __ʒ__   pneumonia __m__   kitchen __tch__

writhe __th__   vision __ʒ__   square __w__

sink __nk__   folk __k__

To identify the third sound in a word, the speaker must segment and count the sounds and then know the difference between a phoneme and a written letter. In the words in Exercise 2.2, the spelling generally does not represent the sounds with a straightforward "one letter equals one sound" principle. Furthermore, speakers may not be aware of or know how to describe the third sound in some of these words, such as the /ŋ/, or /ng/, sound in *sink* or the /ž/, or /zh/, sound represented by *s* in *measure*. Learning a system for transcribing and describing the sounds in a way other than their standard orthographic spellings helps one to clarify the differences between phonemes and the symbols used for writing. When that clarification is achieved, we can make sense of children's early struggles with print far more easily.

Phonetic Transcription

Standard alphabetic writing is unsatisfactory to represent the speech sounds in our language. English spelling uses several hundred graphemes (letters and letter combinations) to represent 40 or so speech sounds;[6] in fact, most spellings for sounds consist of more than one letter. Consider the following sentence: *Daisy weighed in on Thursday to make great strides in horse racing history.* This sentence includes six of the eight spellings of "long *a*" in standard English: *ai, eigh, ay, a*-consonant-*e, ea,* and *a* (it does not include *ey* as in *prey* or *ei* as in *vein*). Although most of the sounds of English have somewhat more predictable spellings, it is not possible to write a transcription of speech sounds unless some standard, consistent method of representation is used.

A writing system is considered phonetic when one sound corresponds to one letter. It is easy to illustrate again that English orthography is not an ideal tool for phonetic transcription. The word *conscience* shows why. In this word, the letter *c* stands for three different speech sounds: /k/, /š/ (or /sh/), and /s/; a vowel team (two vowel letters) is needed to spell the second vowel /ə/; and the final /s/ is represented by *ce*. Phonetically, the same word is written as [kɑnšəns]; there is one symbol for each speech sound. A **phonetic alphabet** represents all of the sounds in the world's languages so that speech can be described with a common symbol system. The International Phonetic Alphabet (IPA) was invented in 1888 for that purpose and was revised by a group of linguists in 1989 and in 1993.[7] The IPA is detailed enough to represent salient linguistic features in each language, but it does not—and should not—represent the minute individual variations in the way two speakers may pronounce the same word. It is sufficient for transcribing the crucial linguistic properties of sounds in English and other languages. An Americanized version of the IPA is used in this book. Readers of this textbook may not be inclined to learn or use a phonetic alphabet and may prefer to transcribe words using the 26 Roman letters only (a phonic or dictionary system; for example, /sh/, /ng/, /th/, /ū/). A phonetic alphabet, however, is recommended for practice with transcription because it unambiguously represents the speech sound system separately from the alphabet symbols of conventional English orthography. Working with the phonetic alphabet requires the learner to differentiate sounds from their conventional spellings.

[handwritten margin notes: phonetic alphabet; common symbol system; IPA - International Phonetic Alphabet]

One can use phonic or dictionary symbols to transcribe the phonetic properties of words, but the disadvantage of such a phonic representation system is that many speech sounds must then be represented with letter combinations (the initial single sound in *chair* must be represented by /ch/). With the phonetic alphabet, only one unique symbol is used for each phoneme. In this book, the major listings of consonants and vowels are given in both symbol systems (phonic representation and phonetic alphabet). Brackets [ ] are used to denote the phonetic form of a word or speech segment, and slashes / / are used to denote phonemes. The distinction between a phonetic segment and a phoneme is clarified in Chapter 3.

Speech sounds are produced with movements of the tongue, lips, and throat. Air is pushed up from the lungs through an opening in the vocal cords (the glottis) and then through the throat, mouth, and nose. Air is more obstructed in consonant production than in vowel production. Thus, we can say for instructional purposes that <u>consonants are "closed" sounds</u> and vowels are "open" sounds. Figure 2.1 shows the speech apparatus.

Air is more obstructed in consonant production closed

vowels open sounds

Consonants and Their Distinguishing Features

Consonants are a class of speech sounds that are not vowels and that are formed with the <u>mouth partially closed and the airflow obstructed by the lips, teeth, and tongue.</u> Not all consonants, however, involve obstruction of the air stream to an equal degree; some consonants have vowel-like qualities (for example, the [r] in *word*), which in turn cause them to be somewhat more ambiguous or difficult to identify in running speech.

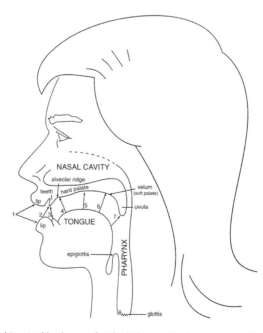

Figure 2.1.   The vocal tract with places of articulation marked: 1) bilabial, 2) labiodental, 3) interdental, 4) alveolar, 5) alveopalatal, 6) velar, 7) uvular, and 8) glottal. (Figure from *AN INTRODUCTION TO LANGUAGE, Sixth Edition* [p. 222], by Victoria A. Fromkin and Robert Rodman copyright © 1998 by Holt, Rinehart & Winston, reproduced by permission of the publisher.)

Consonants are distinguished by place and manner of articulation. **Place of articulation** refers to where the sound is made, or the position of the lips, teeth, and tongue in the front, middle, or back of the mouth. **Manner of articulation** refers to how the sound is made, or the production of airflow through the mouth. Where and how each sound is made constitutes a set of **distinguishing features.**

In English, some of the major distinguishing features for phonemes are voicing, continuancy, and nasality. Consider the following contrasts:

sip, zip

fan, van

chump, jump

pad, mad

sag, sang

Some consonants, such as /z/, /v/, and /j/, are made with the vocal cords engaged or buzzing, and some consonants, such as /s/, /f/, and /ch/, are made with the vocal cords disengaged and quiet. This distinguishing feature is called *voicing*. Consonants may be **voiced** or **unvoiced.**

Other consonants differ in continuancy. Some consonants, such as /p/ and /k/, are stops. We say them with one explosion of sound. Others, such as /m/ and /s/, are **continuants.** We can say them until we run out of breath.

Some consonants, such as /p/ and /g/, send the air through the oral cavity, and others, such as /ŋ/, send the air through the nose. This featural contrast is described as the *oral-nasal contrast*. These and other distinguishing features determine how phonemes are produced and perceived.

You may find it helpful to fill in a blank consonant chart based on your knowledge of the speech sounds (see Figure 2.2) before looking at the charts of consonant sounds that are provided in Figures 2.3 and 2.4. A basic 25 consonants are identified in these two tables, classified by place and manner of articulation. Two symbol systems are given—phonic symbols (see Figure 2.3) and phonetic symbols (see Figure 2.4)—that are likely to be used in classroom reading and spelling instruction. The linguistic terms that appear in these two tables are explained in the next section.

Exercise 2.3

Try to discover and label as many consonants as you can, using the blank chart provided in Figure 2.2. Categorize the consonants by the place in the vocal tract where you think they are articulated. Then, compare the consonants listed on your chart with those that appear in Figures 2.3 and 2.4. Which sounds are difficult to identify? Were any previously unknown to you?

Places of Consonant Articulation   Distinguishing features include the shape and position of the lips, tongue, teeth, and other parts of the mouth. The **bilabial** consonants, as the name suggests, are made by bringing both lips together. Two of these, [b] and [p], are oral stops, and one,

	Lips	Lips/teeth	Tongue between teeth	Tongue behind teeth	Roof of mouth	Back of mouth	Throat
Stops							
Nasals							
Fricatives							
Africatives							
Glides							
Liquids							

Figure 2.2.   Chart for discovering the consonants. List as many consonants as possible, grouping them by where the sound seems to be articulated.

Phonic symbols
American English consonants listed by place and manner of articulation

Manner of articulation	Place of articulation						
	Lips	Lips/teeth	Tongue between teeth	Tongue behind teeth	Roof of mouth	Back of mouth	Throat
Stop (voiceless) (voiced)	/p/ /b/			/t/ /d/		/k/ /g/	
Nasal	/m/			/n/		/ng/	
Fricative (voiceless) (voiced)		/f/ /v/	/th/ /<u>th</u>/	/s/ /z/	/sh/ /zh/		/h/
Affricate (voiceless) (voiced)					/ch/ /j/		
Glide (voiceless) (voiced) *Semivowels*					/y/	/wh/ /w/	
Liquid				/l/	/r/		

Figure 2.3. Phonic symbols: American English consonants listed by place and manner of articulation.

Phonetic symbols

American English consonants listed by place and manner of articulation

Manner of articulation	Bilabial	Labiodental	Interdental	Alveolar	Palatal	Velar	Glottal
Stop (oral)							
voiceless unaspirated	p			t		k	
voiced	b			d		g	
Nasal (stop)	m			n		ŋ	
Fricative							
voiceless		f	θ	s	š		
voiced		v	ð	z	ž		
Affricate							
voiceless					č		
voiced					ǰ ǰ		
Glide							
voiceless					j	ʍ	h
voiced					ɣ	w	
Liquid				l	r		

Figure 2.4. Phonetic symbols: American English consonants listed by place and manner of articulation.

Handwritten margin notes (left column):

voiced and unvoiced

unvoiced	voiced
θ	ð
th	th
thin	then

behind teeth (alveolars)
t d
s z

velars
back of mouth
k g ŋ

palatals
middle mouth
[č] [ǰ]
[š] [ž]

glides
[j] or [y]
yes jester
joy

oral/nasal
b m

---

[m], is a **nasal (stop).** Stops are noncontinuous phonemes. **Labiodental** consonants [f] and [v] are formed with the upper front teeth on the lower lip. If students confuse the words *mad, pad,* and *bad,* then they may not have differentiated the critical features of the three bilabial consonants, and if they write HAF for *have,* then they have confused consonants that are formed similarly except for voicing.

Farther back in the mouth, **interdental** consonants are made with the tongue between the teeth. Two related sounds are made, one unvoiced (vocal cords do not vibrate) and one voiced (vocal cords do vibrate), both of which in English are spelled with *th*: [θ] and [ð]. The unvoiced *th*, [θ], occurs in the words *thin* and *ether*; the voiced *th*, [ð], occurs in the words *then* and *either.*

When the tongue is placed behind the **alveolar** ridge, the ridge of tissue just above the back side of the teeth, five more consonants are produced. The stop consonants [t] and [d] differ from each other only in voicing and otherwise are articulated in the same place and manner. The nasal [n] is articulated in the same position. The [s] and [z] are also alveolars, again differing only in voicing. Alveolar sounds may feel very much the same when they are articulated; thus, if a student confuses *an, and,* and *ant,* then the confusion may originate with the similarity of the final phonemes ([n], [d], [t]) in place of articulation.

Three more consonants are made with the tongue raised against the soft palate in the back of the throat: [k], [g], and [ŋ]. These sounds are **velars** because the soft palate is called the **velum.** The [k] and [g] again differ only in voicing, which often leads to students' misspellings of the ending consonants of words such as *back* and *bag* and substituting [k] or [g] for the nasal [ŋ]. When students write SIG for *sing,* they are not only simply leaving out a letter but they also may be substituting a sound for another that is made in the same part of the mouth.

The **palatals** are made with the front part of the tongue on the hard palate (roof of the mouth) behind the alveolar ridge. They include the pair [č] and [ǰ] and the pair [š] and [ž], which again differ from each other only in voicing, as in the words *chest* and *jest* and the words *fission* and *vision.* The sound [š] can be spelled with an *s* as in *sugar* and *sure* but usually is spelled with *sh* as in *sheep.* The voiced sound [ž] can begin words in French, such as *genre* and *gendarme,* but does not begin any words in English. Most people are not aware it is a phoneme because it has no unique spelling in English orthography. We usually spell [ž] with an *s* as in *vision* or *measure.* The last palatal sound is a **glide,** which has two permissible phonetic symbols for the same sound, [j] or [y]. Notice that [j] is different from [ǰ]. The first represents the first sound in *yes* and *usual*; the second represents the first sound in *joy* and *jester.*

Manner of Articulation   Place of articulation is only one dimension along which consonants are classified and differentiated. The other dimension is the manner in which the air stream is obstructed as it moves through the mouth. For example, the sounds [b] and [m] are voiced bilabial sounds; the manner rather than the place of their articulation distinguishes them. One is an oral sound, and the other a nasal. Likewise, the voiceless alveolars [t] and [s] are different in manner of production, so we can distinguish the words *take* and *sake.*

Stops are to be distinguished from continuants. Stops are aptly named because the flow of air is stopped completely for a short time. Stops may be voiced or unvoiced (voiceless) depending on whether the vocal cords are engaged and vibrate as the air passes through the larynx. The oral stops include three voiced/voiceless pairs including [b] and [p], [t] and [d], and [k] and [g]. These sounds are of short duration when spoken in isolation. They cannot be slowed down and glided into a vowel during **phoneme blending** (add [d] to the beginning of *ate*). In contrast, a continuant sound can be blended smoothly without a break (add [m] to the beginning of *an*).

Are the nasal phonemes stops or continuants? That classification depends on the definition used. The sounds [m], [n], and [ŋ] are the three nasal sounds, as in *sum*, *sun*, and *sung*. Most linguists call these stops because the air flow is obstructed in the mouth or oral cavity, but they can be sustained vocally and blended with other sounds continuously because we can say the sound as long as breath is available. Technically, the nasals are stops; for teaching purposes, they can be thought of as continuants.

All of the **fricatives** are continuants. As the name implies, significant friction is created as the air in the mouth is partially obstructed and forced through a narrow space. If you hold your hand in front of your mouth, then you will feel air coming out in a continuous stream when you say [f], [v], [θ], [ð], [s], [z], [š], and [ž]. These sounds are produced with high-frequency overtones and are difficult for individuals with high-frequency hearing loss to discriminate. More than 300 years ago, during the Elizabethan period, English speakers produced a palatal fricative that remains in our spelling system as the *gh* in *knight*, *enough*, and *right*. This sound, which is no longer a part of English, is pronounced similar to the German *ch* in *Bach*, with the tongue raised as if to pronounce a [g] but not touching the back of the throat.

Affricates [č] and [ǰ] are produced with a stop closure and then an immediate release of the air. Affricates are thus a sequence of a stop and a fricative but are noncontinuant sounds. In English there are only two affricates, which differ only in voicing, as in *etch* and *edge*. Notice that the spellings used for the sounds [č] and [ǰ] after accented short vowels, *tch* and *dge*, include the stop consonants [t] and [d], consistent with the mouth position at the beginning of the production of [č] and [ǰ].

The **liquids,** [l] and [r], are the most problematic speech sounds for English articulation, reading, and spelling. These are among the later developing sounds in the speech production of many children[8] and the most difficult to teach in speech therapy because they "float" in the mouth. The liquids have no clear beginning or end point in articulation. Furthermore, the [r] is articulated quite differently depending on whether it is in the beginning of a word or after a vowel. Usually [l] is described as a lateral liquid, with the tongue raised to the alveolar ridge and the sides of the tongue held down to allow the air to escape out to the side of the tongue. The American English [r] is typically made with the tongue curled back or bunched up behind the alveolar ridge, but there is considerable variation from speaker to speaker and word to word. In some languages, such as Spanish, the liquid phoneme is trilled or tapped with the tongue more forward on the alveolar ridge. In British English, [r] may be flapped (the phonetic symbol for flapping is [ɾ]), with the tongue against the alveolar ridge, as in the British English pronunciation of *very* [vɛɾi]. In English, the liquids are voiced in most positions, but if they follow a voiceless consonant in a blend, then they may be unvoiced, as in *play* or *pray*.

Asian substitution of l and r

Some languages have no liquids at all. Others, notably Cantonese and Japanese, have only one liquid phoneme, pronounced as a flap [ɾ], and thus do not distinguish between [r] and [l]. Speakers of these Asian languages may have difficulty articulating English words with liquids, and they may substitute [l] for [r] or vice versa.

Glides, along with liquids, have vowel-like qualities and are sometimes called **semivowels.** They include [w], [ʍ], [y], and [h]. Glides are similar to vowels and always occur right before vowels. They differ from vowels, however, in that they do not form the peak of a **syllable.** The beginning sounds of *yes* and *went* do not obstruct the air stream in the mouth, and the tongue quickly moves from the glide to the vowel that follows it. Glides are never followed by another consonant in the same syllable and never are the last sound in an English word. Therefore, when the letters *y* and *w* are used in spelling words such as *boy* and *snow*, they are not representing consonant glide phonemes; they work as part of a vowel letter team to represent a vowel sound. *wh*

Voiceless glide

The voiceless glide [ʍ], which is typically spelled with a *wh*, is losing its distinctiveness in American speech. Many Americans pronounce the beginning consonants in the words *witch* and *which* the same way, although British speakers tend to retain the distinction between the voiced [w] and the voiceless [ʍ]. Because [w] and [ʍ] are formed with the lips in a rounded position, they are sometimes classified as bilabial rather than velar.

As mentioned before, [y] is also represented with the symbol [j] in the phonetic alphabet. It is a palatal glide. The position of the tongue as the [y] is formed is very similar to the vowel [i] as in *meet,* but it is not the same as the vowel [i]. When we say [y], the tongue moves quickly into the vowel that follows and does not produce the sound for the same length of time as it does when the vowel [i] is the nucleus of a syllable. Combining the glide [y] with the vowel [u] is very common in English, as in the words *use, refuse,* and *music,* and often is represented with one letter, *u,* in standard spelling. For our purposes, the combination of two phonemes [j] and [u] will be transcribed when phonetic symbols are used in transcriptions of words such as *unicorn* [junəkɔrn].

The glide [h] is formed with the glottis open and no other obstruction of the air stream. Usually the mouth anticipates the following vowel when [h] is formed, as in the difference between the position of the lips in *her* and *he.* Often, [h] is classified as a voiceless glottal fricative instead of a glide; however, [h] is not formed with the same air obstruction as the other fricatives. The [h] is usually voiced when it is both preceded and followed by a vowel, as in *Ahab, cohabitation,* or *antihistamine.*

Glottal stops, represented by [ʔ], are allophonic variations in English; that is, they are not part of the standard phoneme inventory for every speaker, but they do occur in certain dialect variations and in casual American speech. For example, some speakers say the words *bottle* or *button* with a glottal stop instead of a [t] or a flap [ɾ], as in [bɑʔl] and [bʌʔən].

Syllabic consonants are the liquids and nasals that can constitute a separate syllable. Liquids and nasals, including [l], [r], [m], and [n], are continuant consonants with vowel-like features that allow them to act as syllables. The variant or allophone of /r/ that is found on the end of a word, such as *summer* [sʌmɚ], is written as a combination of schwa and /r/. These syllabic consonants are found in words such as *mitten* [mɪʔn̩], [mɪtn̩], or [mɪtən]; *rhythm* [rɪðm̩]; *letter* [lɛɾɚ]; and *Bible* [bajbl̩]. They can also be nonsyllabic single consonants as in *need, mystery, red,* and *laugh.*

The liquids, glides, nasals, and vowels form a class of sounds known as **sonorants.** These are to be contrasted with **obstruents,** the class of sounds consisting of nonnasal stops, fricatives, and affricates. Sonorants are typically the sounds that children have the most trouble spelling, perhaps because they are more difficult to segment or pull out of the speech stream.

Exercise 2.4

Write the symbol for first and last consonants in each word. Pay attention to how the words sound, not how they are spelled.

some [s], [m]   judge [y] [y]   wide [w], [d]

knight [n], [t]   nose [n] [z]   thing [θ], [ŋ]

clear [k], [r]   shoal [ʃ] [l]   rhyme [r], [m]

write [r], [t]   which [w], [č]   phone [f], [n]

once [w], [s]   choose [č], [z]   yawn [y], [n]

thatch [θ] [č]   comb [k], [m]   hymn [h], [m]

guest [g], [t]   quest [k], [t]   gem [y], [m]

gym [y] [m]   whole [h], [l]   rouge [r] [y] [z]

pave [p] [v]   there [ð], [r]   thief [θ] [f]

Vowels and Their Articulation

What is a vowel? Most people will say "*a, e, i, o, u,* and sometimes *y,*" but English has 15 vowel sounds, not 6. *Vowels* are a class of **open,** unobstructed speech sounds that are not consonants. No syllable can be without a vowel. (Sometimes the vowel is contained in a syllabic consonant, as described previously.) The vowel is the nucleus of the syllable; the syllable is formed with consonants surrounding a vowel. Vowels are what we sing. Try singing the song "America the Beautiful" without the vowels! Now try singing it with only the vowels. That should be much easier.

Exercise 2.5

Discover and label as many vowels as you can, using the blank chart provided (Figure 2.5). Record the vowels on the chart according to mouth position. Then, compare the vowels you listed with those that appear in Table 2.1 and Figure 2.6.

Vowels are voiced

The distinguishing features of a vowel are determined by the position of the lips, tongue, and vocal cavity. All vowels are voiced and create resonance in the head. Vowels may be **stressed** or **unstressed,** spoken with tense or lax musculature, carried out for a long or brief duration, and articulated with nasal or nonnasal quality. Tongue and lip positions determine how each vowel sounds. Differences in vowel pronunciation account in large part for dialect differences in word pronunciation, so the "standard" dialect of English that appears in Figure 2.6 may not represent the vowels produced by many Americans. At least the arrangement of vowels on the chart can give us a basis for comparing dialect variations.

The Vowel Chart   Fifteen basic American English vowels can be distinguished from one another on the dimensions of tongue position (front, **mid,** back) and tongue height (**high** to **low**). One way that linguists can tell whether certain vowel phonemes exist in a language is to find two words made with the same consonants and different vowels. This set of words is a **minimal pair.** For example, in English, most vowel phonemes can be put in the blank in [b__t] to create different words (see Table 2.1); thus, we know that these vowels exist in English.

To illustrate more clearly how the vowels are distinguished by subtle changes of mouth position, Figure 2.6 shows them arranged by proximity of articulation to one another. The highest, most front vowel is [i] as in the English *meat* or Spanish *fajita*. Front high vowels are made with the mouth in a smile position. As the tongue drops step by step and the mouth opens to say each vowel in succession, [i], [ɪ], [e], [ɛ], [æ], and so forth, the jaw drops to

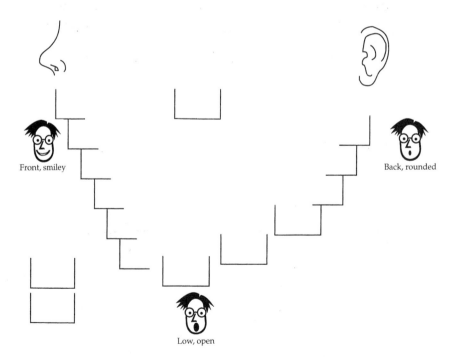

Front, smiley

Back, rounded

Low, open

Figure 2.5.   Chart for discovering the vowels. List as many vowels as possible, grouping them by mouth position.

[i] = long e sound   [a] = octopus
[ʌ] = umbrella

its most open (mid) position for [ɑ], as in the words *father* and *pot*. The diphthong [ɑj] is placed in the sequence before [ɑ] because the mouth is in a position similar to [ɑ] when the vowel is articulated.

The next vowel [ʌ], as in *putt* and *stubborn*, is sometimes perceived as being slightly in front of [ɑ] and slightly higher. It is hard to place and is sometimes referred to as an "accented schwa" [ə], the indistinct mid vowel. As the four **back vowels** are spoken in order, the mouth closes slowly: [ɔ], [o], [ʊ], and [u]. All of the back vowels are made with the lips rounded.

The difference between adjacent vowels in Figure 2.6 is a small adjustment in closure of the jaw and a small shift of tongue height. Beginning with the highest front vowel, [i] as in *beet,* one can say the vowel sequence and watch in a mirror how the mouth changes little by little. One can feel the slight drop of the jaw for each step down the vowel chart by placing one's hand under one's chin.

All of the **front vowels** are unrounded in English. They include the vowels [i] to [a]. The four last back vowels, [ɔ], [o], [ʊ], and [u], are all rounded. The lips are rounded up or shaped like a gentle *o*. (Note that front rounded vowels occur in French, as in *tu* and *vieux*, and in German, as in *Tür* and *Müle*, but not in English.)

The vowels that do not fit in the progression on the vowel chart in Figure 2.6 are the **diphthongs** [ɔj] and [æw] or [aw] (not to be confused with the phonic symbol [aw] as in *caught*) and the **schwa** [ə]. *Diphthongs are vowels that glide in the middle.* The mouth position shifts during the production of the single vowel phoneme. When you say the word *boy* [bɔj], notice how your mouth begins with a back, rounded position and shifts or glides to a front, smiley position. It shifts as well with *bow* [bæw] (as in *take a bow after a performance*) from a front position to a lip-rounded position. A third diphthong, [ɑj], is placed on the main vowel chart because of its relationship to [ɑ]. Children's spellings show that they perceive these vowels as being close together, so they will spell *light* [lɑjt] as *lot* [lɑt]. The mouth also shifts or glides at the end of the vowel [ɑj] as in *pie*. It is important, however, to real-

[ɔj] = oi

[æ] =

[ɑj] = ï
  pie
  light

Table 2.1. American English vowels: phonetic and phonic symbols

Phonetic symbol	Phonic symbol	Spelling
/i/	ē	beet
/ɪ/	ў	bit
/e/	ā	bait
/ɛ/	ĕ	bet
/æ/	ă	bat
/ɑj/	ī	bite
/ɑ/	ŏ	bottle
/ʌ/	ŭ	butt
/ɔ/	aw	bought
/o/	ō	boat
/ʊ/	oŏ	put
/u/	ū	boot
/ə/	ə	between
/ɔj/	oi, oy	boy
/æw/	ou, ow	bough

ize that the glide is a property of the vowel phoneme [ɑj], not a separate vowel, as students sometimes think.

Schwa [ə] is a mid central lax vowel. In English, the vowel in an unstressed syllable often "reduces" to schwa. For example, the base word *commerce* has an [ɑ] in the first syllable, but its derivation *commercial* reduces that first vowel to schwa when the stress shifts to the second syllable. Schwa reduction presents a problem for children learning to spell because schwa can be spelled with any of the vowel letters in standard orthography (*alone*, *effect*, *definition*, *commence*, *upon*), so students must learn the identity of vowels on the basis of other, related words or by memorization. Sometimes in phonetic alphabets a schwa that sounds more like [ɪ], as in *definition* or *squeamish*, is represented as [ɨ]. One way to recognize a schwa is that it cannot easily be "sounded out" for spelling purposes. The mid low vowel [ʌ] sounds similar to an "accented schwa" but is found in stressed syllables only, as in *but*, *butter*, and *supper*, and usually is spelled with the letter *u*.

The terms **long** and **short** are used in the terminology of **phonics** instruction but not in the language of phonetics. The terms, although traditional among teachers, do not directly describe the physical reality of vowel duration. The terms also imply that there are only two categories of vowels, ignoring the third category—diphthongs. Linguists use the terms **tense** for long vowels and **lax** for short vowels, as follows.

Long, or tense, vowels are spoken with more tension in the tongue muscles than are the short, or lax, vowels. The actual duration of the vowel, that is, how long it is spoken, is affected by the consonant that comes after the vowel as well as by the tense/lax distinction. The vowel in *bide* is longer in duration

[handwritten margin note: tense long vowels / lax short vowel]

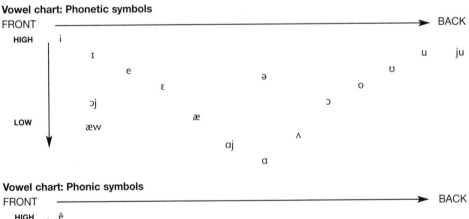

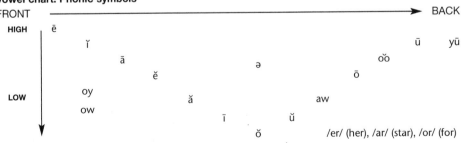

Figure 2.6. Vowel articulation: a) phonetic and b) phonic symbols.*(Sources: Bolinger & Sears, 1981; Fromkin & Rodman, 1993.)

than the vowel in *bite* because of the voiced consonant /d/ after the vowel in *bide*. Therefore, there is no valid linguistic reason for the terms long and short to be used to label vowel sounds. These labels have become part of our standard teaching vocabulary and will continue to be used, but they should not be interpreted literally. If we use these terms, then it is important to remember that the diphthongs make up the third class of vowels and that vowels followed by *r* (*r-controlled* vowels) are a special problem for phonetic transcription.

Exercise 2.6   *Kwestʃan*

1. Write your full name in phonetic transcription. Share your transcription with other people, if possible, and decode other names. For example, [luizə kʊk mots]

2. Now write the full phonetic transcription for these words:

put *ɪpʊt*   putt *pʌt*   puke *pʊk pjuk*

coin *kɔjn*   shower *ʃæwɚ*   sigh *saj*

should *ʃʊrd*   thesis *θisʌs*   chain *ʧen*

sacks *sæks*   sax *sæks*   preppy *prɛpi*

critter *krɪtɚ*   ceiling *silɪŋ*   cymbal *s___*

whether *mɛðɚ*   question *kwesʧən kwɛsʧən*   measure *mɛʒɚ*

3. Translate these words into standard English spelling:

ɔldo ðə prabləm ʌ v dɪslɛksiə ɪz nat ə kəndɪšən ʍerɪn pipl si θɪŋz bækwɚd ðə sɪmptəm ʌ v rivɚsəlz hæz bɪn ovɚpled baj ðə prɛs

Vowels in Other Languages   Many other possibilities exist for vowel production. These possibilities are exploited by languages that use **pitch, intonation, nasalization,** and vowel duration to make different phonemes. Many African, Native American, and Asian languages are tone languages in which the register (tonal quality) of a vowel will determine different meanings. In fact, most languages in the world use tonal systems for making vowels. Thai, for example, has five tones for vowels that might be difficult for an English speaker to distinguish, remember, or use: low, mid, high, falling, and rising. One of the challenges for a speaker of a tonal language learning English is to ignore variations in vowel tone and duration.

Summary

The major distinctions for understanding and teaching speech sounds and their relationship to print include the classes of consonants and vowels. Each of these classes of speech sounds has distinct features or properties, and the sounds' features can be represented by their place and manner of articulation. Identifying the existence of the speech sound inventory is not an easy or obvious task because the sounds we think of as phonemes are buried in the continuous stream of speech that makes words, phrases, and sentences.

English spelling is not a good phonetic representation of speech because it has too few symbols (26) for the more than 40 speech sounds and they are used in complex and varying ways. Therefore, a phonetic alphabet is useful for representing the component sounds in words.

Consonants *Closed Speech*

Consonants, **closed** speech sounds made with an obstruction of air, share features with each other when they are spoken in the same place in the mouth or in the same manner. The major groups of consonants, classified by manner of articulation, are stops, nasals, fricatives, affricates, glides, and liquids. These sounds can be voiced or unvoiced. English has nine pairs of consonants that are produced in the same vocal place but that differ in the presence or absence of voicing. Some phonemes are oral and others nasal. English has three nasal consonants, not two. Consonants can also be described by their placement in the back (glottal), middle (velar and alveolar), or front (interdental, labiodental, and bilabial) of the mouth.

Vowel open speech

A vowel is an open speech sound that forms the nucleus of a syllable. Vowels are classified on the dimensions of front, mid, and back as well as high to low. The front vowels are unrounded, but the back vowels are made with a rounding of the lips. Vowels may be tense, lax, or diphthongs. As the next chapter discusses in greater depth, vowels also may have tone, stress, nasality, and length. English is a nontonal language, but the majority of the world's languages do produce vowels with specific pitch.

Within these general classes of sounds, there is a great deal of both systematic and random variation in how the sounds are produced. Random variation occurs from speaker to speaker depending on individual characteristics and dialect. Systematic variation occurs when **phonological rules,** shared by speakers of the language, determine how speech sounds are produced. The rule system for speech production is the subject of the next chapter.

Supplementary Exercises

2.7   Determine what these groups of speech sounds have in common:

    a)   [t], [d], [n], [s], [z]

    b)   [m], [n], [ŋ]

    c)   [r], [l], [y], [w], [h], [m], [n], [ŋ]

    d)   [k], [g], [ŋ]

    e)   [t], [g], [d], [k], [p], [b]

    f)   [u], [ʊ], [o], [ɔ]

2.8   Write an example of the following type of speech sound:

    a)   Rounded back high vowel

    b)   Mid front lax vowel

    c)   Voiced velar nasal

    d)   Unvoiced interdental fricative

    e)   Voiced affricate

    f)   Lateral liquid

    g)   Diphthong that begins with lip rounding

2.9   Contrast the sounds in the following minimal pairs of words. How do the sounds differ from one another, and how are they alike?

    a)   tee<u>th</u>, tee<u>the</u>

    b)   c<u>o</u>ne, c<u>o</u>n

    c)   ri<u>ch</u>, ri<u>dge</u>

    d)   lea<u>f</u>, lea<u>ve</u>

    e)   <u>p</u>ap, <u>m</u>ap

2.10   Write the phonetic symbol for the last phoneme in the following words. (Avoid being fooled by the spelling!)

cheese _____	laugh _____	enjoy _____
attached _____	baby _____	collage _____
Xerox _____	aglow _____	
you _____	wealth _____	

2.11   On a separate sheet of paper, write the following poem (from "The World Is Too Much with Us" by William Wordsworth) in phonetic transcription. Brackets are optional in this exercise.

The world is too much with us; late and soon,
Getting and spending, we lay waste our powers:
Little we see in Nature that is ours;
We have given our hearts away, a sordid boon!
This Sea that bares her bosom to the moon;
The winds that will be howling at all hours,
And are up-gathered now like sleeping flowers;
For this, for everything, we are out of tune;
It moves us not.

2.12   On a separate sheet of paper, translate the following poem (author unknown) from phonetic symbols to standard English spelling:

ɑj tek ɪt ju ɔlrɛdi no
ʌv tʌf ænd bæw ænd kɔf ænd do
sʌm me stʌmbəl bʌt nɑt ju
ɔn hɪkəp θʌro slæw ænd θru
so næw ju ɑr rɛdi pɛrhæps
tu lɛrn ʌ v lɛs fəmɪljɚ træps
biwɛr ʌ v hɚd ə drɛdful wɚd
ðæt lʊks lɑjk bird ænd sæwndz lɑjk bɚd
ænd dɛd ɪts sɛd lɑjk bɛd nɑt bid
for gʊdnɛs sek dont kɔl ɪt did

2.13   Here are some spelling errors (followed by correct spellings) made by sixth-grade students. Match the spelling errors to the type of error they represent:

WOSUT/wasn't   CLORER/color   INGLISH/English
LEDR/letter   SINGIG/singing   SGARY/scary
STASUN/station   FOWD/food

a)   Nasal omission or deletion

b)   Liquid confusion

c)   Voiced/voiceless stop substitution

d)   Fricative substitution

e)   Flap for a medial stop

f)   Back vowel substitution

g)   Front vowel substitution

h)   Oral (nonnasal) for a nasal

Endnotes

1.   Ashby et al., 2009; Liberman et al., 1989; Rayner et al., 2001.
2.   Ehri, 2004; National Institute of Child Health and Human Development, 2000.
3.   Fromkin et al., 2003, for example, list 25 consonants and 15 vowels in English; Owens, 1992, lists 24 consonants and 20 vowels.
4.   Balmuth, 2009; Fromkin et al., 2003; Owens, 1992; and Yule, 1996, all use different descriptions of sounds in English, especially for vowels.
5.   Fromkin et al., 2003.
6.   Hanna, Hanna, Hodges, & Rudorf, 1966.
7.   Fromkin et al., 2003.
8.   Owens, 1992.

Additional Resources

Akmajian, A., Demers, R.A., Farmer, A.K., & Harnish, R.M. (1995). *Linguistics: An introduction to language and communication* (4th ed.). Cambridge, MA: MIT Press.

Edwards, H.T. (1992). *Applied phonetics: The sounds of American English.* San Diego: Singular Publishing Group.

Fromkin, V., Rodman, R., & Hyams, N. (2003). *An introduction to language* (7th ed.). Boston: Heinle.

Ladefoged, P. (1993). *A course in phonetics* (3rd ed.). Orlando, FL: Harcourt Brace & Co.

Moats, L.C. (2003). *The speech sounds of English* [video]. Longmont, CO: Sopris West Educational Services.

Moats, L.C. (2004). *LETRS interactive CD: The speech sounds of English.* Longmont, CO: Sopris West Educational Services.

Moats, L.C. (2009). *Language essentials for teachers of reading and spelling: Module 2. The speech sounds of English: Phonetics, phonology, and phoneme awareness* (2nd ed.). Longmont, CO: Sopris West Educational Services.

Phonology
Speech Sounds in Use

By the end of this chapter, you will understand:

- The structure and pronunciation of spoken syllables

- Aspects of phonological processing important for literacy

- The development of phonological awareness

- The use of minimal pairs to contrast phonemes

- Schwas, flapping, and the nasalization of vowels

- The influence of phonology on children's spelling

- General principles for teaching phonological awareness

Phonology is the study of the speech sound system of any language, including the rules and patterns by which phonemes are combined into words and phrases. The word *phonology* refers both to the sound patterns themselves and to the discipline of studying those sound patterns and their mental representations.

The previous chapter describes and classifies the inventory of speech sounds in English, but the description of individual sounds does not account for many other phenomena that are part of the speech sound system of a language. For example, speech sounds are combined only in certain sequences within a language system. We can say [dɑks] but not [dksɑ]. The frequency with which sounds occur within syllables varies. "Short," or lax, vowels are more common in English than are diphthongs.[1] Some speech sounds occur only in certain parts of syllables and in combination with certain other sounds. For example, a glide such as [j] or [h] is always followed by a vowel, and [ŋ] is always preceded by a vowel.

Speakers of a language know that some speech sound sequences seem more pleasing than others, some are "foreign," and some vary considerably from speaker to speaker. Recognizing that a word sounds "foreign" may also coincide with an inability to pronounce the unfamiliar sounds of the word, such as the last sound of *Bach* in German. When we make up new words in our own language, such as words for new products, they are likely to sound similar to words we already know. We change certain sounds automatically in continuous speech without thinking about what we are doing and without changing the meaning. For example, if you say the words *would you* in a normal sentence such as, "Would you run to the mailbox for me?" you probably would say something such as [wʊǰu rʌn]. If each sound were isolated, the utterance would be [wʊd ju]. Finally, we are aware that stress patterns affect the meaning of words such as *contract* and *reject*, which can be either nouns or verbs (e.g., *cóntract* versus *contráct*). This kind of knowledge includes more than the ability to pronounce the individual speech sounds (phonetics); it also encompasses awareness of the sound patterns and the rules by which the speech sounds are combined and spoken (phonology).

Knowledge of phonology and its role in learning to speak, read, and spell is essential for teachers of literacy. Individuals who have reading, writing, and language processing problems often demonstrate weaknesses in this language domain. To teach awareness of speech sounds, the teacher needs to judge what sounds and words to use, in what sequence, for how long, and for whom. The teacher must decide how much of a lesson to dedicate to speech sound awareness, how to interpret student errors, and how to give corrective feedback to students who are confused. Teaching sound–symbol correspondences is much more effective when it includes explicit, accurate information about units of speech and print. This chapter, therefore, is focused on the concepts that are most applicable to teaching the connection of spoken to written language. It also considers the broader context of phonological processing and its role in learning to read and spell.

Sequences, Syllables, and Stress

When a teacher plays Hangman with a class of children who already know something about spelling, some children will make logical guesses about the letter sequences in words and some will not. The children who make logical guesses not only are better at keeping track of which letters have been asked already but also have a better sense of the order in which sounds and letters occur in words. They realize, often intuitively, that words in their language are formed from certain permissible sequences of phonemes. These possibilities are influenced by ease of pronunciation, but often the sequences are arbitrary and simply part of the grammar of the language.

Suppose that you were asked to create possible or pronounceable words in English using only these four phonemes:

/ŋ/   /l/   /ɛ/   /b/

The only sequence that would be possible is [blɛŋ]. No words in English can start with /ŋ/; no blends start with /l/; no beginning blends have /ŋ/ as the second phoneme; and there is no sequence [ŋb] or [bŋ] in English syllables. So, the only pronounceable option is [bl] in the beginning, with [ɛ] and [ŋ] following.

When words begin with an affricate, a liquid, a glide, or a nasal, the next sound must be a vowel. In English, we cannot create words such as *yburtz*, *lgas*, or *chwot* for this reason. There can be no more than three consonant sounds at the beginning of a word, and these are limited to the following possibilities in first, second, and third position: /s/ + /p, t, k/ + /l, r, w, y/. Thus, we have the words *sprain* [sprẽn], *strain* [strẽn], *square* [skwer], and *spew* [spju] beginning with these three-consonant sequences. (*Note:* The tilde [˜] over the vowel denotes nasalization.) Not all sequences of these elements are possible, however; we can say the word *strict* but not the word *stlict*.

A regular, predictable sequence of sounds occurs whenever a nasal phoneme comes after a vowel and before another consonant. Consider these words (note that the [ŋ] in the third column of words is spelled with *n*):

[m]	[n]	[ŋ]
jump	gentle	jungle
jumble	gender	junk
symbiotic	sentinel	singular
sympathy	send	sink

From the examples, can you determine which consonants follow each of the nasal consonants [m], [n], and [ŋ]? Sound sequences in spoken words are often arranged so that the sounds are articulated in the same place in the mouth. Similarity of placement contributes to ease of pronunciation. Try the next exercise to discover this rule.

 **Exercise 3.1**

Find at least nine more examples of words that have a nasal consonant before another stop consonant within a syllable. These sequences will be in syllable-ending blends or clusters. Sort them into those that have /m/, /n/, or /ŋ/ after the vowel, and look at the consonant that follows each nasal sound. What is the principle that governs how these sounds are sequenced?

Examples: /m/: gli<u>mp</u>se   /n/: de<u>nt</u>al   /ŋ/: la<u>ng</u>uish

In all English words, the bilabial nasal phoneme [m] precedes the bilabial stop consonants [p] and [b]; the alveolar nasal phoneme [n] precedes the alveolar stop consonants [t] and [d]; and the velar phoneme [ŋ] precedes the velars [k] and [g]. When children say "punkin" [pʌ̃ŋkĭn] for *pumpkin*, they are applying this rule automatically. After deleting the elusive [p], they must articulate a nasal consonant, [ŋ], that is in the same mouth placement as the consonant that follows it, [k].

Syllables

Words comprise phonemes, but those phonemes are organized into coarticulated units—syllables—that always have a vowel sound. A word always has at least one syllable because it always has at least one vowel sound. The number of syllables is equivalent to the number of vowel sounds in the word.

Simple and Complex   As mentioned in Chapter 2, phonemes are an abstraction. We do not pronounce separate phonemes when we speak. We coarticulate them as an unbroken unit. For this discussion, syllables are not units of print but are units of speech organized around a vowel, and they may be simple or complex. A **simple syllable** has a vowel that may be preceded and/or followed by a single consonant (*me* [mi], *at* [æt], *pipe* [pɑjp]; a **complex syllable** has two or more consonants in a cluster before or after a vowel (*act* [ækt]; *blimp* [blɪmp]; *squeeze* [skwiz]). Syllables may have any of the following combinations of consonants (C) or vowels (V), in progression from most simple to most complex (C and V refer to *phonemes*):

Syllable structure	Example	Syllable structure	Example
V	I	CVCC	cans
CV	me	CCVCC	stops
VC	ice	CCCVC	scream
VCC	ask	CCCVCC	squeaks
CVC	sack	CCVCCC	starts
CCV	ski	CCCVCCC	scrimped
CCVC	skin		

Note again that the examples listed here demonstrate sequences of consonant and vowel sounds, not letters; therefore, *ice* [ɑjs] is two phonemes, a
vowel and a consonant.

Complex syllables that contain consonant clusters (blends) are more difficult for children to read and spell than simple syllables because many of
their errors involve omitting or substituting sounds in consonant clusters,
especially the internal sound in a cluster.[2] When consonants exist in clusters
before or after vowels, they are difficult to segment because the phonemes
tend to be stuck tightly together in articulation. Phonetically, the duration of
consonant pronunciation is often shorter within a cluster.

Children's ability to identify all of the sounds in consonant clusters
tends to develop after reading instruction is started, after kindergarten for
many typical 5- and 6-year-olds. Therefore, the complexity of syllable structure is important to consider in choosing words for phoneme awareness,
decoding, and spelling instruction. The word *blast* is not simply a word with
more sounds than the word *bat*; it is linguistically more difficult to pronounce and learn because of the presence of two blends. Words with three
sound blends are more challenging than two sound blends, and two sound
blends are more challenging than single consonants before or after a vowel.

Syllable Boundaries in Speech and Print   Most people who
understand the definition of a syllable will have little trouble identifying
how many syllables are in a word. The boundaries between syllables, however, may be cause for disagreement because the natural breaks between syllables do not correspond to the syllable division rules used by editors and in
dictionaries and because syllable boundaries are simply ambiguous, even to
linguists. The word *yell* is one syllable, and the word *yellow* is two, but where
is the boundary in the second word? Is the [l] part of the first syllable, part
of the second, or part of both? (The doubled letter is a spelling convention,
not a reflection of phonological reality; there is only one segment [l] in *yellow*.) There are rules that tell us where to divide words in print (see Chapter
4), but our judgment—and that of linguists—about where spoken words
divide often differs from those conventions.

Onsets and Rimes   Although scholars may disagree about where
syllables begin and end, they do agree on a few basic ideas about these natural linguistic units. First, every syllable must have a vowel, and each separate vowel constitutes the **peak** of a syllable. When two vowel sounds are
adjacent, as in *idiot, poetry,* or *idea*, there is a syllable division between the
vowels (*id-i-ot; po-et-ry; i-de-a*). Second, consonants tend to cluster at the
beginning of a stressed syllable rather than at the end of an unstressed syllable. In the word *astringent*, the *str* begins the stressed syllable; therefore,
speakers who are asked to find the natural boundaries in the word are likely
to divide the word like this: *a-strin-gent*. Finally, sequential order rules for
allowable consonant sequences govern our perceptions of syllable boundaries. The word *only* has to be divided between the /n/ and the /l/ because
these two consonants cannot form a cluster within a syllable; they can only
be adjacent across a syllable boundary. Similarly, *pumpkin* has to be divided

between the /p/ and the /k/ because /pk/ is not an allowable consonant cluster. The existence of these phonological properties of syllables can assist children in deciding where the boundaries of multisyllabic written words are located.

Syllables are much more than strings of phonemes. They have an internal structure composed of the **onset** (what, if anything, comes before the vowel) and the **rime** (the vowel and what comes after it). Words do not always have an onset; for example, the words *egg* and *itch* do not have an onset and are structured as rimes. A word always has a rime because it includes the vowel. The vowel belongs to a part of the rime that is the peak. The peak is the part of the syllable with the most sonority or resonance. The consonants that follow the vowel in the rime are usually called the **coda.** For example, the syllable *trust* has an onset [tʰr] and a rime with a peak [ʌ] and a coda [st], as shown in the following tree diagram:

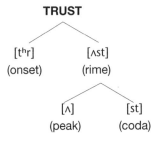

TRUST

[tʰr] [ʌst]
(onset) (rime)

[ʌ] [st]
(peak) (coda)

Linguists debate whether a sonorant consonant following a vowel can also be part of the syllable peak. In the word *went* [wɛ̃nt], the vowel is nasalized, and the nasal consonant is closely bonded to the vowel. Some argue that the nasal consonant coheres with the vowel so much that it, too, is part of the syllable peak, not the coda, which would be /t/ alone. In contrast, the /t/ in *wet* does not adhere to the vowel and is clearly the coda, not part of the peak. Thus, the internal structure of the word varies according to the features or properties of the phonemes and their sequences. The syllable peak includes an inseparable combination of a vowel and a following consonant when the consonant is a liquid /l/ or /r/, such as in *bell, will, fur, her,* and *bird.* That is why children so often confuse the letters in words such as CLOD for *cold,* BRID for *bird,* and GRIL for *girl.* The vowel and the following liquid operate as a unit in the syllable peak, and the printed form of words containing such sound combinations is deceptive. Vowels followed by /r/ are even more cohesive units than those followed by /l/ because the sonority of /r/ is only slightly less than the sonority of a vowel and is greater than that of any other consonant.[3] Nasals seem to adhere both to the peak and to the coda of the rime, spreading out their features in both directions, but other consonants (stops, fricatives, affricates) adhere clearly to the coda.

Even if this discussion seems somewhat abstract, it will make more sense when children's spelling and reading are analyzed closely. When a child spells BRID for *bird* or GRIL for *girl,* the child is making a very sensible linguistic choice. There is no auditory discrimination problem in such instances; the child is writing what, in fact, is in the word—a vowel and a liquid consonant that have become one unit. Therefore, the teacher cannot say, "Sound it out," and expect to get better results. The teacher must teach the spellings of *r*-controlled vowels as units (*er, ir, ur, ar, or*) and teach groups of words with each spelling pattern while offering students much practice reading and writing the words in meaningful sentences.

How to Teach Syllable Awareness   A few time-honored techniques can help students detect the number of syllables in spoken words. Ask students to hold their lips together while saying a multisyllable word aloud, such as *window, porcupine,* or *elevator.* Each vocalization required to say a vowel sound will be an audible syllable. Or, ask them to say the word with their hand placed under their chin. Each drop of the jaw is a syllable.

Prosodic Features: Stress and Intonation Patterns

The phonological layer of language also encompasses intonation, phrasing, and stress patterns on words, phrases, and sentences. English does not have a tonal system for vowel production, but the intonation of a phrase does help determine its meaning and resolve any ambiguity that may ensue from the order of words. These sentences may illustrate the importance of intonation and phrasing:

Marcia did say she was going, didn't she?
Marcia did say she was going, didn't she.

I *expect* her to show up later.
I expect *her* to show up later.
I expect her to show up *later.*

The phrase stress in a sentence will determine which of a number of possible meanings is intended by a single word string. Stress will occur on the nouns, verbs, adjectives, and/or adverbs that should carry the central meaning. Whole phrases and sentences are changed by stress and intonation patterns in which one syllable (usually the most meaningful word) is stressed more than the others. A sentence that ends with a downward contour in English can affect how well children remember or process sentences during writing or speaking. Sometimes a child's writing will contain clear examples of his or her "losing" the unstressed parts of words and phrases (see Figure 3.1).

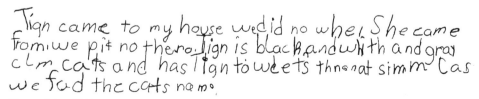

Figure 3.1.   Writing sample from K.T., a second-grade student. When asked to read her writing aloud, K.T. said (with some difficulty deciphering her own writing), "Tiger came to our house. We did not know what to do. We put it on the radio. Tiger is black and white and gray colored cat and has tiger. For two weeks then at swimming lessons we found the cat's owner."

Any multisyllabic word will have a primary stress and sometimes a secondary stress applied as part of the word's form. Individuals with phonological processing weaknesses often have trouble achieving awareness of stress in a word, phrase, or sentence, even though they speak with standard intonation patterns. Some stress patterns may vary according to region or dialect, but most are standard enough to merit a preferred pronunciation by writers of dictionaries. A few are a matter of choice; *eleméntary* and *eleméntary* are two accepted versions of this word. How do you say the word *address*? Pronouncing morphologically related words, such as *philosophy* and *philosophical*, that shift the stress from one syllable to the next are challenging for students with a weak sense of phonology. Chapter 5 provides more information about patterns with phonological shifts.

Aspects of Phonological Processing

Phonological processing is an umbrella term pertaining to all the jobs of the phonological processing system in the brain. Phonological processing is assumed to be an **underlying** component of all language tasks. It encompasses the mental formation, retention, and/or use of speech codes in memory. Speech codes in memory are used during the performance of language operations including listening to and understanding speech; remembering words and phrases; learning and remembering the names for objects and ideas; reading an alphabetic writing system; and writing. Phonological processes are employed unconsciously in listening and speaking. Reading and writing, however, often require conscious awareness of the phonological aspects of speech.

The speech codes, or **phonological representations,** that are used for language operations are mental images of the features of the sounds in words. When we know a word, we know the sequence of speech sounds and the stress patterns (accents) in that word well enough to say it and recognize it as a unique entity. Phonological codes must be detailed to allow us to distinguish similar-sounding words, such as *entomology* and *etymology, reverent* and *relevant,* and *playdough* and *Plato.* Phonological mental codes may be wrongly specified, incomplete, or unstable in students who have phonological processing weaknesses.[4] Those codes may be insufficient to support the sound–symbol matching process necessary to read and write.

Phonological processing is an integral part of oral language processing because words by definition have sound, meaning, and roles in sentences. Phonological processing encompasses three kinds of oral language skills: speech perception and production; phonological memory, retrieval, and naming; and metalinguistic awareness of phonological elements.[5] These oral language functions are the foundation for efficient processing of alphabetic writing systems.

Speech Perception and Production

Speech perception and production are among the unconscious activities carried out by the phonological processor. **Speech perception,** also referred to as a receptive language skill, includes the abilities to distinguish between words that sound almost alike (e.g., *dusk/dust; fill/fail*) and recognize any word that has been spoken. Speech is perceived by the brain as a set of acoustic signals or sound frequencies formed by the vocal actions of a speaker. **Phoneme discrimination** or **speech discrimination** are terms used for the ability to distinguish words that differ only in one phoneme. The term *auditory discrimination* is sometimes used in discussions of speech sound perception, but it is not used in this book because it is too general and does not reference the important differences between linguistic and nonlinguistic processing of sound.

Speech production is an expressive language skill and includes articulating or pronouncing speech sounds and speech–sound sequences. Speech production errors may involve substituting one sound for another (e.g., *weal* for *real; dat* for *that*); omitting a sound (e.g., *mus* for *must*); adding a sound (e.g., *artheritis* for *arthritis*); or distorting a sound (e.g., *shtate* for *state*). Such errors may be driven by faulty phonological processing or by the inability to coordinate the speech articulators at a more peripheral level. SLPs are trained to distinguish these two kinds of expressive language difficulties.

Speech production tasks that tap into phonological processes include pronouncing challenging words such as *specific, Methodist, Episcopal,* and *nuclear catastrophe.* They also include repetition of tongue twisters, such as *Peter Piper picked a peck of pickle peppers,* or fast repetition of a single word that is difficult to say.

Phonological Memory, Retrieval, and Naming

Retaining phonological information in memory, retrieving phonological information from memory, and naming stimuli are also important phonological processes. These memory and naming processes play a substantial role in reading and writing and are often weak in students who experience difficulties with literacy acquisition.

Phonological memory, or **phonological working memory (PWM),** refers to temporary mental storage of speech stimuli. PWM is like a looping tape on an old telephone answering machine. It has limited storage space and holds verbal information only long enough for us to extract meaning. Stimuli are "taped over" constantly as we listen to and comprehend speech. We experience the limited capacity of our PWM systems when we try to remember a telephone number long enough to write it down or recite a series of numbers backward; remember the directions to a destination; hold two words in mind while we compare them; or hold what we just read in mind while we read the next section of a book.

We tax students' PWMs when we ask them to retell what they have heard, follow a series of directions, or repeat sentences before writing them down. Only some of what we hear or read is extracted from PWM and sent to storage in **long-term memory (LTM).**

When speech information is translated into mental representations it is said to be **encoded** into memory. (The term *encode* also has another meaning: to spell by sound.) Tasks that measure the PWM span (amount of speech information that can be held in the memory "loop") include short-term and delayed recall of verbally presented information, including lists of words, numbers, or speech sounds. If an individual is having trouble encoding incoming speech codes into PWM or LTM, then the quality of the mental code may be degraded. Degraded mental representations of speech, in turn, will affect ease and accuracy of word retrieval.

Phonological retrieval, retrieval of the phonological form of a word from LTM, refers to the mental act of formulating and pronouncing the word. When we cannot retrieve words that have been stored in memory, we may experience a "tip of the tongue" phenomenon, or we may "draw a blank" even though we think we know what we want to say. Or, we may retrieve a word that resembles the word we want to say but it is inaccurate. Retrieval problems may originate with poorly specified or degraded phonological codes (representations) in memory or with the retrieval process itself. The speaker may produce often humorous approximations of target words, as in:

Texas is having tarantula rains.
My ear infection is giving me Virgo.
The eye doctor doesn't think I need Cadillac surgery.

Naming is a kind of verbal retrieval that involves extracting a word from the mental dictionary or **lexicon** where words are filed in memory. Naming involves producing a verbal label for a visually presented stimulus, such as a person, object, or picture. Rapid serial naming, or **rapid automatic naming (RAN),** is a structured task used in assessing literacy-related learning problems. In a serial naming task, stimuli such as objects, colors, letters, or numbers are repeated in rows and must be named as quickly as possible within a time limit. **Confrontation naming** is a term used for timed tests of labeling a series of pictures of objects. There has been considerable theoretical debate about what these tasks measure,[6] but they do add predictive power to assessments of early reading ability.

Most people can use language effectively for communication purposes without having to think consciously of the sound, word, or phrase structures they are using. The next set of phonological skills requires conscious thinking about the forms and functions of language and are the most closely related to reading and writing.

Phonological Awareness

Phonological awareness refers to a metalinguistic facility with spoken word analysis.[7] Phonological awareness is the ability to identify, think about, and mentally manipulate the parts of words, including spoken syllables, onsets and rimes, and phonemes. Recognizing and producing rhymes also draws on phonological awareness to some extent. Activities that teach phonological awareness cultivate a student's ability to think about the internal details of the spoken word.

Spoken words can be analyzed, compared, and/or changed at three levels: the syllable, onset and rime, and phoneme. Mental manipulations of these units can involve substituting, deleting, adding, or reordering word parts. Table 3.1 explains and gives examples of the three units of word analysis.

Phoneme awareness and **phonemic awareness** are interchangeable terms that refer to one aspect of phonological awareness. Phoneme aware-

Table 3.1.   Units of word analysis, with examples

Unit of analysis	Sample activity
Syllable	
A unit of speech organized around a vowel sound. *win-ter* *tri-um-phant* *cre-a-tiv-i-ty*	With your hand under your chin, feel your jaw drop as you say each syllable. *o-strich* *el-e-phant* *hip-po-po-ta-mus*
Onset and rime	
Two parts of any syllable. The onset is the consonant(s) that comes before the vowel in a syllable; the rime is the vowel plus any consonant(s) that follows. *-ash* *l-ash* *spl-ash* A syllable must have a rime. An onset is optional. The activity of rhyming involves the recognition and production of words with the same rimes.	Orally blend the two pieces of a syllable together. *st + eam = steam* *z + ip = zip*
Phoneme	
The smallest segment of sound that distinguishes words in a language system. *chose* = /ch/ /ō/ /z/ [čoz] *those* = /th/ /ō/ /z/ [ðoz] *these* = /th/ /ē/ /z/ [ðiz] *threes* = /th/ /r/ /ē/ /z/ [θriz]	Say all the sounds in the word; as you say each sound, hold up one finger for that sound. *etch* = /e/ /ch/ [ɛč] *now* = /n/ /ou/ [næw] *heard* = /h/ /er/ /d/ [hɛrd]

ness is demonstrated by any *oral language* task that requires attending to, thinking about, or intentionally manipulating the individual phonemes in spoken words and syllables. Phonological awareness activities do not involve print. If letters or letter–sound correspondences are part of the task, then the task is one of phonics.

Phoneme awareness is acquired gradually. By the end of kindergarten, most children can segment and blend words with three or four phonemes, especially if they have had some instruction. A substantial number, however, find this apparently simple task very difficult. Of all the phonological skills, the ability to identify, manipulate, and remember strings of speech sounds accounts for a significant portion of the difference between good readers and poor readers.[8] The same relationship holds for learning to spell: Those who learn to spell easily usually have well-developed phoneme awareness, and the poorest spellers usually have phonological processing weaknesses.[9]

The Development of Phonological Awareness

Awareness of subword linguistic units and the ability to consciously manipulate them progresses along a continuum that has been documented in research. Paulson[10] examined the phonological development of eighty 4- and 5-year-old preschool children and documented the relative difficulty of 10 phonological tasks for this age group. The tasks included the following:

Rhyming	Detection (Which words rhyme? *Goat, say, boat*)
	Production (Tell me a word that rhymes with *sock.*)

Alliteration	Detection (Which picture starts with the same sound as *zoo?*)
	Categorization (Find all the things that start with /m/.)

Blending	Syllables (Put this word together: *kan-ga-roo.*)
	Onset/rime units (Put this word together: *s-ink.*)
	Phonemes (Put this word together: *sh-ee-p.*)

Segmenting	Syllables (Say the syllables in *Melanie.*)
	Onset/rime units (Break *van* into two parts.)
	Phonemes (Say three sounds in *mouse*; move a chip into a box as you say each sound.)

Every 6 months, there were significant changes in the developing phonological awareness of the children. Table 3.2 summarizes the order of difficulty of these tasks for children in the study. The developmental continuum of phonological awareness skills, in this study and others,[11] demonstrates two principles that underlie the order in which skills are acquired. First, children can analyze words by syllables at age 4 but only gradually learn to analyze words by their constituent phonemes. Phoneme awareness is relatively more difficult than syllable or onset/rime awareness. Progressive differentiation of the syllable into its smallest units is learned over time. Second, activities that involve matching sounds in words are easier than activities that require isolation, production, or recall of sounds in words. The greater the demand on PWM and the greater the demand on retrieval of vocabulary, the more difficult will be the phonological awareness task.

Table 3.2 identifies the skills for both age groups that were the easiest to the most difficult. Before entering kindergarten, young children certainly were developing phonological awareness skills, but they had *not* yet developed competent levels of phonemic awareness.

Table 3.2. Rank order of phonological awareness tasks from easiest to most difficult, with percentage of students able to complete each task successfully

Rank	Task	4-year-olds	5-year-olds	Both
1	Blending syllables	84%	92%	88%
2	Segmenting syllables	62%	81%	70%
3	Rhyme detection	58%	74%	67%
4	Alliteration categorization	53%	71%	63%
5	Blending onset/rime units	42%	61%	49%
6	Alliteration detection	32%	57%	47%
7	Rhyme production	31%	54%	43%
8	Blending phonemes	13%	29%	21%
9	Segmenting onset/rime	8%	22%	15%
10	Segmenting phonemes	3%	7%	5%

From Paulson, Lucy Hart. (2004). *The development of phonological awareness skills in preschool children: From syllables to phonemes.* Ed.D. dissertation, University of Montana, United States—Montana. Retrieved January 28, 2010, from Dissertations & Theses: Full Text. (Publication No. AAT 3166292).

This kind of evidence confirms the abstract and elusive nature of the phoneme. When we hear speech, the incoming signal is an unsegmented, continuous stream of sound. A spectrogram recording (Figure 3.2) of spoken words shows the production of speech sounds as a coarticulated unit without any actual acoustic divisions between one phoneme and the next. Our minds, however, perceive or interpret the acoustic input in a way that leads us to believe that phonemes are discrete, identifiable segments. To perceive phonemes, our brain must translate an unsegmented acoustic signal into segments that are perceived categorically. For example, we hear one burst of sound if someone says [bɪd], but we classify the acoustic signal as a sequence of three separable speech sounds, /b/ /ɪ/ /d/. The classification process is a consequence of central linguistic processing, a special capability of the human brain.

Phonemes and Minimal Pairs

The phoneme is the smallest segment that is used to create a new word. A minimal pair is when words differ only in one speech sound and all of the others are identical. For example, the following are minimal pairs for the sounds /t/ and /d/:

damper   reteam   rode
tamper   redeem   wrote

Notice that the term *minimal pair* refers to the sequence of speech sounds, not the conventional spellings; the sounds may be similar even though the spellings differ. Phonemes distinguish words or determine the difference between one word and another. If a linguist seeks to document the phonological system of an unfamiliar language, then his or her first test for whether a sound is a phoneme is to identify a minimal pair of words in which a target sound replaces a sound in one word to make a different word.

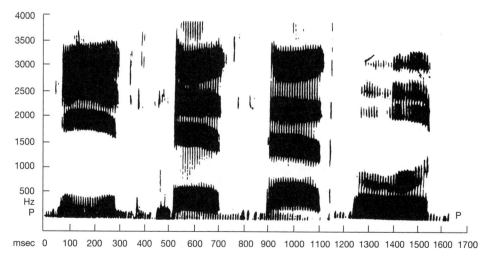

Figure 3.2. Spectrogram of the words *heed, head, had,* and *who'd,* as spoken by a person with a British accent. (*Key:* Hz, hertz; msec, milliseconds.) (Figure from AN INTRODUCTION TO LANGUAGE, Sixth Edition [p. 364], by Victoria A. Fromkin and Robert Rodman copyright © 1998 by Holt, Rinehart and Winston, reproduced by permission of the publisher.)

Phonemes are formally described by linguists in terms of their distinctive features. We identified some of those features in Chapter 2. Each distinctive feature is a controllable aspect of articulation that a phoneme either has or does not have. For example, the feature voiced is either present (shown by a plus sign) or not present (shown by a minus sign). The phoneme [b] is [+voiced] and the phoneme [p] is [–voiced]. Both [b] and [p] share the features [+labial] and [+consonantal]. The phoneme [m] shares the features [+labial], [+consonantal], and [+anterior] with [p] and [b] but is also [+nasal], whereas the others are [–nasal]. Each phoneme is essentially a combination of features such as these and others. A partial description of the phoneme [s] is [–syllabic] [+consonantal] [–sonorant] [–voiced] [+continuant] [–nasal] [+strident] [–lateral] [+anterior]. Here are more examples of minimal pairs and minimal sets of words in English:

Consonant voicing	Place of articulation	Continuancy	Lateral/central
teeth	leaf	leash	seer
teethe	lease	leech	seal

Vowel placement

bowel	bought	pin	cot	put
bile	boat	pen	caught	putt
boil	boot	pan	cut	pout

Minimal pairs are important because they represent the level of precision in word analysis that a person with fully developed phonological awareness has achieved. If students can distinguish the sounds in minimal pairs of words and identify which sound makes one word different from another, then they are likely to have attained a level of awareness that will fully support word recognition, spelling, and vocabulary development. In instruction, minimal pairs of words can be used for sound substitution tasks and word comparisons.

Phonetic Variation and Allophones

The difference between phonology and phonetics, the psychological perception of speech segments and the actual physical production of them, can be illustrated with the concept of phonetic variation. **Allophones** are phonetic variations that are still perceived as part of the same category of sound (phoneme). Allophones are slightly different pronunciations of a phoneme that are still recognizable as the target phoneme. Allophones exist because phonemes are affected by coarticulation or the "saying together" of clusters of phonemes. Whether phonemes occur in initial, medial, or final position in a syllable, their features will change slightly depending on the sounds that surround them. Allophonic variations, however, do not create new words; thus, they are not perceived as separate phonemes.

To illustrate, the words *table, swept, bitter,* and *tray* all have the phoneme /t/; that is, if you were asked to identify the sound represented by the letter *t* in those words, you would say /t/. All of the sounds that we identify or classify as /t/ in our minds are in fact spoken slightly differently. The first sound in *table* is aspirated, or articulated with a push of breath that does not characterize the articulation of the [t] on the end of *swept*, and is notated as [tʰ] to indicate the aspiration. The letters *tt* in *bitter* are pronounced as a tongue flap [ɾ] with the tongue coming up behind the teeth; the tongue taps the alveolar ridge only briefly, and the vocal cords keep vibrating throughout. The /t/ before an /r/, as in *tray*, is pronounced with affrication, close to the sound of [č]. Many children in fact will spell *tray* as CHRA until they are deliberately taught that the *tr* blend sounds as though it should be spelled *chr* but is to be recognized as *tr*. But we would not think that the word *tray* pronounced with [t] was a different word from the *tray* pronounced with a beginning sound close to [č]. We would not think that the word *swept* pronounced with an aspirated [tʰ] was a different word from the *swept* pronounced without an aspirated [tʰ].

Some phonetic variations are nonsystematic. That is, not all speakers of a language change the phonemes in the same way. For example, in northern New England, some people say [ɛ́ləmɛnteri] instead of [ɛləmɛ́ntri] for *elementary*, but whether the word is pronounced that way is a matter of choice (nonsystematic variation). Still, regional variation in speech is usually attributable to slightly varying phonological rule systems that are shared by speakers in that region or group. The variations do not affect our understanding of the meaning of the word being spoken. Many people in Boston say [pæk] for *park*. Many people in Texas say [pɪn] for *pen*. *Britches* was a Western American version of the English *breeches*, but both words still refer to pants. If a child puts a glottal stop in the middle of the word *little* and says [lɪʔl], then the meaning is understood. If you say [tʰomɑto] and I say [tʰomeɾo], then the conversation will continue and we will have the same referent in mind. Such variation in utterance is often determined by dialect or by idiosyncrasies in individual speech patterns.

Most variation in individual speech patterns, however, is **systematic allophonic variation.** It is driven by a set of unconscious phonological rules for the production of sounds in words. Every speaker of the language varies his or her speech in these predictable ways. The predictable, rule-based changes in pronunciation are surface expressions (allophones) of underlying phonemes. To clarify the difference, slashes / / indicate phonemes and phoneme representations, and brackets [ ] denote allophones or phonetic realizations of those phonemes. The phonological rules that govern the translation of phonemes into allophones are unconscious and applied automatically by speakers who acquired the language naturally. Explaining these relationships requires us to acknowledge at least two levels of speech codes, an abstract phonemic code and a phonetic code realized in speaking. For example, the word *tempest* is pronounced with an aspirated /t/ in the beginning, but not the end, and the second vowel is reduced to a schwa. The first vowel is also nasalized:

Abstract code: /t/ /ɛ/ /m/ /p/ /ɛ/ /s/ /t/

Phonetic code: [tʰɛ̃mpəst]

The next section explores several predictable allophonic variations that are important for understanding spelling and reading behavior. These systematic variations of speech often cause the spoken word to differ from the printed word. When these are understood, children's speech, reading, and spelling errors make much more sense.

Systematic Variation in Speech Sound Production

As just described, speech sounds exist at an abstract, psychological level and a concrete, physical level. On the abstract level, each speech sound that contrasts with other speech sounds has an identity that is determined by a set of features, such as voicing, nasality, or stopping. For example, the final sounds of *his* [hɪz] and *hiss* [hɪs] share some overlapping features: Both are alveolar fricatives. They differ, however, in the critical feature of voicing. The same is true of the plural in *cubs* [kʌbz] and *cups* [kʌps]; however, in this case, we must account for the fact that the plural units represented by *s* have the same meaning and different phonetic forms. To account for this phenomenon, we could state that there is a plural morpheme, {PLU}, whose form is similar to an abstract phoneme /s/. Realizing the spoken plural, however, depends on applying a rule that governs how this plural morpheme is pronounced when it follows specific sounds. A phonetic description is one that describes how the abstract plural form /s/ is spoken in *cats*, *dogs*, and *wishes*. The phonetic production of a plural ending is the result of a systematic phonological translation process that converts an abstract linguistic construct (or category of features that distinguish a phoneme) into a physical reality, as in

cat + {PLU} = /kæt/ + /z/ or /s/ = [kʰæts]

We unconsciously and automatically choose which pronunciation to use because we know the rule. We add a voiceless ending [s] to all words that end in a voiceless consonant, such as [t]. Several of these regular phonological alternations come up again and again in teaching language skills to children. Some of the most important allophonic variations are discussed here in more detail because children's spellings often show that they are sensitive to these variations in speech.

Reduction of Vowels to Schwa

In multisyllable words, one syllable gets primary stress and the others are either unstressed or given secondary stress. Often, vowels will be pronounced as a neutral schwa [ə]. Schwa itself has allophones, sometimes sounding like "short *u*" and sometimes sounding like "short *i*," as in *picnic*, especially in words of Latin origin. The schwa is the most commonly spoken vowel in English, accounting for 20% of all vowels uttered.[12] Schwa has no special letter in spelling, although the letters *a*, *i*, and *o* are used most often for the sound, as in *about*, *definition*, and *wagon*.[13] When the phonemes in the word *tempest* are spoken as [tʰɛ̃mpəst], the second syllable is unaccented and the second vowel becomes a schwa. This occurs by phonological rule; we do not have to think about where to place stress or how to pronounce the vowel.

Consider the differences among the following words: *photograph, photography,* and *photographic.* The stress pattern in each word shifts to accommodate the new syllable structure. When we speak, we apply the changes in stress automatically because we know not only the specific words but also the way the pattern of stress works in English. If we were asked to read nonsense words that follow the same pattern, then we would apply stress and reduce vowels to schwas by the same set of stress rules: *milograph, milography,* and *milographic.*

 ## Exercise 3.2

Underline the unaccented vowels that have lost their distinctiveness in pronunciation (schwas). Write other forms of the words, if any, in which the vowels recover an identity (see example). Your perceptions may be different from someone else's.

imitate _____   expository _____

blossom _____   argumentative _____

about _____   orthographic _____

application ____*apply*____   competent _____

complexity _____   deleterious _____

narrative _____   beautiful _____

Vowel Nasalization

Every time a vowel is spoken before a nasal consonant, that vowel is automatically nasalized. Vowel nasalization is nondistinctive in English; that is, nasalization of a vowel does not create a different phoneme and a different word. It is difficult, however, to avoid nasalizing the vowel before a nasal consonant because we do this automatically. With each pair of words in the following list, you should be able to feel the channeling of resonance through the nose on the vowels preceding nasal consonants and the lack of nasal resonance on the other vowels that are not followed by a nasal consonant. To detect this phenomenon, hold your nose and say the following pairs of words:

and   add
limb   lib
bunk   buck
went   wet
gang   gag
don't   dote

The nasalization phenomenon becomes important in understanding one of the most common characteristics of children's early spelling and the spelling errors of children who are not good spellers. Frequently, these children omit the nasal consonant in a word when the nasal comes before a final stop consonant and after a vowel, as in WOT for *want*, FED for *friend*, SAD for *sand*, SIG for *sing*, and JUP for *jump*. These omissions often occur even in compositions in which the nasal consonants /m/, /n/, and /ŋ/ are spelled correctly in the beginnings or ends of words.

Why does the omission of nasals after vowels and before final consonants occur? In essence, the nasal phoneme in the spoken word becomes absorbed by the vowel before it and the final consonant after it, especially when the final consonant is a voiceless stop. Say the word *can't*. Phonemically it is /kænt/; phonetically it is [kæ̃t]. There is no separate, distinct speech gesture for the nasal phoneme /n/. The nasal quality becomes part of the preceding vowel because that vowel is automatically nasalized by a phonological production rule, and the place of articulation for [n] was unified with the articulation of the final consonant [t]. Thus, if a child were to spell the word *can't* as CAT, then the child's phonetic spelling would be very close to phonetic reality. Note that the presence of a nasal consonant before a vowel has no effect on the vowel that follows it. For example, the word *net* does not have a nasalized vowel.

Here are other spelling errors that are attributable to vowel nasalization and the disappearance of the consonant following the nasal:

FROT = front
COMET = comment
TRUK = trunk
DAP = damp

Consonant Aspiration

Experienced teachers know that children make more errors with consonants at the ends of words than with other consonants during phoneme awareness, reading, and spelling instruction. But why should the endings of words be more difficult? The answer may have more to do with the properties of sounds at the ends of words than with the fact that the consonants are the last letters of a sequence.

Aspiration is characteristic of voiceless stop consonants in certain positions only. That is, voiceless stop consonants /k/, /p/, and /t/ have at least two allophonic forms: an aspirated form, [kʰ], [pʰ], and [tʰ], and an unaspirated form, [k], [p], and [t]. The aspirated forms of these sounds are detectable if you put your hand about an inch from your mouth. When a consonant is aspirated, you should feel a small explosion of breath against your palm. Say the following phrases, and try to detect where that push of breath occurs:

Candy canes make good presents.
Let's play Star Trek.

The push of breath can be felt at the beginning of *candy, canes, presents, play*, and *Trek*, as denoted in the phonetic transcription of the sentences:

[kʰændi kʰɛ̃nz mek gʊd pʰrɛzãnts]
[lɛts pʰle stɑr tʰrɛk]

It is possible to determine when aspiration occurs and whether it is a predictable variation—one that occurs by phonological rule in the speech of anyone who uses the language. We can do this by observing what is similar about all of the occurrences of an aspirated /p/, /t/, or /k/ and what is true about the instances when /p/, /t/, and /k/ are not aspirated:

Aspirated	*Unaspirated*	
(Beginning of syllable)	(Second consonant)	(Word-final)
<u>p</u>lace	s<u>p</u>end	soa<u>p</u>
ap<u>p</u>alled		
<u>c</u>lean	s<u>c</u>are	soc<u>k</u>
ac<u>c</u>ountant		
<u>t</u>ame	s<u>t</u>able	kno<u>t</u>
at<u>t</u>end		

These observations could be summarized as follows. When a voiceless stop consonant occurs in the beginning of a stressed syllable, it will be aspirated. Under other conditions, these stops are not aspirated, such as when they are the second sound in a blend or when they come after the vowel in a syllable. Alternating these allophones is predictable; thus, they are said to be in **complementary distribution** because each of the two never occurs in the same phonemic environment as the other. Predictably, the aspirated and unaspirated forms of the consonants occur in specific places in a word.

The unaspirated forms of the unvoiced stops can sometimes sound or feel like their voiced equivalents. That is, /p/ can be confused with /b/, /t/ with /d/, and /k/ with /g/. Children's spelling errors often show their tendency to confuse these sounds. It is common to see substitutions such as the following:

S<u>B</u>OYDR = s<u>p</u>ider
CU<u>B</u> = cu<u>p</u>
S<u>G</u>OL = s<u>ch</u>ool
HOS<u>BIDL</u> = hos<u>pita</u>l
SI<u>G</u> = si<u>ck</u>

Notice that these confusions are much more likely to occur when the sounds are in the second part of a blend or in word-final position; that is, when they are not aspirated.

 **Exercise 3.3**

Write these words phonetically, using the aspiration sign ['] for aspirated voice-less stops, the schwa [ə] for unaccented vowels, and the tilde [~] above nasalized vowels that precede nasal consonants.

kitchen _____   steam _____

purchase _____   challenge _____

tender _____   approve _____

problem _____   snap _____

skate _____   threat _____

spirit _____   solution _____

Vowel Lengthening

The terms *long* and *short* to describe the sets of vowels in English are mis-nomers. There is such a thing as vowel length, but it is not synonymous with the duration of vowel articulation; that is, how many milliseconds are needed to pronounce a vowel. Consider the following words:

seize	cease		sped	speck
bed	bet		live	lift
keel	keep		hag	hack
heed	heat		rise	rice

In these pairs, the vowels in the first column are actually spoken with slightly longer duration than the vowels in the second column. Can you determine what causes this variation?

The consonant in front of the vowel obviously has nothing to do with the length of the vowel sound because each of these pairs begins with the same consonant. The consonant after the vowel, however, does determine its length. As you may have guessed, the voicing of the consonant following the vowel determines its length. Therefore, it is important to tell children that the labels *long* and *short* are quite arbitrary. At one time in history, the labels were directly descriptive of vowels as they were spoken in Middle English, but many of those distinctions have since been lost. The vowels have changed so much that the labels have little meaning. But the lengthening of a vowel in coarticulated words is another predictable phenomenon, governed by phonological rule, that pertains to the sequences of sounds in words and the effect of some sounds on others.

Flapping of Medial /t/ and /d/

Say the following words naturally, as you would say them in a phrase or a sentence:

putting	pudding		tally	dally
writer	rider		temple	dimple
little	Liddy		tire	dire
latter	ladder			

The sounds /t/ and /d/ in the first two columns are pronounced very similarly to one another and differently from the initial /t/ and /d/ in the words of the last two columns. In each of the first two columns, the medial /t/ and /d/ are pronounced as an alveolar flap, or tongue flap, [ɾ]. This is not lazy speech because most American English speakers change these sounds in medial position by a predictable phonological rule. The /t/ and /d/ are pronounced as a tongue flap when they occur between two vowels and the second vowel is not stressed, as in *photograph* [foɾəgræf]. Notice that flapping does not automatically occur in words such as *rooster* and *panda* because the /t/ and /d/ in those words occur between a consonant and a vowel.

Affrication

The affricates are the phonemes [č] and [ǰ] that comprise two vocal gestures: a stop of breath followed by a fricative. In some phoneme environments, /t/ and /d/ are affricated; that is, before certain speech sounds, [t] is articulated like a [č] and [d] is articulated like a [ǰ] because of the influence of the phoneme that follows. Say the following words:

take	train	attack	actuary
desk	dress	actor	furniture
addict	educate	could he	could you

In the right-hand word in each pair, the [t] or [d] that is affricated is followed by an [r] or the glide [j]. The mouth must pucker in anticipation of the [r] or the [j]. The glide after the [č] or [ǰ] in the examples *educate, actuary,* and *furniture* is hidden. Spelling does not show the presence of [j] directly; the letter *u* in those three words stands for the combination of the glide [j] and [u], as it does in the word *you*. Sometimes this combination is called *long u* in phonics texts; sometimes the combination is classified as a diphthong in phonics systems. At any rate, the affrication of alveolar stops before [ju] is automatic for most American English speakers. When children spell words with *tr* or *dr* blends, such as *train* or *dress,* or when they spell words such as *educate,* they are likely to write CHRAN, JRS, or EGUKAT until they learn consciously to ignore the concrete phonetic details of speech. Teachers can reassure children that their perception is correct: Their mouths do say what they are writing, but pronunciation is not spelled so literally. Their mouths are fooling them.

Vowel Raising Before a Velar (Back) Consonant

Say the following words:

Lax vowel	*Lax and raised vowel*
bat	bag, bank
etch	egg, Engle
icky	igloo, ink

In the first column, the words contain front, lax ("short") vowels in their pure form. In the second column, the vowels sound slightly different. The subtle changes in the vowels in the second column occur because the tongue is raised to anticipate the velar consonants [k], [ŋ], and [g]. Thus, in each word in the second column, the lax vowel comes out sounding more like the tense vowel next to it on the diagram showing vowel articulation (see Figure 2.6). When children write the word *bag* as BAEG, the word *egg* as AG, or the word *igloo* as EGLOO, they are demonstrating awareness of the literal phonetic characteristics of the words. They have yet to learn about the more abstract nature of English orthography.

Exercise 3.4

What allophonic variation is reflected in children's spelling of each set of the following words (invented spelling in capital letters before the target word)?

a) LAG = leg   ENK = ink   EGLU = igloo

b) CHRIK = trick   GRAK = drink   CHRA = tray

c) SWEDR = sweater   PUDING = putting   PEDE = pretty

Phonology and Spelling

With this background, we can evaluate how closely children's spelling errors approximate the sound patterns in speech. The following spellings are typical of students at the 4- to 5-year-old level who do not yet know the conventional spelling system and of older poor spellers who rely on immature strategies to spell. The spellings look odd until we consider the strategies the student is using. The following spellings indicate very good awareness of the sounds in spoken words, even though the student may be using letter names to spell.

- **Errors consistent with good phoneme awareness but underdeveloped knowledge of conventional spelling:**[14]

  1. Long vowels spelled with letter name.
     DA = day   KAM = came   FEL = feel

  2. Short vowels: spelled with letter name closest in articulation. (Reference the vowel chart.)
     a for /e/   BAD = bed   i for /o/   GIT = got
     e for /i/   FES = fish   o for /u/   SOGH = sugar
     i for /u/   KIT = cut

  3. Nasals omitted after vowels, before consonants (vowel is nasalized, and nasal consonant is "lost" in articulation).
     JUP = jump   AD = and   ED = end

4. Syllabic consonants /m/ /n/ /l/ /r/.

   LIDL = little   BIGR = bigger   OPN = open

5. Inflections spelled phonetically (-ed, -s).

   WAKT = walked   DAWGZ = dogs   LITID = lighted

6. Vowel spellings showing phoneme features or phonetic detail.

   SOWN = soon   GOWT = goat   BOE = boy

7. Affrication of *tr* and *dr*.

   CHRA = tray   CHRIBLS = troubles   JRAGN = dragon

8. Intervocalic flaps shown as *D*.

   LADR = letter   WODR = water

9. Letter names *Y* for /w/ and *H* for /ch.

   YOH = watch   YL = will   HRH = church

- **Common spelling errors indicating underdeveloped awareness of phoneme sequence or identity**

  These error types are common in students with underdeveloped phoneme awareness, both normally progressing students who have not been taught and older students who are having trouble learning. Distance from the target phoneme should be noted, with reference to the vowel and consonant charts. Substitutions of sounds that share most features with the target phoneme are more positive indicators than substitutions that share few or no features with the target phoneme.

  1. Omission of consonants within consonant blends or clusters.

     MIKE = milk

  2. Confusion of consonants because student is unaware of critical features that differentiate them (e.g., voicing, nasality).

     INEMS = items

  3. Omission of unaccented (schwa) syllables.

     CIMMON = cinnamon

  4. Omission, substitution, or phonetic spellings of inflections (-ed, -s).

     FRIGHTINGLY = frightened   FRIGHTING = frightened

  5. Omission, confusion, or mis-sequencing of nasals (*n, m, ng*) and liquids (*l, r*).

     CLOREL = color   MD = bed

  6. Vowel substitutions, far from target.

     DRONCK = drink

Children's spelling attempts are very good diagnostic indicators of phoneme awareness[15] and are sensitive indicators of response to instruction.

Teaching Phonological Awareness—General Principles[16]

1. Follow a progression of phonological skill development (see Table 3.2) and recognize the relative difficulty of each task. The goal of instruction is progressive differentiation of the *internal details* of the *spoken word* for deep, accurate representation in memory.

2. Focus students' attention on speech sounds before focusing on letters. Work with phonemes, not letters, until you are sure they can "tune in to" speech. Then transition to letters.

3. Encourage mouth awareness. Phonemes are speech gestures as well as speech sounds. Use mirrors. Ask students to determine whether their mouths are open or closed and whether they are using their tongue, teeth, or lips when they make the sound.

4. Include all English phonemes in the instruction. All phonemes can be taught, including all vowel sounds (e.g., /ʊ/ in *foot*) and sounds represented by digraphs (e.g., /č/ as in *itch* or /ð/ as in *that*).

5. Think *multisensory*. Involve students' hands, eyes, bodies, and mouths whenever possible.

6. A few brief activities—about 5–10 minutes per day—for 12–20 weeks are all that most young students need to improve speech awareness.

7. Show students what you want them to do [**I do**]. Practice together [**we do**], and then let students take turns while you supervise [**you do**].

8. Give immediate corrective feedback (e.g., if a student gives a letter *name* instead of a *sound*, then explain the difference to the student and elicit the correct response).

9. Use letters to represent sounds as soon as young students are ready. Letters reinforce phoneme awareness and support it once students have learned to attend to sounds.

Sample Activities for Preschool or Beginning Kindergarten Level

These activities are the easiest, the starting point for phonological awareness instruction. They are appropriate for 4- and 5-year-olds who are just learning to pay attention to speech or older students with severe phonological processing difficulties. They include rhyme identification, syllabication, and mental manipulation of onsets and rimes within syllables.

Rhyme Judgment

Say, "Words rhyme if the last part of each word sounds the same. *Cake* and *bake* rhyme; so do *merry* and *cherry*. Listen while I say the poem, and get ready to say the rhyming word. Jack and *Jill* went up the *hill*. What words rhyme?"

Rhyme Matching

Say, "Listen carefully. Rhyming Robot wants to find a match for each of his favorite words. If one of his favorite words is *shake,* then which of these words can he have: *meat, steak,* or *corn*?"

Alliteration

Say, "Peter Piper picked a peck of pickled peppers."

Say, "Let's make a silly sentence with /n/ words. *Neat Nancy . . .*"

Syllable Blending

Say, "Silly Caesar speaks very slowly. What word is Silly Caesar saying?"

ta-ble	hos-pi-tal	tan-ger-ine
roll-er-blades	fire-truck	play-ground

Syllable Deletion

Say, "Let's play a game with words. We're going to break some long words into parts and leave a part out. If I say *toothpaste* and then leave off the *tooth,* then what's left? That's right: *paste.* Let's try some more."

What's *baseball* without *ball?*	What's *butterfly* without *butter?*
What's *paddleboat* without *boat?*	What's *Sunday* without *day?*
What's *power* without *-er?*	What's *telephone* without *tele-?*

Syllable Counting

Say, "Inside this treasure chest are lots of things with names that you know. When it's your turn, reach in and take something out. Then tap the syllables as you say the word."

balloon	cricket	calculator	eraser
sharpener	stapler	candlestick	napkin

Initial Sound Matching

Say, "Let's see whose name starts with the same sound as someone else's name. They can stand together. *Tanya* and *Timmy.* What sound begins each of your names? Let's think of another name that starts with /t/."

Onset-Rime Division

Say, "Let's say some words in parts. I'll say the whole word. Then you say the whole word and divide it into two parts. Touch a syllable square [colored felt square] for each part, like this." [Model the technique first.]

c-ar   sh-ip   w-ave   p-ie   sk-ate   d-esk

Rhyme Production

Say, "Let's play a game. I'll say three words that rhyme, and they sound alike at the end. You say one more word that rhymes. It can be a silly word. Let's start: *hinky, pinky, slinky,* _____ ."

Say, "Say a word that sounds like (rhymes with) *star*."

Sample Activities for First-Grade and Older Students

These activities are most appropriate for the last part of kindergarten and first grade, when proficiency in phoneme segmentation and blending is the necessary underpinning for learning to read and spell words. Older students with phonological processing weaknesses, including many poor readers and spellers, will benefit from activities at this level of difficulty. A few exercises, practiced for a just a few minutes daily, can produce growth in phoneme awareness. (*Note:* Phonic symbols are used in these exercises.)

Final Sound Matching

Say, "Listen while I say two words. If they end with the same last sound, then repeat the sound."

moon, pen	/n/
bridge, page	/j/
wish, mash	/sh/
brick, steak	/k/

Blending Phonemes

Say, "I'm going to say a name sound by sound. If you hear your name, then stand up."

/k/ /r/ /ĭ/ /s/ /t/ /ə/ /n/

Teaching Sound Blending (Phonic symbols used to denote sounds.)

(I do) Say, "I'm going to say some sounds slowly and you'll help me put them together to make a word. Listen." Put two colored squares on the board a few inches apart while you say, "/s/ /ē/." Push the colored squares together. Say, "Say it fast: *see!*"

(We do) Say, "Now you do it. Put out two colored squares that are not touching. Touch your colored squares while you say the sounds with me: /s/ /ē/. Now, push them together and say the word fast: *see!*"

Try a few more words with two sounds: /t/ /ō/ = *toe;* /ā/ /k/ = *ache;* /z/ /ū/ = *zoo.* Say the sounds; then blend the word. Have students touch their squares and say the sounds while you model on the board. They can sweep a finger left to right while they "say the sounds fast."

(You do) Students can practice as a group. Then, give each student a turn to repeat blending phonemes, using tiles to "touch and say" and blend the word.

Two-phoneme words	Three-phoneme words (no consonant clusters)	Four-phoneme words with consonant clusters
/g/ /ō/ (go)	/k/ /ē/ /p/ (keep)	/l/ /ă/ /m/ /p/ (lamp)
/ā/ /p/ (ape)	/g/ /ā/ /m/ (game)	/f/ /ĭ/ /s/ /t/ (fist)
/ē/ /ch/ (each)	/ch/ /ĭ/ /p/ (chip)	/m/ /ō/ /l/ /d/ (mold)
/ĭ/ /n/ (in)	/sh/ /ou/ /t/ (shout)	/g/ /r/ /ă/ /b/ (grab)
/ī/ /s/ (ice)	/b/ /ă/ /g/ (bag)	/k/ /l/ /ō/ /z/ (close)
/y/ /ū/ (you)	/k/ /oi/ /n/ (coin)	/s/ /t/ /ŏ/ /p/ (stop)
/sh/ /ī/ (shy)	/y/ /ĕ/ /l/ (yell)	/k/ /l/ /ow/ /n/ (clown)
/ar/ /t/ (art)	/s/ /ĭ/ /t/ (sight)	/f/ /l/ /ă/ /g/ (flag)
/ou/ /t/ (out)	/t/ /er/ /n/ (turn)	/w/ /aw/ l/ /z/ (walls)
/b/ /oi/ (boy)	/r/ /ē/ /ch/ (reach)	/sh/ /ĕ/ /l/ /z/ (shells)

Say-It-and-Move-It[17] (Phoneme Segmentation)

Say, "Listen to this word: *chick.* Say the word sound by sound while you move the counters in the boxes. Watch me first: /ch/ /ĭ/ /k/. Let's do some together. Good. Which one is /k/? Which one is /ĭ/? What is the word?"

Say, "Now, it's your turn. Let's try some silly words (nonsense words)."

pem   zer   uff   zone   cheed

Initial and Final Sound Substitution

Say, "Let's see if we can make some new words by changing just one sound. If I change /b/ in *bat* to /r/, then what new word do I have? (*rat*) If I change

/w/ in *wag* to /t/, then what new word do I have? (*tag*) If I change /l/ in *shell* to /f/, then what new word do I have? (*chef*)."

poodle–noodle   witch–win   race–rays

Middle Vowel Substitution

First, move same-colored chips to show the segmentation of the word. As the vowel is changed, show which chip is changing.

Say, "Now we'll make some new words by changing just one sound in the middle—the vowel sound. Here is *moose*: /m/ /ū/ /s/. Let's change *moose* to *mouse*. Which sound is changed? Only the middle one right here— the vowel sound."

moon–man   fawn–fin   soup–sap   boot–beet

Track Sound Changes with Colored Blocks (Sound Chaining)

Use colored blocks to show what sound has changed in each new word in the chain.

1. day, date, dot, pot, spot, spit, sit, sits
2. me, mean, men, zen, zin, zip, chip, pitch, titch, stitch
3. ouch, out, shout, shoot, shoes, use, dues, twos, stews

Sound Deletion

Syllable: "Say *potato* without the *po*."
Initial sound: "Say *peas* without the /p/."
Final sound: "Say *sheet* without the /t/."
Initial blend: "Say *stop* without the /s/."
Final blend: "Say *wild* without the /d/."

Transition to Letter–Sound Correspondence

During the Say-It-and-Move-It[18] phoneme segmentation activity, introduce a first set of six to eight grapheme tiles, such as *b, p, m, f, ee, v, t,* and *d*. (Note that *ee* and other two-letter combinations can be put on one movable tile because they are one sound-spelling unit. A grapheme represents a phoneme.)

Teach the difference between "quiet" and "noisy" sounds that feel very much the same (i.e., /p/, /b/; /f/, /v/; /t/, /d/) as well as that /m/ goes through the nose.

Use a guide word on a sound-spelling card to teach phoneme–grapheme associations. Reinforce associations through games and drills. Be sure that students can point to the right symbol for each sound as the sounds are dictated, and then use the symbol to build simple words.

Pig Latin

Make a sentence by removing the first consonant from each word, putting the consonant at the end of the word, and adding the vowel *ay* to it (e.g., "Ello-hay, y-may, ame-nay, is-ay, teve-say"—*Hello, my name is Steve*).

Summary

Phonology is the study of the speech sound system of a language. It includes but is not limited to the study of phonetics, the physical description of the inventory of speech sounds. The phonological system of any language includes rules or constraints about the order and place of speech sounds in words and the specific ways they should be articulated. Languages differ not only in their inventory of phonemes but also in the rules that specify how these phonemes can be combined. Pitch, stress, and intonation all are part of the phonological system.

Speakers of a language actually produce many subtle variants of phonemes called *allophones*. Allophonic variation occurs according to phonological rules. Phonemes are really groups or classes of speech sounds that are perceived to be similar because they share distinctive features. When those segments are spoken in patterns governed by systematic rules, they are in complementary distribution and their forms are predictable according to their place in words and phrases. For example, /t/ and /d/ are always affricated before /r/ and /j/ but not before other consonants. A phoneme can be used in combination with others to make a word. Its existence is verified by the existence of minimal pairs of words that differ only in one phoneme.

The *syllable* is a suprasegmental, or overarching, unit with a hierarchical internal structure. Every syllable must have a vowel that serves as the syllable nucleus. Syllables may have an onset, or a consonant or consonant cluster before a vowel, and must have a rime, or the vowel and any consonants that follow it. These are natural segments that have psychological reality. The vowel and sometimes a following consonant form the syllable peak. The coda is the consonant or consonant cluster following the vowel.

A large proportion of students who have trouble learning to read and spell demonstrate early difficulties with phoneme awareness and related phonological processes, including speech–sound pronunciation, word pronunciation, memory for verbal information, and/or retrieval of names and words. These problems inhibit the ability to decode and spell words and to remember names and word forms. Before children can learn phoneme–grapheme mapping for phonics and spelling, they need to be aware of the phonemes to which the symbols correspond. Phoneme awareness instruction should help students progressively differentiate syllables, onsets and rimes, and phonemes in initial, medial, and final position so that they recognize and remember subtle differences between and among spoken words.

Supplementary Exercises

3.5   Reverse the sequence of speech sounds in each of these words, or say them backward. Think of the sounds, not the letters.

teach _____   lip _____   palm _____

sigh _____   easy _____   cash _____

cuts _____   judge _____   snitch _____

pitch _____   speak _____   face _____

3.6   Do this exercise with an adult partner. Say each word. Then ask your partner to say the word again without the part marked in parentheses ("Say the word *man*. Now say it again without the [m]").

(m)eat   ma(ke)   st(r)eam   off(er)ing

(b)and   (s)kill   sc(r)am   dri(v)er

sol(d)   (g)lass   boa(s)t   in(ve)stigate

3.7   In each of the following minimal pairs of spoken words, two phonemes contrast to form different words. Identify by number, from the right-hand column, the primary feature by which each contrasting phoneme pair differs.

tick, chick _____   1.   voicing

seek, sick _____   2.   nasalization

rich, ridge _____   3.   front/back placement

keel, cool _____   4.   tenseness/laxness

whet, when _____   5.   affrication

3.8   Automatic aspiration of /p/, /t/, and /k/ in the beginning of words is the result of an unconscious phonological rule in action. When does aspiration occur? What difference might aspiration, or lack of it, make to the ease with which students learn to decode and spell these phonemes?

3.9   Write concise definitions for the following terms:

Phonology

Phonetics

Phoneme

Allophone (phone)

3.10   Think of minimally contrasting pairs of words that differ only in the target sounds in initial, medial, and final position.

Example: /p/, /b/   pest, best   scrapple, scrabble   cap, cab

	Initial	Medial	Final
/k/, /g/			
/ǰ/, /č/			
/t/, /n/			
/s/, /š/			
/f/, /v/			
/ŋ/, /n/	n/a*		

*It is not possible to start a word with /ŋ/ in English.

3.11   Given these four phonemes, how many possible words (real and nonsense) can you make with the set that conform to the order rules of English phonology? (Words should be pronounceable.) Which words have complex syllable structures?

$$/r/, /s/, /k/, /ɑ/$$

Example: [rɑks]

3.12   Some consonant sounds in English never begin a word. List them.

List the consonants in English that must always be followed by a vowel if they are in the beginning of a syllable. These consonants would never be followed by another consonant to make a blend. (Look back at the consonant inventories in Figures 2.3 and 2.4.)

3.13   Here are some phonological rules that affect word production in English. Find a spoken word that is an example of each of these rules.

a) Automatic nasalization of a vowel before a nasal consonant

b) Reduction of an alveolar stop to a voiced flap when preceded by a stressed vowel and followed by an unstressed vowel

c) Elongation of a tense vowel before a voiced final consonant and shortening of a tense vowel before a voiceless final consonant

d) Raising of a lax vowel before a voiced velar consonant

3.14   What do the three words in each of these sets of spelling errors have in common? What phonological processing problems might they represent?

a) JELE = chili   GARASH = garage   SBENT = spend

b) POIT = point   KINCHEN = kitchen   FRUT = front

c) SPEAS = spears   COLOL = color   TEE = tree

Endnotes

1. Edwards, 1992.
2. Kibel & Miles, 1994; Treiman, 1997.
3. Treiman, 1997.
4. Brady, 1997.
5. Scarborough & Brady, 2002.
6. Goswami, 2000; Scarborough & Brady, 2002; Wolf & Bowers, 1999.
7. Ehri, 2004; Gillon, 2004.
8. Schatschneider, Fletcher, Francis, Carlson, & Foorman, 2004.
9. Cassar, Treiman, Moats, Pollo, & Kessler, 2005; Pennington, 2009.
10. Paulson, 2004; Paulson & Moats, 2009.
11. Gillon, 2004.
12. Hanna et al., 1966; Yule, 1996.
13. Hanna et al., 1966.
14. What the student wrote is in capital letters; what the student meant is in lowercase letters.
15. Cassar et al., 2005; Tangel & Blachman, 1995.
16. *Source:* Moats, 2009.
17. Blachman, Ball, Black, & Tangel, 2000.
18. Blachman et al., 2000.

Instructional Programs for Phonological Awareness Development

Adams, M.J., Foorman, B.R., Lundberg, I., & Beeler, T. (1998). *Phonemic awareness in young children: A classroom curriculum.* Baltimore: Paul H. Brookes Publishing Co.

Blachman, B.A., Ball, E.W., Black, R., & Tangel, D.M. (2000). *Road to the code: A phonological awareness program for young children.* Baltimore: Paul H. Brookes Publishing Co.

Dodson, J. (2008). *50 nifty activities for 5 components and 3 tiers of reading instruction.* Longmont, CO: Sopris West Educational Services.

Lindamood, P., & Lindamood, C. (n.d.). *The Lindamood phoneme sequencing program for reading, spelling, and speech* (LIPS). Austin, TX: PRO-ED.

O'Connor, R.E., Notari-Syverson, A., & Vadasy, P.F. (2005). *Ladders to literacy: A kindergarten activity book* (2nd ed.). Baltimore: Paul H. Brookes Publishing Co.

Resources for Professional Development of Teachers

Moats, L.C. (2009). *Language essentials for teachers of reading and spelling: Module 2. The speech sounds of English: Phonetics, phonology, and phoneme awareness* (2nd ed.). Longmont, CO: Sopris West Educational Services.

Moats, L.C., & Farrell, L. (2006). *Teaching reading essentials: Video demonstrations of small-group interventions. Program guide.* Longmont, CO: Sopris West Educational Services.

The Structure of English Orthography

By the end of this chapter, you will understand:

- The history of writing systems
- Anglo-Saxon, Latin, and Greek influences on the English language
- Correspondence between phonemes and graphemes in English
- English orthographic conventions
- The predictability of written English

The word **orthography** refers to a written language system. Humans have invented many kinds of orthographies: Some read left to right; others right to left or up and down. Some use symbols for meaning units, and others use symbols for syllables or speech sounds. The alphabetic writing system of English, although sometimes maligned as crazy, irregular, or unduly complex, can be explained if its history is taken into account. Most of the time we can explain why words are spelled the way they are, but to do so, we need to look at words from several interesting angles.

This chapter and the next explain the structure of the English writing system from the perspectives of:

- Word origin and history

- Phoneme–grapheme correspondences

- Position constraints, or the effect of the position of a phoneme on its spelling within a word

- Patterns of letter sequence and use, including syllable spellings

- Morphology—the spelling of meaningful parts

A Brief History of Writing

Many literate cultures have invented myths about the origins of writing, attributing the development of written language to acts of the gods. Writing seems almost too miraculous to have been invented by mere mortals. History tells us, however, that over several millennia, writing systems slowly evolved from early drawings to abstract symbol systems. The first known form of written communication, dated to 20,000 years ago, contained signs and pictures (**pictograms**) that portrayed the objects, events, and ideas of daily life without assigning either meaning or sound to a symbol. Modern pictograms, such as signs for "no bicycles," "leash your dog," and "quiet area," are used today as signs in parks or public places because they can be understood by anyone.

Ideographic writing systems evolved simultaneously in China and Sumeria more than 5,000 years ago. *Ideograms* were stylized pictograms used to represent ideas and words rather than concrete depictions of events (see Figure 4.1). Li Si decreed the first standardization of 3,000 basic Chinese characters in 213 B.C., aiming to eliminate redundancies and simplify the complex system then in use throughout China. Each ideogram had to be memorized, however, because it did not bear a direct relationship to sound.

The Sumerians of Mesopotamia left an archive of clay tablets with commercial and historical records written in cuneiform script, a system more abstract than ideograms (see Figure 4.2). Cuneiform symbols were stylized, simplified representations of words and

Figure 4.1. Classical Chinese script. (Reprinted from Wikimedia Commons.)

Figure 4.2. Ideographic script, Sumerian cuneiform. (From Pedersen, H. [1959]. *Linguistic science in the 19th century.* Cambridge, MA: Harvard University Press.)

ideas. When adopted by other cultures, including the Assyrians and Persians, the Sumerian symbols were used to represent each syllable of speech. Cuneiform scripts became the first **syllabaries,** although Wolf[1] pointed out that sounds, syllables, and meaning units were all shown in these very early writing systems. (A modern example of a *syllabary,* wherein each symbol represents a consonant–vowel combination, is the writing system developed by Chief Sequoia of the Cherokees early in the 19th century; see Figure 4.3).

The **hieroglyphics** of the Egyptians developed in parallel with cuneiform writing and flourished around 4000 B.C. Gradually, hieroglyphics came to symbolize the syllables of Egyptian words. Many other trading partners of the Egyptian and Sumerian civilizations borrowed hieroglyphic symbols to use in their writing systems. The Phoenicians, who resided on the eastern shore of the Mediterranean, created a system of 22 syllabic symbols that represented consonant–vowel combinations and some consonants alone. The Greeks then adapted Phoenician symbols around 1000 B.C. but found that they were inadequate for representing the complex syllables of Greek. Taking the final step toward creating a true **alphabetic** writing system, the Greeks assigned a symbol to each consonant and vowel. (*Alpha* and *beta* were the first two letters of the Greek symbol system.) The Romans, who acquired the Greek alphabet through contact with the Etruscans, also adapted and refined the Greek alphabetic system, used it to transcribe Latin, and spread it throughout the world.

Thus, alphabetic writing represents a late evolutionary development and an advanced discovery acquired over several thousand years. Only gradually did humans become aware of the separate segments of speech (phonemes) that could be represented in a writing system. Why did alphabetic writing evolve so recently? Because the insight that words can be broken into phonemes, which, in turn, can be represented with symbols, was and still is elusive for the human brain. This insight is by no means self-evident, as we demonstrated in the previous chapters. In many ways, the individual development of children who are discovering the alphabetic principle in English writing recapitulates human history and reflects the unnatural and effortful learning process that underlies learning to write.

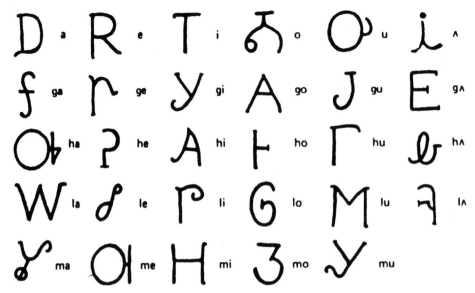

Figure 4.3. Syllabic script. (From Akmajian, A., Demers, R.A., Farmer, A.K., & Harnish, R.M. [1995]. *Linguistics: An introduction to language and communication* [4th ed., p. 542]. Cambridge, MA: MIT Press; reprinted by permission.)

Meaning and Sound

Alphabetic writing systems, including English, represent the speech sounds of language but vary in the extent to which the correspondences are predictable, consistent, and a one-to-one match between sound and letter. Alphabetic writing systems exist on a continuum from **transparent** to **opaque,** or from shallow to deep. Finnish and Serbo-Croatian are among the most phonetically predictable or transparent written languages because each symbol of their alphabetic systems corresponds to a speech sound. English, however, is known as a deep or opaque orthography, one in which the spellings represent not only phonemes and syllable patterns but also morphemes. English orthography is most accurately described as a **morphophonemic** system (see Figure 4.4) because it represents both sound and meaning.

The linguists Carol Chomsky[2] and Chomsky and Halle[3] even described English as an optimal system for a reader. Meaningful parts of words are spelled consistently, although pronunciation may not be easily recovered from print. At times, the meaning of a word may be deciphered from print more easily than from speech. For example, we know that the words *education* and *induction* share a meaningful Latin root (*duc, duct*—to lead) that is preserved in spelling even though the spoken forms of the root differ considerably. The words *anxious* and *anxiety* have a consistently spelled root (*anx*) that is pronounced quite differently in each word. The alphabetic system represents phonemes abstractly without the kind of detailed phonetic representation that might, for example, be used to show whether the /d/ in *educate* is affricated (pronounced as "ejukate"). Our orthography is phonemic, not phonetic; it represents phonemes, not allophones.

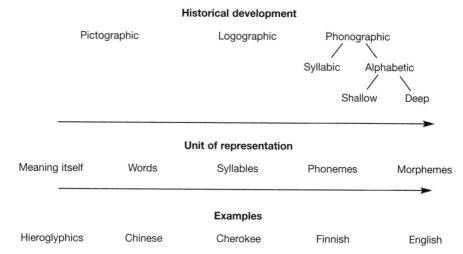

Figure 4.4. Classification of orthographies. (From Seymour, P.H.K. [1992]. Cognitive theories of spelling and implications for education. In C. Sterling & C. Robson [Eds.], *Psychology, spelling, and education* [p. 53]. Clevedon, England: Multilingual Matters, Ltd.; adapted by permission.)

Anglo-Saxon, Latin, and Greek Layers in English Orthography

One way to categorize and explain the spelling patterns in English words is by their language of origin (Anglo-Saxon, Latin, and Greek) and the units of sound, syllable, and morpheme that are represented systematically in each base language (see Table 4.1).[4]

Anglo-Saxon and its Roots

Have you ever wondered why the most common words in English, such as *many, does, said, they,* and *enough,* seem odd and irregular? The answer lies in their history.

The most common words in English are from its oldest layer, Anglo-Saxon, also known as Old English. Anglo-Saxon, in turn, evolved from primitive Indo-European and primitive Germanic roots. Indo-European languages are believed to have descended from a common ancestral language more than 20,000 years ago.[5] This ancestral language was spoken by tribes residing in Eastern Europe before the isolation of migrating groups allowed different languages to evolve. Similarities in the vocabulary, grammatical patterns, and phonological features of all the Indo-European languages attest to their common origin. Words for animals, family members, numbers, emotions, and universal daily activities tend to be similar across related language groups with a common language ancestor. A Germanic language family comprises one group of languages with such similarities, including Danish, German, Swedish, Dutch, and English; a Latin family comprises another, including French, Italian, Portuguese, Romanian, and Spanish.

Table 4.1. Features of English orthography by language of origin

Language of origin	Features of words	Examples
Anglo-Saxon (Old English)	Often one-syllable words; use of vowel teams, silent letters, and digraphs in spelling; words for common, everyday things; irregular spellings; function words and the most common words in English; new words formed as compounds	*sky, earth, moon, sun, water, sheep, dog, horse, cow, hen, head, arm, finger, toe, heart, shoe, shirt, pants, socks, coat, brother, father, mother, sister, hate, love, think, want, touch, does, were, been, would, do*
Norman (Old) French	*ou* for /ū/, as in *soup;* soft *c* and *g* when followed by *e, i, y;* special endings such as *-ine, -ette, -elle,* and *-ique;* words for food and fashion, abstract social ideals, and relationships	*amuse, cousin, cuisine, peace, triage, rouge, baguette, novice, justice, crouton, coupon, nouvelle, boutique, ballet, croquet, coquette, mirage, debut, depot*
Latin (Romance)	Multisyllable words organized around a root, many with prefixes or suffixes; content words found in academic language in social sciences, traditional physical sciences, and literature	*firmament, terrestrial, solar, stellar, aquarium, mammal, equine, pacify, mandible, extremity, locomotion, paternal, maternity, designate, hostility, amorous, contemplate, delectable, deception, reject, refer*
Greek	Spellings *ph* for /f/, *ch* for /k/, and *y* for /i/; constructed from combining forms, similar to English compounds; philosophical, mathematical, and scientific terminology	*hypnosis, agnostic, neuropsychology, decathlon, catatonic, agoraphobia, chlorophyll, physiognomy*

Source: Henry (2003).

The Proto-Germanic language from which Anglo-Saxon evolved was spoken in a territory around Denmark before the first century A.D. Certain words in modern English, including *rain, drink, broad,* and *hold,* probably came from Proto-Germanic because they are different in form and structure from those in the Latin language family. The Germanic language was highly inflected and included derived forms similar to our present day *heal/health, hold/held, sell/sold,* and *bake/baked,* some of which included a vowel shift and all of which included an inflected ending pronounced with the tongue behind or between the teeth. Gradually, the unaccented inflections on verbs became shorter in duration; eventually, they were dropped altogether. *Ride/rode, stand/stood,* and *choose/chose* are Proto-Germanic descendants in which a vowel shift was maintained in the past-tense verb form after a final inflection was dropped. Proto-Germanic words were always stressed on the first syllable with the exception of compound verbs such as *abide* and *begin.* The evolution of Indo-European languages is depicted in Figure 4.5.

West Germanic, an offshoot of Proto-Germanic, had evolved by the fourth century A.D. The isolation of migrating tribal groups again allowed the evolution of more branches of Germanic, including, by the sixth century, dialects spoken by Angles, Saxons, and Jutes living on the west side of the waters separating what are now the British Isles from Germany and Denmark. During the fifth and sixth centuries, Germanic tribes steadily invaded Britain, pushing to the west the Celtic peoples who lived there. Celtic and Latin forms, some of which were introduced by early Christian missionaries,

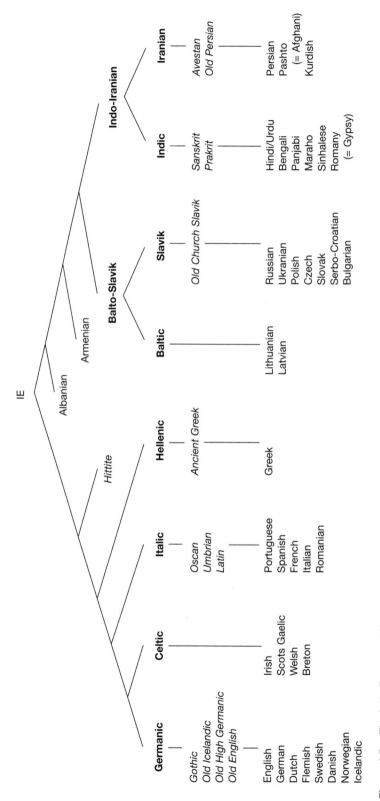

Figure 4.5. The Indo-European (IE) language family. Families are listed in bold type. The oldest attested forms of each family are given in italics, and currently spoken languages are listed in plain Roman type. (From Akmajian, A., Demers, R.A., Farmer, A.K., & Harnish, R.M. [1998]. *Linguistics: An introduction to language and communication* [4th ed., p. 311]. Cambridge, MA: MIT Press; reprinted by permission.)

melded with the Low West German languages of the Angles and Saxons, spawning the language now known as Old English or Anglo-Saxon. The Roman alphabet, invented to represent an entirely different language (Latin) with only five vowels, was far from ideal for representing the speech sounds of Old English. The church prevailed, however, and English writing based on the Roman alphabet spread through the monasteries where scribes toiled at producing religious manuscripts. The writings of King Alfred and the Augustine monks, teachers of Roman Christianity in Britain during the ninth century, are among the earliest surviving examples of the Anglo-Saxon language.

Anglo-Saxon words in English include those for work (*shepherd, plough, work*), for numbers (*one, two, hundred*), for body parts (*heart, knee, foot*), for basic sentiments (*love, hate, laughter*), and for animals (*sheep, goat, horse*). All of the 100 words used most often in English can be traced to Anglo-Saxon origins. The grammatical glue words or function words, including **pronouns, articles,** conjunctions, prepositions, and **auxiliary verbs,** are almost uniformly Anglo-Saxon (*the, a, and, you, to, would*). They are often one-syllable words. In Anglo-Saxon or Old English, compounding was the favored way to coin new terms, as it still is in German. Anglo-Saxon compounds stressed the first syllable or word, as in *grandmother, rubberneck,* and *yellowtail.*

Anglo-Saxon vowels were spelled as they sounded, with *a, e, i, o, u, y, ea, eo, ie,* and *ae* used to spell the vowel sounds of the language. Some vowels were shorter in duration than others. (Duration of vowel production is the actual length of time, in milliseconds, that it takes to produce a vowel in a word.) In Anglo-Saxon spelling, vowel lengthening was indicated by doubling the letter (as in *aa*) or by a diacritical mark. As mentioned previously, the labels "long" and "short" used to describe the qualities of vowel sounds have different meanings and do not have the same direct relationship to vowel length that once characterized Old English spelling. "Short" vowels are sometimes long in duration, and "long" vowels are sometimes short in duration. The "short" vowel in *bend* is spoken for a longer duration than the "long" vowel in *beat.* Our descriptions and labels for vowels descend from Old English concepts rather than from modern speech patterns.

In spite of the great shift in pronunciation of vowels that occurred between 1400 and 1600 and many changes in word form that occurred over centuries, spoken and written word relationships such as *foot/feet, tooth/teeth, goose/geese, climb, told,* and *find* have survived in Modern English. Most of the regular consonant and vowel sound–symbol correspondences and patterns are used in the spellings of Anglo–Saxon-based words.

The French and Latin Layers of English

The Latin-based vocabulary incorporated into Anglo-Saxon after the Norman invasion of Britain in 1066 was the language of scholars, nobles, and those of high social class. The Normans, led by William the Conqueror, were a French-speaking people whose scholars wrote in French and Latin—closely related members of an Indo-European language family. These languages contributed thousands of new words to English during the 300 or so years of French domination of England. Words such as *amorous, malevolent, fortitude, maternal,* and *residence* entered the language in scholarly writings.

After the monarchies of France and England officially separated in the 14th century, the upper classes renewed their use of English. British nobility and the educated, both religious and nonreligious, adopted English from the 14th century onward. In the 1300s, the first great works of English literature were written, including those of Geoffrey Chaucer, and by the early 15th century, English became the official language for written communication during the reign of Henry V. Close to Modern English, the form of language used then was an amalgam of Anglo-Saxon, Latin, and French that had undergone rapid evolution and several major shifts of pronunciation.

> With us ther was a DOCTOUR OF PHISIK;
> In al this world ne was ther noon hym lik,
> To speke of phisik and of surgerye,
> For he was grounded in astronomye.
> He kepte his pacient a ful greet deel In houres, by his magyk natureel.
> Wel koude he fortunen the ascendent
> Of his ymages for his pacient.
>
> —Geoffrey Chaucer, *The Canterbury Tales*
> Lines 414–420 of the *Prologue: The Physician*

Translation[6]
phisik = medicine
grounded = instructed
kepte his pacient = cared for and saved a patient
a ful greet deel In houres = many times
magyk natureel = natural science and studying astrological signs
fortunen the ascendent of his ymages = calculate the planetary position to
    improve the state of

The Greek Influence

The Greek influence on Middle English can be traced to the residence of St. Augustine in Canterbury during the 10th century. St. Augustine borrowed Greek words such as *disciple, apostle,* and *psalm*—religious terms with Greek roots. Centuries later, followers of the Greek Orthodox religion exported Greek vocabulary, scholarship, and aesthetics to Italy during the Renaissance of the 14th and 15th centuries.

Emanating from Italy, a revival of classical Roman and Greek language, art, and literature reached England in the mid-16th century. Tudor scholars in the mid-16th century deliberately borrowed words from classical vocabulary to embellish and elevate their prose. Words of Greek origin, such as *catastrophe, lexicon,* and *thermometer,* became English words in this way.

Scientific inquiry flourished and the printing of scholarly works proliferated after the 15th century. Scholars needed new words to describe discoveries, inventions, and concepts such as *atmosphere, pneumonia, skeleton, grav-*

ity, and *encyclopedia.* Anatomical and physical scientists coined words such as *chronology, excrement,* and *paradox* to explain their ideas. Of course, the reliance on Greek roots and combining forms continues today in science, mathematics, and philosophy; words recently added to English include *synthesizer* and *cryptogram.*

Greek words can be recognized by their use of combining forms—elements that are somewhat analogous to the parts of English compounds. Each part has equal value in determining the meaning of the word, but, unlike Anglo-Saxon compounds, each part must exist in combination with others before it can make a word in English. For example, the Greek combining form "graph" is found in *graphology, graphophonic, autograph,* and *biographic.* Additional phonic correspondences that characterize Greek-based spelling patterns include *y* for /ĭ/ as in *gym; ph* for /f/ as in *philosophy;* and *ch* for /k/ as in *chorus.*

The coinage by 16th-century scholars of *inkhorn terms*—those borrowed directly from another language to refine or embellish one's writing—continued at a great rate, initially with some public controversy but later with greater acceptance. *Irrevocable, irradiation,* and *depopulation* entered the language in this way. As a consequence, English vocabulary expanded by thousands of words that enhanced writers' ability to communicate meaning with flare and precision. For this reason, English remains the language with the richest vocabulary (more than 600,000 words in the *Oxford English Dictionary*) and the most options for expressing a range of abstract ideas and shades of meaning. For example, the words *wedlock* (Anglo-Saxon), *marriage* (Old French), and *matrimony* (Latin) all refer to more or less the same concept, as do *fear* or *dread* (Anglo-Saxon), *terror* (Latin), and *phobia* (Greek).

Exercises 4.1, 4.2, and 4.3 illustrate the relationship between the origin of a word, its structure, and its spelling. If necessary, check Table 4.1 as you complete these exercises.

Exercise 4.1

Identify whether the following words are likely to be Anglo-Saxon (AS), Latin (L), Greek (G), or other (O). Then, satisfy your curiosity by looking them up in a dictionary.

ball __AS__	orbit __L__	sphere __G__
inspect __L__	eye __AS__	ophthalmology __G__
prophylaxis __G__	protection __L__	guard __AS__
maternal __L__	mother __AS__	matriarch __G__
water __AS__	hydrophobia __G__	aqueduct __L__
elevation __L__	hyperbole __G__	high __AS__
tempestuous __L__	stormy __AS__	catastrophic __G__

Exercise 4.2

All of the following words use the digraph spelling *ch*. Sort the words by the sound that *ch* represents. You should have three groups. What do you think is the original language of each word group? What sound does *ch* represent in each?

chauffer sh	chain ch	chagrin sh	lunch ch	school k
chalk ch	chalet sh	cholesterol k	chaos k	chapstick
character k	cheek ch	chateau sh	chuck ch	chemical k
machine sh	chestnut ch	chlorophyll k	cache sh	chlorine k

sh = ʒ   ch = č

Exercise 4.3

Next are some word parts that can be combined to make real words. Put as many together into real words as you can. Why do you think you can combine some parts but not others?

stage	ic	graph	craft	per	ize
ance	form	fright	in	al	eme
ism	ed	de	choreo	coach	ation

The Evolution of Spelling

During the change from Old English to Middle English in the 14th and 15th centuries, scholars adopted spelling habits that added to confusion and inconsistency in vowel representation. Middle English had seven diphthongs, or vowels pronounced with a glide in the middle, that were spelled with letter combinations including *au/aw, ai/ay, ei/ey, u/eu/ew, oi/oy,* and *ou/ow.* Ten vowels were pronounced without a glide, sometimes long and sometimes short in duration. Doubled letters *aa, ee,* and *oo* were sometimes used to show vowel lengthening. Unaccented vowels were reduced to schwa in pronunciation but were most often spelled with *e* or *i*.

Where did "silent *e*" come from? Several change processes account for the final *e* on the ends of syllables with tense vowels. Old English included more inflections than Middle English and over time they were dropped or reduced, leaving only an unaccented neutral vowel pronounced at the ends of Middle English words such as *time, stake,* and *before.* Thus, what to us is "silent *e*" represented a spoken, final syllable in Middle English. Scribes also added a final *e* to some words that were not inflected, such as *home* and *bride,* just for appearance sake or orthographic consistency. By the 16th century, final silent *e* had become a convention of spelling used as a pronunciation guide not only for long vowels but also to mark soft *c* and *g* (*page, chance*) and to prevent words from looking like plurals (*false, else*).

[handwritten margin note: tense vowels = long]

After 16th-century spelling conventions developed, rapid pronunciation changes continued, including a phenomenon known as the Great Vowel Shift. During the 15th and 16th centuries, it became customary to pronounce long vowels /ā/, /ē/, /ī/, /ō/, /ū/ (now represented in the phonetic alphabet as /e/, /i/, /ɑj/, /o/, and /u/ to match the way they were spelled and pronounced in Middle English) with a higher tongue position. The shift resulted in our Modern English tense vowel and diphthong pronunciations, but spellings were preserved from eras during which pronunciation was considerably different from today's speech.

Modern English spelling has been fairly well fixed since the mid-17th century. In 1690, the *New England Primer*, the first American primer for children, was published in Boston and was reprinted and used for more than 100 years. Its spelling patterns were similar to present-day conventional English spelling, with several exceptions, such as using the letters *i* and *j*, and *u* and *v*. A long history of letter confusion accounts for the interchangeability of these letters until Noah Webster's 19th-century dictionary. The Romans had adopted the letter *i* from the Greeks but began to use it to represent not only a vowel sound [i] but also to spell two consonants: [y] as in *bunion* and [ĵ] as in *jump*. When the letter *i* was adopted into English after the Norman invasion, scribes elongated it, writing it as *j*. *Y* was also used in Middle English for [i] at the ends of words. Thus, the custom of changing *y* to *i* when suffixes were added to words, such as *stories* and *beautiful*, began. The *u* and *v* were confused because at one time a bottom-rounded *u* was a version of the Latin *v*; this single letter *u/v* represented both a consonant and a vowel, and the letters were not clearly separated in spelling until about 1700.

By the early 1700s, Jonathan Swift and other literary figures began a movement to preserve and defend the integrity of English against the rampant experimentation and **assimilation** of the Elizabethan period. Writers were literally afraid that their works would drift into oblivion because English lacked standard usage and was so vulnerable to rapid change. A committee of the Royal Academy assumed the duty of purifying English by declaring right and wrong usage. Although the Royal Academy never succeeded in its task, Samuel Johnson volunteered to bring order to chaos by single-handedly writing a dictionary of English with definitions for 40,000 words. Johnson worked for 9 years, finally publishing his work in 1755. This was the first document of standard, Modern English that fixed orthographic patterns, usage, origin, and meanings of words.

Excerpts from Samuel Johnson's dictionary.[7]

Distiller: One who makes and sells pernicious and inflammatory spirits.

Dull: Not exhilarating; not delightful; as, to make dictionaries is dull work.

Excise: A hateful tax levied upon commodities, and adjudged not by the common judges of property, but wretches hired by those to whom excise is paid.

Far-fetch: A deep stratagem. A ludicrous word.

Lexicographer: A writer of dictionaries; a harmless drudge, that busies himself in tracing the original, and detailing the signification of words.

Network: Any thing reticulated or decussated, at equal distances, with interstices between the intersections. [See how he defined reticulated.]

Oats: A grain, which in England is generally given to horses, but in Scotland supports the people.

Patron: One who countenances, supports or protects. Commonly a wretch who supports with insolence, and is paid with flattery.

Pension: An allowance made to any one without an equivalent. In England it is generally understood to mean pay given to a state hireling for treason to his country.

Politician: 1. One versed in the arts of government; one skilled in politicks. 2. A man of artifice; one of deep contrivance.

Reticulated: Made of network; formed with interstitial vacuities.

To worm: To deprive a dog of something, nobody knows what, under his tongue, which is said to prevent him, nobody knows why, from running mad.

English is a system heavily influenced by its word origins in spite of many historical efforts to simplify and standardize its spelling. English continues to adopt words from other languages, assimilating their spellings as well as their meanings (*barbecue, plaza, marijuana,* and *chocolate* from Spanish; *bayou, butte, unique,* and *picayune* from French; *pizza* and *cello* from Italian). For this reason, spelling bee champions may ask, "What is this word's language of origin?" because the answer will provide valuable clues for spelling accuracy.

Phoneme–Grapheme Correspondences in English

The alphabetic writing system of English represents the sounds in spoken words with variable, but teachable, consistency. Although students must know more than the correspondences of letters to sounds in order to read and spell well, phoneme–grapheme relationships are the foundational building blocks of the orthographic code.

What Is a Grapheme?

In this book, the term **grapheme** is an analog to **phoneme**; it refers to any letter or letter combination that corresponds to one phoneme in a printed word. A *grapheme* is a relational or functional unit to represent an element of speech, and it is the symbol for a phoneme.

Why are single letters not our exclusive focus when exploring orthography? Because the alphabet is insufficient for English spelling—we have only 26 Roman letters to spell the 44 phonemes of English. Thus, letter combinations are necessary to spell some consonant phonemes, such as *th, wh, sh, ch,* and *ng,* and many of the 19 vowel sounds, such as *oo, ee, i-e,* and *er.* The alphabetic principle, then, is a concept that students must gain, but they will not know orthography until a few more principles and many specific correspondence patterns are learned.

Graphemes may comprise two, three, or even four letters. The *eigh* in *weight,* the *ough* in *though,* the *igh* in *fight,* and the *tch* in *batch* are multiletter graphemes used to spell a single phoneme. To complicate matters, many phonemes have multiple spellings: The letter combinations *ea, ei, ie, ee, ey,* and *e-e* are all used for "long *e*" ([i]). Although some graphemes have unsounded letters, letter groups form stable configurations that correspond to speech sounds, and most "silent" letters are part of these stable configurations. They are an indispensable part of the grapheme unit, not extraneous letters as some phonics systems teach; therefore, almost all letters have a functional relationship to sound or meaning.

Types of Graphemes

English uses more than 250 graphemes to spell the 44 phonemes of English. Thus, reading is a convergent process whereby we map a limited set of sounds onto various spellings or graphemes. Spelling, however, is a divergent and more challenging process because there are often several ways to spell the same sound.

The grapheme units for spelling consonants include single consonant letters, consonant **digraphs** (two letters that stand for one unique sound), consonant **trigraphs** (three-letter spellings that stand for one consonant sound), consonant **doubles** (doubled *f, l, s,* or *z* in one-syllable words), and silent letter consonant spellings (see Tables 4.2, 4.3, and 4.4). **Consonant blends** are composed of the graphemes for two or three consonant sounds in a cluster that precedes or follows a vowel within a syllable, such as *bl* in *bleak, pr* in *prince, st* in *past, squ* in *square,* and *str* in *street.* **Blends** should not be described as "one sound" in phonics or spelling instruction. Blends can be spelled with combinations of single consonant letters or with combinations that include digraphs, such as *thr* in *three, shr* in *shrimp,* and *phr* in *phrase.*

Table 4.2.   Consonant graphemes

Simple letters	Doublets	Digraphs/trigraphs	Silent letter combinations	Oddities
p, b, t, d	*ff*	*ch/-tch*	*-bt*	*qu* = /kw/
k, c, g	*ll*	*ph*	*gn-*	*x* = /ks/ or /gz/
f, v, s, z, x (/z/)	*ss*	*sh*	*kn-*	
h	*zz*	*-gh*	*-lk*	
m, n		*th*	*-lm*	
w, y		*-ng*	*-mb*	
r, l		*wh*	*-mn*	
j		*-ck*	*ps-*	
		-ge/-dge	*rh-*	
			wr-	

Table 4.3. Vowel graphemes

Lax (short) vowels, single letters	Tense (long) vowels, single letters	VCe pattern	Vowel teams for lax, tense, diphthong, and vowel-*r* sounds	Vowel-*r* combinations
a = *mad*	s*e*-cret	th*eme*	ee, ea, ei, ie, ey	er
e = *mess*	b*a*-by	b*ide*	ai, ay, ei, eigh, ey	ar
i = *bit*	t*a*-ble	m*ade*	ea (for /e/)	or
o = *rob*	d*i*-graph	r*obe*	ie, igh	ur
u = *cut*	cr*y*	c*ute*	oa, ow, oe, ough	ir
u = *put*	r*o*-bot	r*are*	ue, ui, ew, ou, ough	
y = *gym*		h*ere*	au, aw, augh	
		f*ire*	oo (book)	
		st*ore*	ou, ow	
		s*ure*	oi, oy	
			ear, eer, air, oar, our	

Exercise 4.4

Underline the consonant blends and put a box or paretheses around the consonant digraphs in the following words. Be careful and think about the sounds the letters are representing. Some words do not have blends or digraphs. Refer to Table 4.2 if in doubt.

shirt	debt	whole	strength	zilch	Ethernet
track	illness	squeeze	Grinch	decoy	psychology

Vowel graphemes include single vowel letters, **vowel-consonant-*e* (VCe)** patterns, **vowel teams,** and vowel-*r* combinations, also known as *r*-controlled vowels. *Vowel teams* are combinations of letters that correspond to single vowel sounds, such as *oa, ay, ee,* and *ou.* Therefore, the combinations *igh* in *sigh, eigh* in *weigh, augh* in *daughter, ough* in *though, eig* in *reign,* and *eau* in *beauty* are vowel teams. The letters work together to spell a vowel phoneme. (Note that we are avoiding the term *vowel digraph* because vowel teams may be more than two letters and to avoid confusion with consonant digraphs.)

Some letters in English orthography are used as markers; that is, they have no direct relation to sound themselves, but they signal the sound of other letters. Examples include the *k* in *picnicking* that keeps the *c* from sounding like [s]; the *e* that always follows *v* at the ends of words such as *have* and *love;* the *e* in *continue* that keeps the word from ending in a plain *u;* the *u* in *guess* that keeps the *g* from sounding like [j], and, of course, the *e* in *date* that marks the long vowel. (Note that graphemes are spellings for individual phonemes; those in the word list [see Table 4.4] are among the most common spellings, but the list does not include all possible graphemes for a given consonant.)

Table 4.4. Spellings for consonant phonemes

Phonetic symbol	Phonic symbol	Examples	Graphemes for spelling
/p/	p	*pit, spider, stop*	*p*
/b/	b	*bit, brat, bubble*	*b*
/m/	m	*mitt, slam, comb, hymn*	*m, mb, mn*
/t/	t	*tickle, mitt, sipped*	*t, tt, ed*
/d/	d	*die, loved, handle*	*d, ed*
/n/	n	*nice, knight, gnat*	*n, kn, gn*
/k/	k	*kite, crib, duck, chorus, walk, quiet*	*k, c, ck, ch, lk, q*
/g/	g	*girl, Pittsburgh*	*g, gh*
/ŋ/	ng	*sing, bank, English*	*n, ng*
/f/	f	*fluff, sphere, tough, calf*	*f, ff, gh, ph, lf*
/v/	v	*van, love*	*v, ve*
/s/	s	*sit, pass, science, psychic*	*s, ss, sc, ps*
/z/	z	*zip, jazz, rose, dogs, Xerox*	*z, zz, se, s, x*
/θ/	th	*thin, breath, ether*	*th*
/ð/	th	*this, breathe, either*	*th*
/š/	sh	*shoe, sure, charade*	*sh, s, ch*
/ž/	zh	*measure, azure, garage*	*s, z, ge*
/č/	ch	*cheap, etch, nature*	*ch, tch, t*
/ǰ/	j	*judge, wage, educate*	*j, ge, dge, d*
/l/	l	*lamb, call, single*	*l, ll, le*
/r/	r	*reach, wrap*	*r, wr*
/j/, /y/	y	*you, onion*	*y, i*
/w/	w	*witch, queen, (which)*	*w, (q)u, (wh)*
/ʍ/	wh	*where, when*	*wh*
/h/	h	*house, rehab, whole*	*h, wh*

Note: Graphemes are spellings for individual phonemes; those listed are among the most common spellings, but the list does not include all possible graphemes for a given consonant. Hanna, Hanna, Hodges, and Rudorf's (1966) tables are recommended for lists of all possible spellings.

Some Odd Consonants

The spelling system of English sometimes assigns letters to odd or unusual roles. The system does, at times, break patterns or rules by recruiting vowel letters to protect consonants (the *u* in *guest*), consonant letters to protect vowels (the *d* in *fudge*), or letter combinations that serve to differentiate similar words (*loose, lose*).

Versatile Letters *x, w, u, y*   A few letters in English orthography play multiple or unique roles in the print mapping system. These puzzlers all occur toward the end of the alphabet sequence.

- The letter *x* can correspond to [z] as in *Xerox,* to [ks] as in *mix,* or to [gz] as in *exact.* It is the only single letter that represents two phonemes. The voiceless correspondence [ks] occurs when the *x* lies between a stressed and an unstressed vowel as in *exit* and *excellent,* and the voiced equivalent [gz] occurs when the *x* is between an unstressed and a stressed vowel as in *examine* and *exist*.

- The letter *u* has three roles. It is used as a consonant when it corresponds to [w], as in *quack*, *assuage*, and *language*. It is used as a vowel unit by itself as in *cut* and *unknown*, or as part of a vowel team as in *sausage*, *blue*, and *fruit*. It also serves as a marker in *guest* and *vague*, serving to keep the *g* from being softened by the *e*.

- The letter *w* acts as a consonant when it represents [w], as in *water* and *beware*. It can be part of a vowel team spelling as in *snow*, *few*, or *saw*, where it marks lip rounding, but it is never a vowel by itself.

- The letter *y* is a consonant when it represents [y], as in *yes* and *beyond*. It can represent one of three vowel sounds when it is used alone ([i], [ɪ], [ɑj], as in *baby*, *gyp*, and *cry*). Or, it can be part of a vowel team spelling as in *toy*, *key*, *buy*, or *stay*.

Soft *c* and *g*   The phonemes [s] and [ǰ] are often spelled with the letters *c* and *g*, followed by the letters *e*, *i*, and *y*. These consonant sounds are described as "soft" *c* and *g*, whose use we can attribute to the Old French influence on English.

- Examples of soft *c*: *cent, face, cedar, city, cider, cymbal, cytoplasm, cynicism*

- Examples of soft *g*: *gentle, gyrate, gigantic, gesture, wage, college*

Many words, such as *give*, *gift*, and *get*, break the soft *g* rule; it is not as predictable as the soft *c* rule.

Spellings (Graphemes) for Vowel Phonemes

Vowel graphemes have a more variable relationship to phonemes than consonant graphemes do. Graphemes for short vowels are more predictable than those for long vowels and diphthongs. In Figures 4.6 and 4.7, vowel phonemes are arranged by place of articulation, from front to back and high to low, and the list of words below each vowel contains examples of the most common spellings for each vowel. The first table uses phonic symbols for the vowels, and the second uses phonetic symbols.

Phoneme–Grapheme Mapping

Once we understand the basic correspondence principle—that letters or letter groups represent phonemes—then phoneme–grapheme mapping is possible. Phoneme–grapheme mapping is the process of matching letters and letter groups to the phonemes they represent. Methods for teaching phoneme–grapheme correspondence include manipulating grapheme tiles to spell words or circling the graphemes in a printed word. In Exercise 4.5, we use a grid to place graphemes into boxes.

96

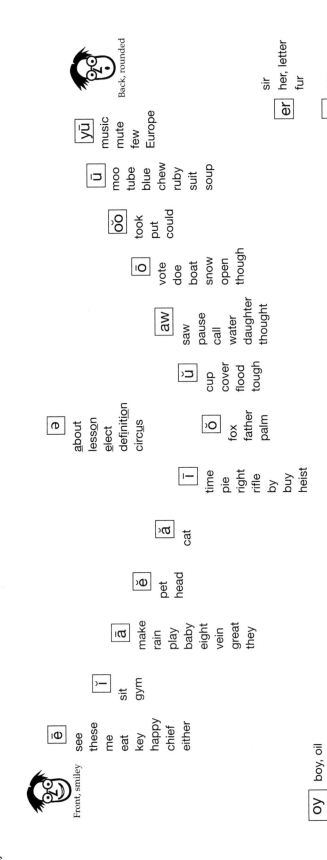

Figure 4.6. Spellings for vowels (phonic symbols) positioned by place of articulation.

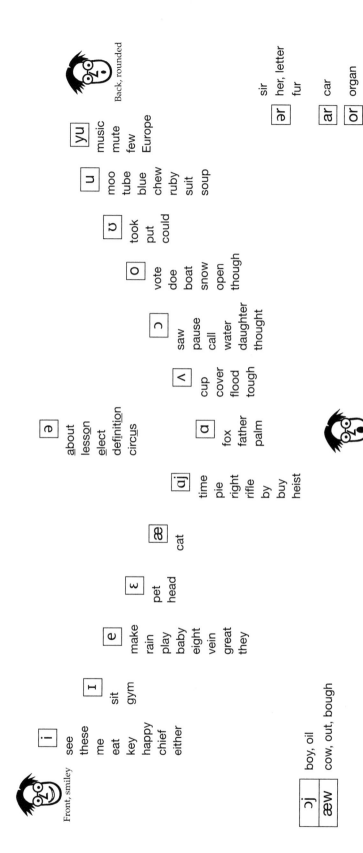

Figure 4.7. Spellings for vowels (phonetic symbols) positioned by place of articulation.

Exercise 4.5

Each box in the following grid stands for a phoneme. First, count the phonemes in each word and determine how many boxes you will need to map the word. Next, identify the letters or letter combinations (graphemes) that correspond to the phonemes in the following words and write them in the boxes. For example, the graphemes in *shriek* are sh / r / ie / k.

Word	First sound	Second sound	Third sound	Fourth sound	Fifth sound
shriek	sh	r	ie	k	
sow					
slew					
shoe					
batch					
eight					
neighbor					
sharp					
Jell-o					
tough					
through					
thought					
drought					
draught					

Phoneme–grapheme mapping requires that we know how the letters work. While practicing phoneme segmentation in Chapter 2, we learned that we needed to identify and categorize phonemes and distinguish them from allophones. Similarly, we should take the guesswork out of the correspondence system through explicit and systematic teaching.[8]

Spellings Determined by Position of a Phoneme in a Word

The position of a phoneme in a word, the letter sequences in a word, and the stress patterns in syllables affect how phonemes are spelled. Grapheme correspondences, although numerous, are constrained by these aspects of word structure. For example, there are many ways to spell the phoneme /k/, as listed in Table 4.4, but some spellings are used only in some positions. Sorting words into groups that use a common spelling is a good way to investigate these constraints on graphemes, as in Exercise 4.6.

 Exercise 4.6

These one-syllable words have been sorted by the spelling of the phoneme /k/, which can be spelled *c, k, ck,* or *q* in the *qu* combination. What can you discover about the pattern? Answer the questions. Add words to each category to see if the pattern holds.

count	kick	stack	quest
cab	keg	mock	queen
cull	keep	fleck	quit
comb	kind	buck	quaint
cusp	kiss	wick	quote

a)   Letter *c* is followed by which vowels?

b)   Letter *k* is followed by which vowels?

c)   *Ck* is preceded by what kind of vowel phoneme?

d)   *Qu* stands for which two phonemes?

At the end of a syllable following an accented short vowel, *ck* is the preferred spelling for /k/, as in *decks, sticker,* and *bucket.* The *qu* combination, which represents the two phonemes /k/ + /w/, always occurs before a vowel. (Words borrowed from French that end in /k/, spelled *que,* such as *antique,* are the exception.) Whether the letter *k* or *c* is used to spell /k/ at the beginnings of syllables depends on the letter or phoneme that follows it. When /k/ is followed by vowels spelled with *a, o,* or *u,* the letter *c* is used, as in *cat, cushion,* and *cozy;* when /k/ is followed by vowel letters *i* or *e,* the letter *k* is used, as in *kite, ketchup,* and *keen.* In consonant blends, /k/ followed by /r/ or /l/ is always spelled with a *c,* as in *clean* and *crazy.* As we explored in the beginning of this chapter, word origin also determines spelling: *ch* for /k/ is used almost exclusively in words of Greek origin, such as *chorus* and *orchestra.*

Short Vowels Attract Consonants   Three other "choice" spellings

for consonants are similar to the *ck* pattern. Syllables with short vowels crave the protection of consonants. Extra consonants wrap a vowel inside a closed syllable and prevent it from bursting forth with its name (long sound).

The **floss rule** or *f, l, s* letter doubling pattern is the first example of the attraction between short vowels and extra consonant guardians. Note that a short vowel, spelled with one letter, precedes the double *f, l,* or *s* in these words:

f	*l*	*s*
stiff, cliff	spell, well	mess, chess, guess
staff, chaff	spill, fill	miss, kiss, hiss
stuff, muff	shall*	mass, class, pass
scoff, doff	cull, mull, dull	moss, gloss, toss
		muss, fuss, truss

*Note that the *all* pattern of *ball, wall,* and *call* is a not a short vowel pattern but an exception or oddity.

This consonant doubling pattern extends to some short vowel words ending in /z/, as in *fizz, jazz,* and *fuzz.*

The short vowel's need for extra consonant protection also explains why and when we use *tch* for /č/ and *dge* for /ǰ/. Let's explore these one at a time. In the following exercise, sort the words and confirm for yourself what is going on with this pattern.

Exercise 4.7

Sort these words into three groups by the spelling for the final consonant /č/: those that end in *ch*; consonant + *ch*; and *tch*. When does *tch* represent /č/? When is *ch* used at the ends of words? (The words *such, much, rich, which, sandwich, bachelor,* and *ostrich* do not follow this rule; they are exceptions.)

blotch	wrench	scratch	mulch
squelch	fetch	crutch	arch
hatch	haunch	screech	ouch
pooch	wretch	zilch	patch

The examples for the *ch, tch* alternation in Exercise 4.7 were all one-syllable words. By definition, the vowels are accented in one-syllable words. What happens in multisyllable words when schwa often occurs in the unaccented syllable(s)? Here is a pattern in which syllable stress or de-stress is an additional factor that determines which grapheme a word will contain (Exercise 4.8).

Exercise 4.8

These words are sorted by the way in which the final phoneme /ǰ/ is spelled. What is going on here? Write a header for each one of these columns.

dodge	wage	village
wedge	gouge	appendage
budge	scrooge	advantage
lodge	siege	steerage
ridge	huge	college
badge	gauge	bandage

a)   Is the letter *j* ever used to spell /j/ at the ends of words in English?

b)   Why is *g* followed by *e* at the ends of words?

c)   What purpose does *d* serve in the first column of words?

Vowel Alternations or "Choice" Spellings

The variation of sound–symbol correspondences based on phoneme position can also be illustrated with vowels. For example, the diphthong [ɔj] is spelled *oi* in the middle of a syllable, as in *boil, void, coin,* and *hoist,* but is spelled *oy* at the end of a syllable, as in *toy, annoy,* and *loyal.*

Spellings for the long vowel [o] are more complex. When we learn to spell words such as *boat, coat; potato, tomato; toe, foe, Joe, woe;* and *snow, stow, bow, throw,* part of what we learn implicitly is the probability of certain spellings for sounds in certain positions. Of the 20,000 words most commonly used in English, those ending in the phoneme [o] use a plain *o* spelling 140 times, *oe* 12 times, and *ow* 74 times.[9] Only two words with unaccented final syllables ending with [o] spell it with *oe: mistletoe* and *oboe.* Just for good measure, it is also interesting to note that when /t/ and /d/ follow [o], the preferred spelling is *oa,* as in *boat, float, goad,* and *load.* Finally, [o] in the middle of accented syllables at the ends of words is most often spelled *o*-consonant-*e* as in *abode, enclose,* and *alone.* This is the sort of information most of us learn by exposure to multiple examples rather than through conscious memorization of a rule system. Preferred spellings for some vowels depend on whether they come at the beginning, middle, or end of a word. Table 4.5 summarizes some of the most common vowel spelling alternations.

Table 4.5.   Common vowel spellings by position in a syllable or word

Vowel	Middle of a syllable	End of a word	Examples
long *e*	ee, ea	y	creep, eat, baby
long *a*	a_e, ai	ay	race, rain, ray
long *i*	i_e, igh	y	ice, sight, spy
long *o*	o_e, oa	ow	vote, boat, bow
long *u*	u_e	ew, ue	rude, dew, blue
diphthong /ɔj/	oi	oy	spoil, soy
diphthong /æw/	ou (ow before n, l)	ow	cloud, clown, cow
/ɔ/	au (aw before n, l)	aw	fraud, dawn, saw

Spelling Requires Pattern Recognition

Learning to decode print and spell it is not a rote visual memory process. Memory for the letters in print is mediated by pattern recognition, and print images are networked into the language system of the brain. Orthographic patterns are internalized through exposure to multiple examples, opportunities to sort and compare words, and explicit instruction in the most dependable patterns. The goal of instruction should be to enhance students' attention to orthographic detail so they know what to look at and think about as they decipher print. Once students understand that graphemes map to speech in predictable ways, they will have strategies for analyzing and making sense of orthography. Word study activities, however, must also respect the diversity, complexity, and multilayered nature of language organization. In addition to knowing the spellings that are most likely given the sequence of phonemes in a word and spelling by position, students also need to know about spelling conventions for syllables, how syllables are assembled in longer words, stress patterns in words with two or more syllables, and conventions for adding suffixes.

Orthographic Conventions

Orthographic conventions include patterns of correspondence larger than or independent of phoneme–grapheme relationships. In English, conventions established by scribes often determine letter sequences and letter doubling. In addition, letter patterns may represent sequences of phonemes or may indicate whether a vowel is long or short.

Constraints on Letter Use

In addition to the sound–symbol rule system, the orthography embodies constraints on permissible letter sequences and letter uses, many of which were settled by the writers of dictionaries and primers for children in the 18th and 19th centuries. Some letters in English can never be doubled within a syllable or between syllables, such as *j, y, i* (exception: *skiing*), and *k* (exception: *bookkeeper*). Consonant *digraphs* (*sh, th, wh, ch, sh, ng, ph, gh*) act as relational units and spell single speech sounds; they also cannot be doubled. A doubled consonant or its substitute must intervene between a stressed short vowel syllable and an inflected ending beginning with a vowel, such as *grabbing* or *drugged*. The complex spellings *ck, dge, tch,* and *x* replace or act similar to doubled consonants after short or lax vowels, in words such as *picnicking, dodger, pitching,* and *boxer,* signaling that the preceding vowel is lax. Tense vowel sounds can never be spelled with single vowel letters before complex consonant graphemes.

Some letters in English are never used in word-final position, particularly *j* and *v*. Thus, the permissible spellings for word-final [ĭ] are *dge* and *ge*. In words ending with [v], such as *love, have, sieve, live, dove, leave,* and *salve,* the marker *e* is placed at the end of the word so that it does not violate the "*v* rule," regardless of the pronunciation of the vowel. In this way, then, all the *v* words are predictable—not according to sound–symbol correspondence necessarily, but according to orthographic convention.

The letter *e* has several uses in orthography. Sometimes it acts a relational unit, that is, it represents phonemes directly, as in *we* and *bet*, and sometimes it acts as a marker within a larger orthographic pattern, as in *rose* and *enrage*. The letter *e* indicates when a vowel is long, as in *drape* and *probe*. It indicates when a *c* or a *g* should have its "soft" sound, as in *stooge, receive,* and *nice*. As mentioned before, the letter *e* was also placed at the ends of words with [s] to keep them from looking like plurals, not to mark the vowel (*please*, not *pleas; horse*, not *hors; mouse*, not *mous*). No wonder the letter *e* is the most overworked letter in English spelling!

Six Types of Written Syllables

English has six basic spelling patterns for syllables. Noah Webster regularized these to justify the division of words in his 1806 dictionary. The syllable types are useful to know for two reasons: 1) they help explain spelling patterns such as doubled letters, and 2) they help students recognize and recall longer printed words more efficiently. Students who notice redundant patterns in print can develop automatic word recognition and spelling skills.

The syllable chunks that students can learn to identify in print are a contrivance of scholars—a tool for attacking longer unknown words—but they do not correspond directly to the natural syllable breaks in speech. Compare the natural break between syllables in speech with the rule-based division of syllables in the following words.

Spoken language	Written language
mi-ddle	mid-dle
a-ffec-ta-tion	af-fect-a-tion
va-len-tine	val-en-tine
li-fting	lift-ing
com-bi-na-tion	com-bin-a-tion

In speaking, we tend to place consonant phonemes at the beginning of the next syllable, instead of tacking them on to a vowel. (Linguists call this the *maximal onset* rule.) We naturally break our voice right after vowel sounds. The print conventions for spelling syllables, therefore, pertain to orthography—not to speech. It is important to make this distinction during instruction so that students will attend to printed letter sequences when they are reading and spelling. They will not be able to resolve syllable division questions by appealing to pronunciation alone.

The six syllable spelling types are organized around the vowel in the nucleus of the syllable. They help the reader identify the vowel sound in an unknown word. The closed syllable is the most common spelling unit in English. A closed syllable has a short vowel, spelled with one letter, which is

Table 4.6.   Types of syllable spelling patterns

Syllable type	Examples	Definition
Closed	*dapple* *hospital* *beverage*	A syllable with a short vowel, spelled with one letter, ending in one or more consonants
Vowel-Consonant-e	*compete* *despite* *conflate*	A syllable with a long vowel spelled with one vowel, one consonant, and final silent *e*
Open	*program* *table* *recent*	A syllable that ends with a long vowel sound, spelled with a single vowel letter
Vowel team	*awful* *trainable* *congeal* *spoil*	Syllables with long, short, or diphthong vowel sounds that use a letter combination for spelling
Vowel-*r*	*intern* *report* *starter*	A syllable with a single vowel letter followed by *r* (*or, er, ur, ar, ir*). Vowel pronunciation changes before /r/.
Consonant-*le*	*bible* *beagle* *little*	An unaccented final syllable containing a single consonant, *l*, and silent *e*.

always followed by one or more consonants. Three other syllable types can spell long vowels—VCe, open, and vowel team syllables (see Table 4.6).

What syllable patterns do not fit these categories or patterns? Many final, unaccented syllables have schwas in them. Suffixes and final syllables, such as act*ive*, cott*age*, natur*al*, and nat*ion*, do not clearly fit the standard syllable patterns. Unaccented syllables with schwas must be dealt with at another level—**morphology**—which is the subject of Chapter 5.

Vowel-*r* patterns are also confusing. Instead of using the traditional term *r-controlled vowel*, this book uses the more explicit term *vowel-r* to designate the *ar, er, ir, or,* and *ur* combinations in spelling. The vowel phonemes [ɛr], [ɑr], and [or] are spelled with other syllable types as well. *Poor, four, hear, peer, flour,* and *stair*, for example, are all spelled with vowel teams. *Bare, here, fire, pure,* and *more* are all spelled with the VCe pattern. So, vowel-*r* syllables are found in words such as *girl, her, burn, for,* and *star*.

Try the next exercise; refer to Table 4.6 as necessary.

Exercise 4.9

Classify the syllables in the words into the seven columns, one for each syllable type. List the syllables in columns. Look out for the schwa; put it aside. A few samples are done for you.

re-sent	hu-mid	mi-nor	jun-gle	in-spect
ab-cess	ta-ble	lex-eme	ti-tle	ea-ger
im-pale	re-mark	com-pete	few-er	a-mong
ab-surd	com-bine	boast-ful	ail-ment	hair-cut

Closed	VCe	Open	Vowel team	Vowel-*r*	Consonant-*le*	Schwa
sent	*eme*	*re*	*ail*	*nor*	*gle*	*a*

When Doubled Letters Occur Between Syllables

The consistency of these written syllable types explains, in many cases, why letters are doubled between syllables, such as *ladder, better,* and *poppy,* and why we have a consonant doubling rule for adding endings that begin with vowels, such as *humming, beginner,* and *popped.* Closed syllables must end in at least one consonant. Consonant doubling within a word lessens the ambiguity for the reader because the vowel that precedes the doubled consonant must be short if the consonants that follow are doubled. Consider the differences between the following word pairs.

A	B	A	B
writing	written	stable	scrabble
rabies	rabbits	needle	nettle
butane	button	super	supper
prefix	suffix	motel	mottle

Syllable types are particularly useful for understanding what happens when words with closed or open syllables are connected to consonant-*le* syllables. If the vowel of the first syllable is short, then the syllable will be closed and will end in a consonant. If the first syllable is followed by a consonant-*le,* then a doubled consonant will result, as in *scrabble, little,* and *goggle.* If the first syllable is open, then it will end with a long vowel sound; there will be no consonant to close it and protect the vowel. When an open syllable is followed by a consonant-*le,* there will not be a doubled consonant between the syllables, as in *able, title,* and *ogle.*

When the Vowel Is Ambiguous in Longer Words

Syllable patterns in English are not completely transparent or predictable. Sometimes, longer word recognition requires flexibility and educated guesswork.

The VCV Syllable Juncture   Unfortunately, syllable patterns do not resolve all ambiguities of pronunciation when we read an unknown word. We cannot tell if the vowel in the first syllable of a longer word should be long or short if it is spelled with only one consonant between the syllables and we have no idea what the word means. The words in Exercise 4.10 illustrate why we sometimes must try different vowel sounds when adjacent syllables are separated by only one consonant letter.

Exercise 4.10

Divide these words at their syllable boundaries. Which group of words begins with closed syllables? Which group begins with open syllables?

ever _____	even _____
lemon _____	lemur _____
wagon _____	wager _____
comic _____	coma _____
polish _____	Polish _____
relish _____	relax _____

All of the words have a VCV sequence between the first and second syllables. What should we tell our students? To guess thoughtfully! Chance favors a long vowel pronunciation in the first syllable (V-CV division). About 75% of the time, the long vowel will be correct because the first syllable will be open. Students should learn to recognize the VCV syllable juncture pattern and try the long vowel first to see if the word makes sense. If it does not, then try the short vowel (VC-V division). One of these strategies will work.

When Schwa Happens   Syllable types are useful, but something happens in longer words that complicates spelling—schwa. The vowel in an unstressed syllable often loses its stuffing. The vowel sound becomes indistinct or neutral—it has no clear identity. During reading, students can "flex" and produce a schwa as they pronounce a word correctly, but during spelling, they cannot as easily tell what a vowel spelling ought to be. This is one major reason why phonetic spelling may be inaccurate.

Pronounce the following words naturally. Could you spell the vowels by sounding out?

*a*ffect   wag*o*n   lem*o*n   c*a*tastrophe   c*o*mmence   s*a*lute

Syllable types and juncture patterns are helpful for reading and spelling longer words, but are an incomplete set of principles for learning words. Ultimately, students will need to learn the graphemes, syllables, and morphemes within words, as well as something about their meaning and origin. Following is a basic, teachable strategy for reading longer words.

1. Locate and put a line under each vowel grapheme in the word (not final silent *e*). Vowel teams are one vowel sound. If necessary, mark the vowel and consonant sequences with *v* or *c* under neighboring graphemes.

2. Box any familiar endings, such as *ing, ed,* or *ful.*

3. Circle any familiar beginning word parts, such as *re, un,* or *mis.*

4. Use knowledge of syllables to decode the vowel sounds. Scoop the pencil under each syllable, blending the sounds left to right.

5. Say the whole word and see if it makes sense. Flex the accent—try it different ways if it does not sound right.

6. Check the context for clarification. Ask if you do not know it.[10]

Identifying syllables and how they join together becomes important to students at about third grade because they must independently decode words of greater length. If they are not taught to perceive the larger chunks of written words and to associate vowel pronunciation with syllable structure, then they may be stymied by longer words encountered in reading. Yet, if they are aware of syllable units and where to divide them, then they can read words such as *detective, insulation, fantastic,* and *accomplishment* with little trouble.

Three Principles for Dividing Longer Words by Syllable

1. VC-CV—two consonants between two vowels. When syllables have two adjacent consonants between them, we divide between the consonants. The first syllable will be closed (with a short vowel).

   sub-let   nap-kin   pen-ny   win-some

2. V-CV and VC-V—one consonant between two vowels. First, try dividing before the consonant. This makes the first syllable open and the vowel long. This strategy will work 75% of the time with VCV syllable division.

   e-ven   ra-bies   de-cent   ri-val

   If the word is not recognized, then try dividing after the consonant. This makes the first syllable closed and the vowel sound short. This strategy will work 25% of the time with VCV syllable division.

   ev-er   rab-id   dec-ade   riv-er

3. Consonant blends usually stick together. Do not separate digraphs when using the first two principles for decoding.

   e-ther   spec-trum   se-quin

Orthographic Rules for Adding Suffixes

There are three major rules that govern addition of suffixes to base words. They are much easier to learn and teach if students are familiar with the vowel spelling patterns contained in the basic syllable types. Before reviewing these rules, notice that some suffixes begin with consonants and some with vowels. This will be important for understanding when the ending rules apply.

Examples of suffixes beginning with vowels are *ing, es, ed, en, y, ist, ish, al, ence, ance, ible, able, ous, er, est, ity, ic, age,* and *ary.* Examples of suffixes beginning with consonants are *ful, ment, ly, ness, tion, hood,* and *less.*

Consonant Doubling   When a one-syllable word with one vowel ends in one consonant, double the final consonant before adding a suffix beginning with a vowel, as in *wettest, sinner,* and *crabbing.* Do not double the consonant if the suffix begins with a consonant.

 Exercise 4.11

Fill in the missing words or endings.

begin + ing = _____	pat + _____ = patted
sad + ness = _____	_____ + er = runner
beg + er = _____	step + _____ = stepped
bad + ly = _____	_____ + ing = skipping

Advanced Consonant Doubling   When a base word has more than one syllable, and if the final syllable is accented and has one vowel followed by one consonant, then double the final consonant when adding an ending beginning with a vowel, as in *inferred, permitted,* and *embedded* versus *signaling, worshiped,* and *traveler.*

 Exercise 4.12

Why is the consonant doubled or not doubled in these words?

infer	inference	inferred	inferring
remit	remitted	remittance	remitting
repel	repelling	repelled	repellant
travel	traveling	traveled	traveler
worship	worshiper	worshiping	worshiped

Drop Silent *e*   When a base word ends in a silent *e*, drop the *e* when adding a suffix beginning with a vowel. Keep the *e* before a suffix beginning with a consonant, as in *blaming, confinement, extremely,* and *pasted.*

 Exercise 4.13

Fill in the blanks.

Base word	+	suffix	=	affixed word
grime	+	y	=	grimy
rude	+	ly	=	_____
grate	+	ful	=	_____
secure	+	ity	=	_____
shame	+	ful	=	_____

rose	+	y	=	_____
poke	+	ing	=	_____
late	+	est	=	_____
state	+	ment	=	_____
fare	+	ed	=	_____

Change *y* to *i*   When a root ends in a *y* preceded by a consonant, change *y* to *i* before a suffix, as in *tried*, except when adding *ing* as in *crying* and *hurrying*. Note that *y* changes to *i* even if the suffix begins with a consonant, as in *happiness*. If the base word ends in a *y* preceded by a vowel, as in *ay, ey, uy*, and *oy*, then just add the suffix.

 ## Exercise 4.14

Take these words apart into the base word and the suffix, and explain what happened to make these spellings.

studious	beautiful	stories	studying
keyed	sillier	sorriest	happiness
uglier	praying	buying	partying

Is English Orthography Predictable or Unpredictable?

As this chapter and the next explain, the correspondence system used to spell the individual speech sounds in words is predictable to a great extent, as long as several factors are considered. Among these are the position of a sound in a word ([f] cannot be spelled with a *gh* at the beginning of a syllable but can be at the end, as in *rough*), the sounds that come before or after a given sound (the [f] in *sphere* must be spelled with a *ph* because it comes after [s]), the letter sequences that English allows (we can double *f* but not *ph*), and the history of a word in the evolution of Modern English (*ph* spells [f] in words of Greek origin).

English words cannot be divided simply into two categories—regular and irregular—and materials or tests that classify words in this way are oversimplifying linguistic reality. The psychological or cognitive factors that enable people to remember words include the intensity of emotional associations with a word (*sex*), its frequency in an individual's writing (*they, of, said*), whether it follows a pattern at all (*colonel*), and whether it is so unusual that its oddity makes it memorable (*ski*). In addition, some word spellings are less probable in the overall rule system but are members of a small family of common words that can be learned the same as words that conform to a domain-inclusive rule. For example, *he, she, be*, and *we* all share the spelling for [i] and are among the most common words in the language, even though they violate the rule for spelling [i] at the ends of words (*ee* is more often used, as in *bee, fee, glee, thee, tree, free, knee, agree, tee, flee*, and *scree*). If we construct a predictability scale that represents a continuum of absolutely predictable spellings (0) to spellings that recur as part of a family but are less common than the alternative graphemes for the same sound (5), then it might look like the following.

0	1	2	3	4	5
tin	quit	care	catch	pie	hurt
pup	beck	hope	dodge	tea	weigh
bad	crab	kite	child	put	feud

0, no other way to spell the sounds; 5, low-frequency choice, still in a "family"

How faithfully does the English spelling system represent speech sounds, however, given all the "rules" of correspondence that can be identified? The first definitive analyses of English orthography were accomplished by Venezky[11] and Hanna, Hanna, Hodges, and Rudorf[12] who were commissioned by the (then) U.S. Office of Education to resolve the question of regularity in the English spelling system. Venezky wrote a classic paper on the structure and nature of English orthography, explaining the levels at which correspondences operated. Hanna et al. selected the 17,000 most often used words in English print and analyzed them by computer for sound–symbol regularities. Hanna et al. identified 52 speech sounds, including r-controlled vowel variations, coded the words by their constituent phonemes, and then asked the computer to list the spellings for each sound by the position of the sound in the word. The program identified more than 170 spellings for phonemes in specific positions (initial, medial, final).

Hanna and colleagues demonstrated that at least 20 phonemes had spellings that were more than 90% predictable, and 10 others were predictable more than 80% of the time. Vowels were less consistent than consonants. Only 8 phonemes out of 52 that were analyzed had individual predictability of less than 78%, and 5 of these were vowels.

Facts About English Predictability

Consider the following facts:

- Fifty percent of English words are spelled accurately by sound–symbol correspondence rule alone.

- Thirty-six percent more are spelled with only one error.

- Ten percent more are spelled accurately if word meaning, origin, and morphology are considered.

- Fewer than 4% are true oddities.

If multiple layers of language organization are taken into account, then English is a predictable and rule-based spelling system. Using the 17,000 words from which rules were generated, Hanna et al. found that 50% of English vocabulary could be spelled with no errors, and another 36% could be spelled with one error, using only phoneme–grapheme correspondence rules. Only 14% of the words were "irregular" in that the sound–symbol algorithm spelled them with two or more errors, but many of those errors could be easily corrected by a person (or computer) who knew the word's origin and meaning.

There are a few sound–symbol relationships in English that are predictable and invariant. The computer algorithm produced correct spellings for these sounds almost every time. These include the spelling for [ʍ] and [θ], which are always spelled with *wh* and *th*. In addition, except for the word *of*, the sound [v] is always spelled with a *v*, and *v* is always marked with a silent *e* at the ends of words, regardless of the vowel sound, as in *dove, have,* and *live*.

As one would predict, the computer did not do well at spelling compound forms, such as *caretaker* and *daybreak* (they became *cartaecer* and *dabrake*). The sound–symbol algorithm did not account for morphological structure, such as assimilated prefixes in <u>ir</u>*rational* and <u>ab</u>*breviate*. Word families that represent spelling generalizations, such as the "*f, l,* and *s* doubling rule" (*mess, stiff,* and *grass*), and those that use the *old, ild, ind,* and *ost* patterns were also missed by the computer. Adopted foreign language spelling patterns, such as *chaise, buffet, beige, croquet,* and *machete* also caused mix-ups because they do not conform to the same rule system.

There were a few words whose spellings were unique or truly unpredictable. Some were compounds, affixed forms, or foreign words. Others were of Latin or Greek derivation with complex morphological structure, such as *philosophize, psychology, semicircular, officiate, schizophrenia, polysyllabic,* and *accommodating*. Others were the high-frequency, Anglo-Saxon words for common things and ideas, including *said, does, were, who, one, two, their, lose, gone,* and *done*. Most of those were at one time pronounced in a way that is consistent with their spelling. It is safe to say that only about 4% of the words in English spelling are true oddities.

Morphology and Orthography

The last principle for understanding and explaining the spelling of English words is that spellings represent meaning as well as sound, which will be the subject of Chapter 5. After exploring phoneme–grapheme correspondences and orthographic patterns, we are ready to shift focus to the many ways that orthography represents the meaningful units of language.

Summary

English orthography is a morphophonemic system. It represents phoneme–grapheme correspondences and meaningful word parts. Thus, it is said to be a "deep" orthography and it is more difficult to read and spell than other languages whose orthographies directly represent the correspondences between sound and print.

English, however, is not as irregular or problematic as its critics contend. Most words can be explained on the basis of sound patterns, spelling conventions, word sense, or word history. Spellings in English are influenced by the historical languages from which words originated. Words that evolved from the oldest, Germanic, base language—Anglo-Saxon—have the least direct relationship with sound although those words are the most common. Words that evolved from French use special spellings for some consonants (e.g., soft *c* and *g*) and vowels (e.g., *ou* as in *soup*). Words that evolved from Latin preserve consistent spellings of prefixes, roots, and suffixes, as in *expression, defensible,* and *rehabilitate.* Greek-based words use special spellings for the sounds [k], [f], and [ɪ], as in *chlorophyll,* and often combine common meaningful parts that are spelled consistently (*arthritis, arthroscopic, arthrometer*).

Phoneme–grapheme correspondence is the core structure of English orthography. A grapheme is a unit of spelling that corresponds to a phoneme. A grapheme in English may be one to four letters in length (*so; sew; though*). Grapheme types for consonants include single letters, digraphs, trigraphs, doubled letters, and silent letter spellings. Grapheme types for vowels include single letters, the VCe pattern, vowel-*r* combinations, and vowel teams.

In one-syllable words, grapheme choice is sometimes governed by the position of a sound in a word or by conventions of letter use. For example, accented short vowels are often followed by doubled consonants, but unaccented ones are not, as in the two spellings for final [k] in *attack* and *attic.* The final vowel sounds in *boy* and *stay* are spelled differently from the medial vowel sounds in *boil* and *stain.*

Vowel pronunciation in longer English words is often indicated through conventions of syllable representation. There are six basic syllable types in English, plus a few odd final syllable spellings for unaccented suffixes. Closed syllables, with short vowels closed in by one or more consonants, are the most common syllables in English. Long vowels are spelled with vowel-consonant-*e* patterns, vowel teams, or single letters in open syllables. Vowel-*r* combinations are among the most variable spellings in English, as in the spellings for [ɛr] in *her, girl, turn, word,* and *onward.*

Three rules for adding suffixes to base words are very reliable in English. These include the consonant doubling rule (*humming, begged*); the drop silent-*e* rule (*shaved, skating*); and the change *y* to *i* rule (*happiness, studious*).

English orthography, when subjected to formal analysis, proves to be more predictable than often believed. We can make sense of most spellings of English words. Instruction, however, must take into account the multiple layers of language organization that characterize this orthography and help students understand the structure of words they need to recognize or remember.

 # Supplementary Exercises

4.15   Map the graphemes in the following words to the phonemes. First, count the number of phonemes in the word on the right. Next, write the word phonetically. Finally, write the graphemes that represent the phonemes.

Word	Phonetic transcription	Graphemes for phonemes				
		First sound	Second sound	Third sound	Fourth sound	Fifth sound
bread						
wretch						
chrome						
sling						
single						
sank						
village						
geared						
create						

4.16   Underline the consonant blends (not every word has a blend).

dumb   first   squawk   shrink
known   muskrat   scotch

4.17   Underline the consonant digraphs (not every word has a digraph).

whether   shepherd   daughter
church   wrack   physic

4.18   Using the following words, write the syllables under the appropriate column for each of the six syllable types. In the right hand column, put the syllables that have a schwa.

	Closed	VCe	Open	Vowel team	Vowel-*r*	Consonant-*le*	Other (schwa)
re-bel							
as-sem-ble							
cel-e-brate							
ex-plor-er							
ser-vant							
boy-cott							
pil-grim-age							
bat-tle							
ab-ol-ish							
per-ox-ide							

4.19   Sort the following words into groups by the sound of the letter *c*. Explain when the letter *c* has a "soft" /s/ sound and when it has a "hard" /k/ sound.

	/s/	/k/
caught		
cereal		
receive		
pecan		
sauce		
incidence		
coagulate		
cuff		
civilization		
Rule:		

4.20   Given the following list of words, explain what happens to "silent *e*" when suffixes are added to base words.

careless	driving
basement	rising
homely	cloned
lately	invitation
useless	using
ninety	simply

Note: Some exceptions include *advantageous, noticeable, awful,* and *judgment.* You do not need to explain those exceptions.

4.21   What are the two phonemes represented by the letter *n* in the following words?

English	bank	ingot	trunk	_____
errand	band	input	trundle	_____

4.22   Are the vowel sounds in these words the same (S) or different (D)?

few	grief	m<u>ea</u>dow	build	cr<u>ui</u>se	boil
feud	sheaf	b<u>e</u>tter	gild	cr<u>u</u>cial	boy
_____	_____	_____	_____	_____	_____

4.23   Consider this poem from Walt Whitman, and answer the following questions.

I Hear America Singing

I HEAR America singing, the varied carols I hear;
Those of mechanics—each one singing his, as it should be, blithe and
    strong;
The carpenter singing his, as he measures his plank or beam,
The mason singing his, as he makes ready for work, or leaves off work;
The boatman singing what belongs to him in his boat—the deckhand
    singing on the steamboat deck;
The shoemaker singing as he sits on his bench—the hatter singing as he
    stands;
The wood-cutter's song—the ploughboy's, on his way in the morning, or at
    the noon intermission, or at sundown;
The delicious singing of the mother—or of the young wife at work—or of the
    girl sewing or washing—Each singing what belongs to her, and to none
    else;
The day what belongs to the day—At night, the party of young fellows,
    robust, friendly,
Singing, with open mouths, their strong melodious songs.

Find examples of the following orthographic patterns in the poem's words.

a) Three examples of Anglo-Saxon compound words

b) Two examples of the "change y to i" spelling rule

c) An example of a Greek-derived word

d) An example of a Latin-based word with a prefix, root, and suffix

e) Three examples of VCe syllables

f) Three examples of open syllables

g) Five examples of vowel team syllables

h) Three examples of vowel-r syllables

i) Three examples of schwa syllables

j) Three words with consonant blends

Endnotes

1. Wolf, 2007.
2. Chomsky, 1970.
3. Chomsky & Halle, 1968.
4. Henry, 2003.
5. Comrie, Matthews, & Polinsky, 1996.
6. Librarius (n.d.).
7. McAdam & Milne, 2005.
8. Grace, 2007.
9. Venezky, 1970.
10. See REWARDS (Archer, Gleason, Vachon, & Isaacson, 2000); Phonics Blitz (Farrell & Hunter, 2007); and Calhoon (2005) for examples of explicit instructional programs for teaching decoding of multisyllabic words.
11. Venezky, 1967.
12. Hanna et al., 1966.

Recommended Supplementary Reading on Orthography and the English Spelling System

Balmuth, M. (2009). *The roots of phonics: A historical introduction* (Rev. ed.). Baltimore: Paul H. Brookes Publishing Co.

Bryson, B. (1990). *The mother tongue: English and how it got that way.* New York: Avon Books.

Henry, M.K. (2003). *Unlocking literacy: Effective decoding and spelling instruction.* Baltimore: Paul H. Brookes Publishing Co.

McCrum, R., Cran, W., & McNeil, R. (1986). *The story of English.* New York: Viking.

Orton, J.L. (1976). *A guide to teaching phonics.* Cambridge, MA: Educators Publishing Service.

Winchester, S. (1998). *The professor and the madman: A tale of murder, insanity, and the making of the Oxford English Dictionary.* New York: HarperCollins.

Morphology

By the end of this chapter, you will understand:

- The importance of teaching morphology for reading, spelling, and vocabulary

- Categories of morphemes

- Anglo-Saxon, Latin, and Greek influences on morphemes

- How words change when suffixes are added

- How to identify a morpheme in an unknown word

- How to teach morphology to students of different ages

Why Morphology Is Important for Reading and Spelling

This chapter concerns units of meaning called **morphemes**—linguistic entities that may be whole words, parts of words, or single phonemes. Morphemes are the smallest meaningful units in language. As we discussed in Chapter 4, English is a "deep" orthography—it represents both sound and meaning. The morpheme structure of words is often represented in English spelling patterns.

Knowing morphemes enhances reading, vocabulary, and spelling. Awareness of morphemes is one aspect of a verbally proficient person's word knowledge. Since the demise of Latin in the high school curriculum, however, it is uncommon for instructional materials to systematically teach and explain these structural components of language. Such an omission is unfortunate because rapid word recognition, independent discovery of word meaning, and spelling accuracy are all associated with knowledge of word structure at the level of morphemes. Teachers must be familiar with morphology if they are to teach advanced word study in the intermediate grades and beyond.

People who read, spell, and comprehend well are typically able to distinguish between words that sound similar, such as *fiscal* and *physical*, *illicit* and *elicit*, *illusion* and *allusion*, and *specific* and *pacific*. Good readers attend to the internal details of words, both spoken and written. They use strategies to distinguish and remember the meanings of words that sound alike, including recognizing meaningful parts. For example, someone with a deeper knowledge of word structure might know that *il* in *illicit* means "not," and the *e* in *elicit* means "out of." Furthermore, students with better awareness of morphemes can recognize when words might be related even when the words are pronounced differently, as in *resign* and *resignation*, *legal* and *legislate*, *litigate* and *litigious*, and *please* and *pleasant*. With morphological knowledge, a good reader can guess at a definition for a word first encountered in text, such as *exposition*: It comes from *expose*, which has two morphemes, *ex* meaning "out of" and *pose* meaning "put or place." Thus, an exposition puts out information.

Incomplete knowledge of morphology accounts for some of the most amusing speech and spelling errors children produce. Children ages 5–7 commonly use word parts creatively and inaccurately as they are trying to learn the rules and components of word building.

- After going to the circus, a child said, *"That was a great deformance!"*

- Leaving the class for tutoring in intensive phonics, one student said, *"It's time for offensive phonics!"*

- After being asked about his aspirations for creating things, a boy said, *"I want to be a preventor!"*

- Complimenting her mother who complained about feeling pudgy, a girl said, *"Mom, you're a completely unpudgable person! My stomach is unholdable inable!"*

The ability to use words well depends on levels of linguistic knowledge that are gained slowly with much exposure to text—knowledge of words' sound structures, grammatical categories, meanings, and spellings.

Morphemes: The Smallest Meaningful Units

Morphemes are distinct from phonemes, syllables, and words. They can be categorized by their language of origin and by their grammatical role.

Categories of Morphemes

A *morpheme* is the most elemental unit of grammatical form that has both sound and meaning. *Morphos* means "form or structure" in Greek; *eme* means an element or little piece of something. A morpheme may be one or more syllables, as in *red*, *indigo*, and *crocodile*, or a word or a part of a word, as in *full*, a word, versus *ful*, a suffix.

Morphemes can be sorted into two basic categories—**free** and **bound** (see Figure 5.1). Free morphemes can stand alone as words and do not have to be combined with other morphemes, as in *spite*, *woman*, and *elephant*. The term **base word** is used when we talk about free morphemes and usually refers to words of Anglo-Saxon origin. Base words may be made up of one or more syllables. Free morphemes, in turn, can be sorted into two broad syntactic categories that determine how we use the words in sentences— **function words** and **content words.** Function words are free morphemes and include conjunctions (*but*), prepositions (*below*), pronouns (*he*), auxiliary verbs (*was*), and articles (*a, an*). Function words are a closed class of words because languages typically do not add words to these categories, or if they do, the additions or changes occur very slowly. Function words are limited in number, learned early, and function as the grammatical glue of sentences.

Content words, in contrast, are free morphemes that carry the meaning of a sentence. Content words include nouns, verbs, adjectives, and adverbs. These are by far the largest categories of words in any language. Unlike function words, content words are invented frequently as a language evolves. The meanings of content words also change with time. Thus, content word categories are open, not fixed. Most of the new words we encounter during reading are content words.

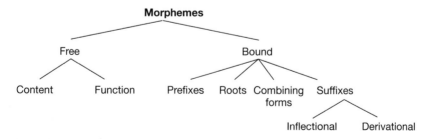

Figure 5.1.   Morpheme types.

Bound morphemes work as meaningful units only in combination with other morphemes. These include **roots** (primarily from Latin) and **combining forms** (from Greek), **prefixes,** and two kinds of **suffixes.** Roots do not stand alone; thus, we do not talk about "word roots" because roots (e.g., *fer, duc, vis, ject*) are not words. To confuse matters, however, some roots have also become free morphemes as language has evolved, such as *port, form,* and *tract.* A prefix is added before a root or base word, such as *pre, peri, ex,* and *bi.* A suffix is added after a root or base word, such as *ous, ity, ible,* and *ment.* A combining form is a Greek-based word part that combines with others to form whole words, like the parts of a compound.

There are two kinds of suffixes—**inflectional** and **derivational.** This distinction is important in several ways. Inflectional suffixes are a closed category of grammatical endings that cannot change the part of speech of the word to which they are added. They include tense markers for verbs, such as *ed, s,* and *ing;* plural markers for nouns, such as *s* and *es;* and comparative markers for adjectives, such as *er* and *est.* Inflectional suffixes are learned early and are unavoidable in early reading and spelling instruction.

In contrast, derivational suffixes are added to base words or roots and do mark or change the part of speech of the word to which they are added; in fact, one of their primary functions is to designate a word's part of speech. Consider these examples of derivational suffixes.

- Noun suffixes: *ment (encouragement); ness (illness); age (verbiage); ity (rarity); ion (action)*

- Adjective suffixes: *ive (selective); al (natural); ous (numerous); ic (stoic); ful (mindful); ible/able (detectible)*

- Verb suffixes: *ate (cogitate); ize (generalize); ify (indemnify)*

- Adverb suffix: *ly (beautifully)*

Morpheme Structures by Language of Origin

Before going on, try the following word-building exercise. You will discover the relevance of knowing something about the origin of English words.

 ## Exercise 5.1

Build as many whole words as you can with these word parts.

re	geo	earth	tract	bio	port
graphic	quake	ex	worm	able	logy

What patterns do you notice?

In the exercise, the parts of words that combined came from the same base language of English. *Quake, earth, earthquake,* and *earthworm* are from

Anglo-Saxon. *Export, report, extract,* and *retractable* are from Latin. *Geology, geographic, biology,* and *biographic* are from Greek. The morphological structure of English words is related to their language of origin (see Table 5.1). Each layer of language uses somewhat different word-building processes.

Anglo-Saxon Compounds   In the Anglo-Saxon layer of English, new words are often formed by adding free morphemes together. Most compounds are combinations of Anglo-Saxon words or two free morphemes, such as *tattletale, lighthouse,* and *blackboard.* Note that Anglo-Saxon is historically related to German, a language that relies heavily on compounding to build new words (*Anwendungsprogrammschnittstelle:* "application program interface"). Many combinations of word types are allowed as we build English compounds.

Adjective with adjective: *bittersweet*
Adjective with noun: *highchair*
Noun with noun: *barnyard*
Noun with verb: *sea-kayaking*
Verb with verb: *sleepwalk*

The grammatical category of the compound will be determined by the last word, not the first. *Hotdog* is a noun, *sleepwalking* is an action, and so forth. Compounds are characterized more by their stress pattern than by their spelling. Stress almost always occurs on the first word of the compound. Spelling, however, may include a hyphen or a space. There are no hard and fast rules about spelling compounds, and often there is more than one acceptable way to write a compound. *Ice cream* and *White House* are compounds by pronunciation but not by visual joining of the components. Sometimes more than two words are combined to make a compound, such as *two-time winner, mother-of-pearl,* and *six-dog sled.* Yet, many compounds are self-defining, such as *turnstile, hardwood,* and *tap dance.*

Table 5.1.   Morpheme structures by language of origin

Historical layers of English	Morpheme structures with examples
Anglo-Saxon layer	Base words (*neighbor, eat, heaven, sky*)
	Compounds (*daylight, crabapple*)
	Inflections (*ed, s, es, er, est, ing*)
	Prefixes (*a, be, en, un, mis, fore*)
	Suffixes (*hood, en, ly, ward, ness, less, most, ish*)
Latin, French (Romance layer)	Prefixes (*un, dis, re, pre, inter*)
	Roots (*form, spect, gress, ject, vis*)
	Suffixes (*ment, ible, ion, ful, ity*)
	Latin plurals (*alumnus, alumni, alumnae; datum, data*)
Greek layer	Combining forms (*neuro, psych, ology, dys, lex, chloro, phyll*)
	Plurals (*crisis, crises; metamorphosis, metamorphoses*)

See Henry (2003) for more information on the historical layers of English.

Exercise 5.2

The meaning of a compound is not always the same as the sum of its parts. Give a definition for the following words.

redcoat

laughing gas

looking glass

blackboard

turncoat

bigwig

rubbernecking

A few prefixes are from Anglo-Saxon, such as *be* (*besmirch, begotten, behave, beset, before, behind*), *a* (*asleep, awake, alone, amuse*), and *en* (*engender, enable, endure*). Suffixes from Anglo-Saxon include *hood* (*neighborhood, parenthood, knighthood*), *en* (*embolden, frighten, enlighten*), *ly* (*heavily, smartly, childishly*), *ward* (*inward, forward, leaward*), *less* (*hopeless*), and *ness* (*hopelessness*).

Latin-Based Prefixes, Roots, and Suffixes   Content words from the Latin layer are built around a root. The root is usually the accented part of a longer word. The vowel is either short or long—not schwa. Because roots are bound morphemes, they are combined with prefixes and/or suffixes. Latin roots have definable meanings, many of which have remained consistent with their original meanings from ancient Rome. Thousands of content words in English are constructed from Latin roots and affixes. Table 5.2 lists some of the most common Latin roots, their meanings, and words in which they are found.

Table 5.2.   Common Latin roots, their meanings, and examples

Root	Meaning	Example
agri	field	*agriculture, agrarian*
alter	other	*alternative, alternation*
ang	bend	*angle, angularity*
anim	life, spirit	*animation, animal*
ann, enn	year	*annual, biennial*
aqua	water	*aquifer, aquatics*
art	skill	*artisan, artful*
aud	hear	*audition, auditorium*
belli	war	*bellicose, belligerent*
brev	short	*brevity*
cap, cip, ceive, cep, ceit	to take, catch, seize, hold	*receive, deception, capacity, accept*
capit, capt	head or chief	*decapitate, captain, capitalism, capitulation*
cede, ceed, cess	go, move, yield	*recede, recess, necessary, concede*

Root	Meaning	Example
cide, cise	cut, kill	*excise, patricide, decide*
claim	shout, declare	*exclaim, clamant, proclamatory*
clar	clear	*clarify, declaration*
claus, clus, clos	shut or close	*closet, claustrophobic, occlusion*
corp	body	*corporal, incorporate*
cred	belief	*credible, accredit, incredulous*
dic, dict	speak, tell	*dictate, interdiction, edict*
duc, duct	lead	*induce, product, educate*
fac, fact, fect, fic	make or do	*ineffective, beneficiary, infection, satisfactory*
fer	yield, bear, carry	*infer, confer, refer, transfer, difference*
fin, finis	end	*finite, final, definitive, refinement*
flect, flex	bend, curve	*deflect, flexion, reflexive*
flu, flux, fluc, fluv	flow	*effluent, influx, fluid, flume*
form	shape	*perform, conformist, reformation*
cog	know	*cognitive, cogitate, incognito*
grad, gred, gress	step, degree, walk	*graduation, regress, ingredient, biodegradable*
grat, gre	pleasing	*gratitude, agree, grace, gratuity*
hom	alike, same	*homosexual, homophobia, homogenous, homogeneous*
jact, ject, jac	throw, lie	*interject, dejection, trajectory*
jud, jur, jus	law, right	*jurisprudence, jury, justify, adjust*
lect, leg, lig	choose, pick, read, speak	*dialect, lectern, neglect, legible*
loc, loqu	speak, talk, say	*interlocution, loquacious, soliloquy*
man	hand	*manual, amanuensis*
mar	sea	*maritime, marine*
mis, mit	send	*dismiss, permit, mission, commitment*
mob, mot, mov	move	*mobile, motive, remove, motion, motivate*
mor	death	*mortal, mortician, mortify*
nat	born	*native, natural, nativity, nation*
nav	ship	*navy, navigate*
nov	new	*novel, novice*
pater, patri	father	*patrician, patriot, paternal*
ped	foot	*pedestrian, pedestal, pedicure*
pel, puls	drive or push	*compel, repulsion, expel, compulsory*
pend, pens	bang or weigh	*appendage, pendulum, suspense*
port	to carry	*export, deportation, report, portal, support*
pos, pon	place, set	*opposite, dispose, component*
rect, recti, reg	straight, right	*correct, erect, irregular, direction*
rupt	break, burst	*interrupt, rupture, corrupt*
scrib, script	write	*proscribe, postscript, scribble*
sec, sect, seg	cut	*dissect, segment*
spec, spect, spic	see, watch, observe	*spectator, inspect, suspect, suspicious, speculate*
spir, spire	breathe	*inspiration, perspire, spirit*
sta, sist, stat, stit	stand	*circumstance, station, standard, substance*
stru, struct	build	*construction, obstruent, indestructible*
tact, tag, tang, tig, ting	touch	*tangible, tactician, contingency*
ten, tain, tin, tinu	hold	*detain, pertinence, tenable, tenant*
tend, tens, tent	stretch, strain	*tension, tendon, attention, superintendent*
tract	pull, draw	*traction, intractable, protractor, contract*
ven, veni, vent	go, come	*adventure, prevention, convene, avenue*
vers, vert	turn	*vertical, inverted, versatile, universe, conversation*
vid, vis	see	*video, visible, improvise, visual*
voc, vok	call	*invocation, vocal, vocabulary*

Exercise 5.3

Underline the root in each of these low-frequency—but real—words, and take a stab at defining the word's meaning on the basis of the parts you know.

retrocede

mellifluous

incisor

quadrennium

incredulity

factotum

gratuitous

interlocution

pedomotive

nonsectarian

Prefixes from Latin were prepositions whose meanings have remained consistent over several millennia. Prefixes generally show relations in space and time, such as *re, trans, inter, sub, ob,* and *ad.* They also negate and reverse, such as *dis, un, non,* and *anti.* Sometimes they intensify the meaning of the root, such as *con* and *re.* The most common Latin prefixes and their translations are in Table 5.3.

Table 5.3.   Common Latin prefixes and their definitions

Prefix	Definition	Prefix	Definition
a	without	*intra*	within
a	from, away	*intro*	in, inward
ad	to, toward	*mal*	bad, abnormal
ambi	both	*multi*	many, much
ante	before	*non*	not, negative
anti	against	*ob*	down, against, facing, to
bene	well, good	*per*	through, completely
circum	around, about	*post*	after, behind
com	with, together	*peri*	around
con	against	*pre*	before
contra	against	*pro*	forward, earlier, prior to
de	down, away	*re*	again, back
dis	not, absence, apart	*retro*	back, backward
e, ex	out of	*se*	apart, aside, without
in	in, into, not	*sub*	under, below, secondary
inter	between	*trans*	across, beyond

Assimilated Prefixes   The prefix-root-suffix structure of many Latin-based words accounts for the prevalence of doubled consonants in which the first and second morphemes are joined. Many prefixes alternate their forms to match the beginning sound of the root to which they are added. The prefix is **assimilated** phonologically; its last sound melds with the first sound of the root for the sake of **euphony,** or ease of pronunciation. It is easier, for example, to say "ap-proach" than to say "ad-proach" or to say "sup-pose" rather than "sub-pose." Doubled consonants near the start of a Latin-based word usually signify the presence of an assimilated prefix and root and can be remembered with reference to the word's structure and meaning. The most common examples of these forms, also called chameleon prefixes, are in Table 5.4.

Table 5.4.   Common chameleon prefixes with their variants

ad (to, toward)	
a	accommodate, accessory
af	affection, affluent
ag	aggression, aggravate
al	alleviate, alliance
an	annoyance, annexation
ap	approach, apportion
ar	arrangement, arrival
as	assimilate, assembly
at	attend, attract
com (with, together)	
co	cohabitation, cooperate
col	collaborate, collusion
con	consist, conclude
cor	corrupt, correlate
dis (not, absence, apart)	
dif	different, diffuse
ex (out of)	
e	evacuate, eject
in (in, on, toward)	
il	illuminate, illustration
im	import, immigrate
ir	irrigation, irrupt
in (not)	
il	illegal, illiterate
im	impossible, impairment
ir	irreplaceable, irreverent
ob (down, against, facing)	
oc	occult
of	offense
op	oppose, oppress
sub (under, below, secondary)	
suc	succeed, succumb
suf	sufficient, suffix
sug	suggestion
sup	suppress, supplant
sus	suspect, suspend

Exercise 5.4

Identify the prefix in each of these words and the meaning of the prefix.

antidepressant

contractual

contradict

expected

imbalance

impress

intramural

peroxide

reapplication

subtext

Greek Combining Forms   Modern scientific and mathematical terms incorporated into English in the past 600 hundred years have most often been constructed from Greek morphemes. Greek-derived words are constructed somewhat differently from Latinate words. Greek-derived morphemes are not necessarily assigned specific roles as prefixes, suffixes, or roots; many can combine with other bound morphemes of equal importance in flexible order. So, for example, we can have *psychoneurosis, neuropsychological, parapsychology,* and many other words with *psych.* Although *psych* has not been a free morpheme in the past, it is becoming a verb in American English, as in, "I'll *psych* him out before making the offer." *Photograph* is a Greek compound; so are *graphology, lithograph, photosynthesis,* and *telephoto,* which use the morphemes in variable order or position. Table 5.5 lists examples of common Greek combining forms in English.

Exercise 5.5

Using a separate piece of paper, give yourself 3 minutes to generate as many words as you can that use any one of these Greek-derived morphemes.

scope   phon   chrom   cycle   therm

Inflectional and Derivational Suffixes

The distinctions between the two kinds of suffixes, inflectional and derivational, are important; only derivational suffixes can change the part of speech of the words to which they are added. Each type of suffix should be introduced in a word study curriculum, but inflectional suffixes must be learned early, before derivational.

Table 5.5. Selected Greek combining forms with definitions and examples

Form	Meaning	Example
aero	air	*aerodynamic, aerodrome*
andro, anthro	human	*philanthropy, anthropology*
arch	chief, ruler	*anarchy, architecture, hierarchy*
archi, arche	primitive, ancient	*archeology, archaic, archivist*
ast, astro	star	*astrophysics, astronomer, bioastronautics*
biblio	book	*bibliography, Bible, bibliotherapy*
bio	life	*biology, biomechanics, macrobiotic*
chrom	color	*monochromatic, chromosome, achromatic*
chron	time	*anachronistic, chronology, synchronize*
cosm	universe	*cosmic, cosmos*
crat, cracy	rule, power	*democracy, autocractic, aristocracy*
cycl, cyclo	circle	*bicycle, unicycle, cyclical, cyclotron*
dem, demo	people	*democratic, pandemic, demography*
derm	skin	*dermatologist, hypodermic, epidermis*
dyn, dynamo	force, strength	*dynamic, hydrodynamic, dynamometer*
eco	house, home, environment	*ecological, economy, macroeconomics*
gen	birth	*genetics, geneology, biogenetics*
geo	earth	*geology, biogeographical, geothermal*
gno	know	*gnostic, agnostic, agnosia, prognosticate*
gram, graph	write, record	*biographer, spectrograph, graphomotor, pictogram*
hydr, hydra, hydro	water	*hydraulic, hydroponic, hydrate, dehydration*
kine, cine	movement	*kinesthetic, kinesis, cinematic, hyperkinetic*
lex	word	*dyslexia, lexical, lexicon, paralexia*
log, logo, logue	speech, word	*logorrhea, monologue, dialogic*
logy (ology)	science, study of	*archeology, pharmacology, zoology*
mania	obsession, madness	*hypomania, egomania, maniacal*
meter, metr	measure	*chronometer, metric, geometry*
morph	form, structure, shape	*morphology, allomorph, metamorphosis*
nym	name, word	*synonym, antonym, acronym*
pan	all	*pantheon, pantheistic, panorama*
path	feeling, suffering, disease	*pathogen, psychopath, sympathy*
ped	child	*pediatrician, pedophile*
phil, phila, phile	affinity for	*bibliophile, philanthropist, philanderer*
phobia	fear, hatred	*agoraphobia, technophobe, phobic*
phon, phono	sound	*symphony, phonology, morphophonological*
photo	light	*photography, photon, telephoto*
pol, poli, polis	city	*metropolis, police, geopolitics*
psych	mind	*psychosis, psychometrician, psychopathic*
scop, scope	see, watch	*microscope, gyroscope, telescopic*
therm	heat	*thermodynamic, thermos, geothermal*
Greek combining forms usually used as prefixes		
auto	self	
demi	half	
hemi	half	
hyper	over, above, excessive	
hypno	sleep	
hypo	under	
macro	large, great	
mega	huge	
meta	beside, after, beyond	
micro	small, minute	
mono	one	
para	beside, alongside	
poly	many	
proto	earliest, original	
semi	half	
tele	distant	

Inflectional Suffixes   Of the two kinds of suffixes, inflections are learned the earliest for speaking, reading, and spelling. Inflections are bound morphemes that show possession (her*s*), gender (alumn*ae*), or number (wish*es*, cris*es*) if the word is a noun; tense (talk*ed*), voice (he was driv*en*), or mood if the word is a verb (she could have been driv*ing*); and comparison (soft*er*, soft*est*) if the word is an adjective. Possession and degree can be expressed either morphologically or syntactically through word order. One can say, "That boat was hers," or, "That was her boat." One can say, "He wanted more curls," or "He wanted curlier hair." Typically developing children first use inflectional morphology as soon as they begin to combine words into sentences, usually by 2 years of age.[1] For example, children quickly learn to inflect some verbs with the progressive tense marker *ing* or to mark the concept of more than one with *s* or *es*. The rules of grammatical inflectional morphology in speech are typically mastered between 4 and 7 years of age.[2]

A word with inflectional suffixes fits the same slot in a sentence structure whether the suffix is added or not.

> I *act* in an odd manner.
>
> He *acts* in an odd manner.
>
> He *acted* in an odd manner.
>
> He was *acting* in an odd manner.

Most preschoolers have learned the basic inflections for speech purposes before they enter school and before they begin to learn to read and spell, whereas most of their awareness about derivational processes in word building will come from learning to read and spell. Inflections are ever present and obligatory in the oral language patterns to which children are exposed early on. Therefore, it should not be surprising that inflections are learned many years before the derivational forms that children will read, often for the first time in the fourth grade or later. Children learn the system by which the inflections are added before they learn all of the specific inflected forms. Because they are generalizing from an apparent rule, they produce regular or predictable inflected forms before they learn the exceptions. Thus, they are likely to say "goed" for *went*, "taked" for *took*, "keeped" for *kept*, and "mans" for *men* until they learn the specific **suppletive** (irregular) forms that are a legacy from Middle English. As with other dimensions of child language, regular patterns can temporarily overrule the production of unusual forms. The generation of past, plural, and comparative words, such as *bringed*, *mices*, and *bestest*, dominate before children come to terms with the exceptions—*brought*, *mice*, and *best*.

Why Spelling the Past Tense and Plural Forms Is Difficult   The spellings and pronunciations of the past tense morpheme *ed* and the plural morphemes *s* and *es* account for a large portion of children's spelling errors in the primary and intermediate grades. These errors are frequent because spelling these forms requires morphological awareness that many children develop late. The past tense and plural inflections follow the morphophonemic principle of English orthography: We use consistent spellings for these suffixes even though their sounds vary, depending on the phonological properties of the ending phonemes of the words to which they are added.

Meaning is preserved in spelling, but variations in pronunciation are not transcribed in our symbol system.

The past tense *ed* is pronounced variously as [d], [t], and [əd], and only the last form constitutes a syllable. Instruction should start with a word-sorting exercise that helps students realize the three sounds of the past tense, as in Exercise 5.6.

Exercise 5.6

Sounds of the past tense *ed*. Mark the sound of the ending; then, count the number of syllables in the word. Remember, a syllable is a spoken unit organized around a vowel sound.

Word	[d], [t], [əd]	Number of syllables
talked	[t]	1
instituted		
spelled		
rebuffed		
opened		
popped		
offended		
exhumed		
breathed		
approached		
enraged		
prevented		
surpassed		

Now, list all of the words that share a common pronunciation of *ed* in groups together, and determine the reason why some words have a voiced [d] at the end, some have an unvoiced [t], and some have a syllabic [əd]. (*Hint:* What is an important feature of the final phoneme in the base word?)

The linguistic complexity inherent in these structures, and the requirement that the user of written English grasp the multiple levels of language organization on which these spellings are based, accounts for the frequency of inflection errors in children's reading and writing. Students with language insensitivity are likely to omit, misread, substitute, or phonetically spell the past tense and plural endings (Figures 5.2 and 5.3).

Again, inflections do not change the part of speech of the word to which they are added. The plural of *wish* (*wishes*) is still a noun; the past tense of *dance* (*danced*) is still a verb; the superlative of *hard* (*hardest*) is still an adjective. Derivational morphemes, in contrast, often change the part of speech of the word to which they are added. The remainder of this chapter explores

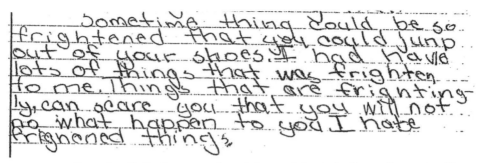

Figure 5.2. Example of inflection errors in an intermediate student's reading and writing.

some interesting features of derivational morphemes and morphologically complex words.

Derivational Suffixes   Derivational word-building processes in English are characteristic of the Latin (Romance) layer of English; Latin-derived words along with Greek-derived words comprise about 60% of the words used in text.[3] Latin-derived words, again, are constructed around a root whose meaning is modified through the addition of prefixes and suffixes (*pro + ject + ion*). Words derived from Latin roots are most common in expository text of a somewhat formal or nonconversational nature. Most derivational suffixes are there to mark or change the grammatical class of the base word to which they are added. For example, *philosophy* is a noun; *philosophize* is a verb; *philosophical* is an adjective; and *philosopher* is a noun.

Exercise 5.7

Identify the part of speech of each word in these pairs. Some words may serve more than one grammatical role (n = noun; v = verb; and a = adjective).

preside	__v__	president	__n__
legislate	_____	legislature	_____
compete	_____	competition	_____
invent	_____	inventor	_____
sign	_____	signify	_____
peril	_____	perilous	_____
disturb	_____	disturbance	_____
active	_____	activity	_____
type	_____	typify	_____
face	_____	facial	_____

All of the derivational suffixes added to the second column of Exercise 5.7 are used to change words predictably from one part of speech to another, and all tend to be used with certain kinds of base words. Words that end in *er, or, cian*, and *ist* are people nouns; words that end in *sion* and *tion* are thing nouns. Nouns can also be made by adding *ment* and *ity*; verbs are made by

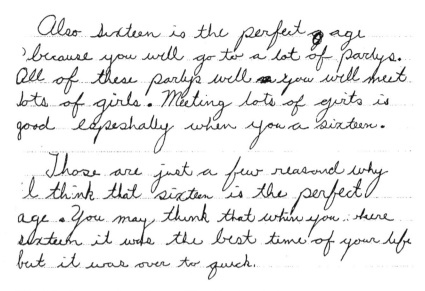

Figure 5.3.   Inflection errors in a 16-year-old's writing (party's for parties, reasond for reasons).

adding *ize* and *ify*; adverbs are made with *ly*; and adjectives are made with *ar, ous, ive, al,* and *ful*. Morphemic knowledge, which may be largely unconscious, includes awareness of the grammatical function of suffixes.

Exercise 5.8

Change the part of speech of a word by adding a suffix. First, identify the part of speech of the word on the left; then, think of a derived form that serves the grammatical function indicated.

Example: generous	_adjective_	noun	_generosity_
decide		adjective	
successive		noun	
extent		verb	
depend		adjective	
occur		noun	
teach		noun	
pretense		verb	
revise		noun	
prevent		adverb	

Schwa Happens in Longer Words   Schwa, the neutralized vowel [ə], is common in unaccented syllables of all etymologies. In morphologically complex words, schwa may occur as a consequence of suffixation. Some derivational suffixes are **neutral,** such as *able* and *ly,* because they do not change the stress or vowel quality of the word to which they are added.[4]

Others, however, are **nonneutral,** such as *ity,* because they often cause shifts in pronunciation of the base word when the suffix is added, as in *generous, generosity; curious, curiosity.* The prevalence of nonneutral suffixes accounts for the frequency with which vowels in unaccented syllables are reduced to schwa, [ə], or otherwise changed. Patterns of pronunciation caused by non-neutral suffixes usually take some time for students to learn because knowing them depends on exposure to enough examples that the student can generalize the phonological patterns to new words.[5]

If your English vocabulary is fairly well developed, then you have stored in memory enough examples of the effects of suffixes on word pronunciation that you can read nonsense words such as the following, changing the stress patterns and vowel pronunciations as necessary.

tupid	tupidity	tupidizable
tupidy	tupiditude	tupidary
tupidation	tupidize	tupidic

Inflectional and Derivational Suffixes Combined   When a word with a derivational suffix is made plural, past, comparative, or possessive, the inflectional suffix is always added to the end of the word and does not come before any derivational suffix. The rule for production is derivation first, inflection last. Thus, we have *uncomplicat<u>ed</u>, deliverable<u>s</u>,* or *summariz<u>ing</u>,* with an inflectional marker at the end of the word. We would not produce words such as *handsful* to mean *handfuls* or *generaledize* to mean *generalized.*

In Middle English, many more inflections were pronounced than are produced in Modern English. Some of our odd spellings are legacies from more than 4 centuries ago; for example, *kept, wept,* and *slept* are contracted forms of old inflectional patterns that at one time were spoken as separate syllables. The form of each word is abstract and includes a base and a past tense morpheme: sleep + {past tense} = slept.

Exercise 5.9

Underline all of the inflections and notice where they occur.

inducements	higher	singing	unhappiest
legalizing	disentangled	tardiest	misunderstood
productions	factors	shoed	lost

Suffixes with Soft *ti, ci,* and *si*   The letter combinations *ti, ci,* and *si* begin a series of final syllables in English that encompass suffixes *ion, ian, ent, ous, al,* and *ence/ance.* Those letters (*ti, ci, si*) spell the sounds [š] or [ž], plus what follows. The letters *ti, ci,* and *si* act as connectors that complete the syllable and link the suffixes to the base word or root. The vowel is reduced to schwa in many Latin-based suffixes. Table 5.6 summarizes these final syllable constructions.

Table 5.6. Final syllable constructions for *ti*, *ci*, and *si*

	a	al	an	ence	ent	on	ous
ti	militia	martial	Martian	patience	patient	notion	fictitious
ci	Marcia	glacial	musician	efficiency	ancient	suspicion	precious
si, sci	dysplasia	N/A	artesian	conscience	prescient	dimension	conscious

Derivational Complexity

Derivational complexity is a term that characterizes the number and type of changes that have been made in the base word or root when it is combined with other morphemes. Some derived words are created without any sound or spelling changes in the base form, as in *forget, forgetful; employ, employment; embark, embarkation*. But more often, changes occur in the way the stem is pronounced, the way it is spelled, or the way it is stressed.

Phonological Changes to the Base Word When Suffixes Are Added   The types of phonological changes that can occur between a stem and a derivation include syllabic regrouping, vowel alternation, consonant alternation, and stress alternation. Syllable regrouping is when *differ* becomes *different*; vowel alternation is when *sane* is changed to *sanity*; consonant alternation explains the difference between *electric* and *electricity*; and stress alternation describes the changes that occur between *philosophy* and *philosophical* and is a common result of derivational word building.

Vowel alternation can occur in many forms. A tense (long) vowel is reduced to schwa between *define/definition* and *compete/competition*. A tense vowel becomes an accented short vowel in *extreme/extremity, precise/precision*, and *profane/profanity*; a schwa becomes an accented lax vowel in *industry/industrious, final/finality*, and *brutal/brutality*. A schwa becomes an accented tense vowel in *labor/laborious* and *injure/injurious*. If words in a derivational family are taught together in a vocabulary or spelling lesson, then students are likely to perceive their relation in spite of these changes in pronunciation.

Consonant alternation is exemplified by each of the following word pairs. Note how consonants change in pronunciation from one form of a word to another, even though most stay the same in spelling.

> bomb, bombardier
>
> crumb, crumble
>
> paradigm, paradigmatic
>
> malign, malignant
>
> anxious, anxiety
>
> incredible, incredulous
>
> perceive, perception
>
> medic, medicine
>
> definite, definition
>
> repress, repression

Orthographic Changes to the Base Word When Suffixes Are Added

Changes can also occur to the spelling of the base word when endings are added. Changes that occur by spelling rule are called orthographic changes in the base form. They include doubling of the final consonant before a suffix that begins with a vowel; dropping a final *e* when the suffix begins with a vowel; and changing *y* to *i* before a suffix, except those that begin with *i*. Examples of these orthographic change rules, which were explained in Chapter 4, are as follows.

Drop *e*	Change *y* to *i*	Double the final consonant
sense, sensible	happy, happiest	win, winning
compete, competition	fury, furious	occur, occurrence

Exercise 5.10

1. Explore the phonological and/or orthographic changes in base words that occur when suffixes are added. From the derived form of the word given, write the base word. Highlight or circle the base words with phonological changes in the derived words, and underline any part of a base word that has undergone an orthographic change.

Example:	division	divi<u>de</u>
	reference	_____
	precision	_____
	dramatic	_____
	theatrical	_____
	possession	_____
	originality	_____
	ridiculous	_____
	sociology	_____
	political	_____
	ritual	_____

2. Decide what kind of change has occurred between the base form and the derived form of these words (1 = no change; 2 = orthographic change only; 3 = phonological change only; 4 = both phonological and orthographic changes).

Examples:	grow, growth	1
	bat, batty	2
	human, humanity	3
	wide, width	___
	differ, difference	___

sun, sunny	_____
athlete, athletic	_____
personal, personality	_____
propel, propeller	_____
combine, combination	_____
idiot, idiotic	_____
usual, usually	_____
extend, extension	_____
ration, rational	_____
define, definition	_____
assist, assistance	_____

Words with Phonological Changes Are More Difficult to Learn

Derivational complexity does affect how easily students learn Latin-based words. One study[6] examined the relationships between oral knowledge of derivational morphology and the spelling development of fourth-, sixth-, and eighth-grade students. Ninth-grade students with learning disabilities were compared with typically developing fourth-, sixth-, and eighth-grade students on both oral and written word generation. Clear developmental trends showed that up to and beyond eighth grade, students continued to learn about derivational rules and relationships. At all age levels, the ability to generate derived forms orally preceded the ability to spell these forms. Furthermore, the complexity of the relationship between the base and the derived form of a word pair affected the ease of spelling. Those pairs with only phonological changes (usually with nonneutral suffixes) and those with both phonological and orthographic changes evoked the most spelling errors at all levels of development. For example, pairs such as *decide* and *decision* evoked more errors than *enjoy* and *enjoyment*.

The implication of this finding is that instruction should begin with base words and affixes that do not involve phonological shifts or spelling changes. Gradually, these complexities can be introduced with examples of typical patterns.

How to Identify a Morpheme in an Unknown Word

When we encounter a new word, the combination of the word's context and its morpheme structure can often guide us to the word's meaning. Several rules of thumb apply in morpheme identification.

Three "Tests" of Morpheme Identity   Identifying morphemes in words without referencing a dictionary can be challenging for students. The meanings of words are sometimes not simply the sum of their parts. If one attempts to identify morphemes without a dictionary nearby, then three minitests are helpful.

1. Can meaningful linguistic units be identified and defined?

2. Can other words be recalled in which that morpheme seems to be used?

3. What is the sense of the whole word in the context in which it is used?

This strategy is not the same thing as "finding the little word in the big word."

To illustrate, *flow* in *flower* and *moth* in *mother* are little words in a bigger word, but in those cases, the smaller words do not function as meaningful units from which the larger words are constructed. In contrast, *spire* in *respiration* does work as a meaningful part. We know other words with that morpheme, such as *inspire, perspire, expire,* and *conspire,* and can surmise from context that *spire* might have something to do with breathing.

The Complex Relationship Between Form and Meaning   The relation of word parts and their function within words is not always transparent; words sometimes contain a letter or sound combination that can be a morpheme in some words but is not a morpheme in others. *Mis* is a morpheme in *misspell,* but is not a morpheme in *missile; sub* is a morpheme in *subdue,* but is not a morpheme in *subtle.* One must think of the structure and meaning of the whole word before deciding whether a part is a morpheme. When questions arise, consulting a dictionary usually yields information about the word's origin, structure, and meaning.

Exercise 5.11

Separate these words into their component morphemes. Check a dictionary, if necessary.

watchdog	telemarketing	consistent
mistletoe	odometer	injection
piped	prevaricate	biodegradable
dodgers	illegal	tower

Just a short exercise on morphological analysis should be enough to demonstrate that the identity of morphemes is not always obvious. How does one divide the word *telemarketing,* a relatively new entry into the English language? There is such a thing as *telemarking,* a type of skiing, but the word *market* does not divide into two morphemes. (*Telemarking* is named after a county in Norway; *telemarketing* is a Greek combining form, *tele,* added to an Anglo-Saxon noun, *market,* transformed into a gerund by adding a grammatical morpheme, *ing.*) The word *illegal* has a prefix, *il,* a root, *leg,* and a suffix, *al,* but *leg* is the same as that in *legislate* and is unrelated to the Anglo-Saxon word for a lower extremity on the body.

More than a spelling unit is necessary to make a morpheme; it has to function as a representation of meaning. The word *tower* has an *er* final syllable, which is often found in nouns, but the ending is not a morpheme in this word; the word *tower* is one free morpheme with two syllables. In some cases, *er* is a comparative inflection, as in *smarter* and *funnier,* and in other cases, *er* is a noun suffix, as in *teacher, player,* and *speller.*

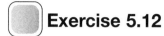

Exercise 5.12

Identify the meaning and part of speech marked by the *er* part of each of these words.

sympathizer

butter

loftier

father

preacher

higher

hirer

water

infer

Limitations on Morpheme Productivity   Prefixes and suffixes can only be added to certain words in English. Thus, we can say that morphemes are only **partially productive.** Their use is confined to specific words or specific types of words. We can add the suffix *ment* to verbs to create nouns such as *enjoyment, refinement,* and *endearment,* but the words *divorcement, rejectment,* or *acceptment* do not exist. We can have *equality* but not *equalness; reddish* but not *cloudish;* and *beautification* but not *uglification.* Some derivational morphemes are more widely applied than others, such as *non,* to negate an adjective, adverb, or noun, but few are applied to all possible base or root forms.

Finally, morpheme combinations do not always mean what the parts suggest. We can say that an event is *unlikely* or that we *dislike* someone, but we cannot say *dislikely,* and if one thing is *unlike* another, then that word means something quite different from an *unlikely* occurrence. *Apartment* may be derived from *apart,* meaning divided, but the relationship is not as obvious to most speakers as that of *place* and *placement.* From *syllabify* we can *syllabificate;* from *syllabicate* we get *syllabication.* All these words exist. Because language evolves, meanings change over time and derivational constructions that were once transparent assume other meanings, such as *unspeakable.* An unspeakable event is often talked about a great deal because it is uncommonly horrific.

Several researchers have estimated that more than 80% of derived words do mean what their parts suggest,[7] as long as multiple meanings of the roots are taken into account. For example, *disengage* can be readily analyzed if several meanings of *engage* are understood. *Scripture* connotes holy or spiritual text, not just any kind of writing, a meaning that is easier to grasp with the historical knowledge that *scribes,* people who could write, translated or copied the Bible and other religious texts. The word *incredible* would be interpreted literally to mean "not to be believed," but it is used to convey a sense of great superiority, as is the word *matchless.*

Exercise 5.13

Mix and match these words parts. Identify which words are possible and which do not exist in English. Use a dictionary, if necessary.

Prefix	Root	Suffix	Words?
inter	spir(e)	(a)tion	_____
dis	cred(it)	icate	_____
non	sect	(i)able	_____
pre	var	arian	_____
in	rupt	ed	_____

Meaning, Pronunciation, and Word Relatedness

Morphological knowledge allows us to judge when words are related in meaning even when they are pronounced differently, as in *wild* and *wilderness, judge* and *judicial, predict* and *predicate.* To a great extent, our knowledge of morphology develops as we learn to read and spell. We could see that words such as *wild* and *wilderness* are related even if we had not thought about this from hearing or saying the words. English orthography often delineates for us the meaningful parts of words, preserving them in spelling even though the pronunciation of the morphemes varies, as in *phone, phonetics,* and *phonics* or *define* and *definition.*[8]

Judging Degree of Word Relatedness

Words that share a morpheme base may be closely or distantly related in meaning. Whether words are related in meaning can be determined by the collective judgment of a community of language users. When speakers of English are asked to judge whether words "come from" each other or are connected in meaning, their opinions generally converge because they are members of a language community. Both semantic and phonetic similarity between words affect whether adults judge them as related. Whether a meaningful connection between words is perceived as close, distant, or non-existent is influenced as much by spelling knowledge as it is by sound similarity.[9] For example, literate adults know that *wise* and *wisdom, doubt* and *dubious, number* and *numerous,* and *please* and *pleasant* are related word forms. They can overlook the differences in pronunciation between the word pairs in deciding whether the words have meaning in common. Exposure to both spoken and written language accounts for developing the ability to tell whether words are related to one another.

Exercise 5.14

Place a 1, 2, 3, or 4 next to the word pairs according to the degree of relatedness or similarity you perceive. Words with a 1 are definitely related in meaning; words with a 2 are related but somewhat less closely; words with a 3 seem to have a more distant connection; and words with a 4 do not have a meaningful connection.

_____ doubt, dubious	_____ scribble, scripture
_____ deep, depth	_____ iris, iridescence
_____ ham, hamburger	_____ amnesty, amniotic
_____ bomb, bombard	_____ serene, serenity
_____ holy, holiday	_____ hand, handkerchief
_____ joy, join	_____ catch, ketchup
_____ sheep, shepherd	_____ cap, capture

Individual Differences in Using Derivational Morphology

The language proficiencies of good readers and the language weaknesses of poor readers extend beyond phonology to other levels of language organization, including morphology. To understand individual differences in morphological skill, it is necessary to appreciate the connectedness of words to one another.

How We Remember Words

There is considerable evidence that words, both spoken and written, are remembered in relation to other words, and word meanings are not stored in our memory as isolated wholes that resemble separate entries in a dictionary. Whenever possible, we learn words in connection to others that we already know. Each word is part of a network of related meanings. One of the ways that word family networks are constructed in memory is by their morphological relationships.[10] When one word in the family is accessed, the other words in the family are activated for possible retrieval. The stem of words in a known high-frequency word family, such as *decide, decision, decided, undecided,* and *decisive,* will be recognized more quickly during reading than will the stem of words in a low-frequency word family such as *amnesia, mnemonic,* and *amnesty.*[11] These connections between words in memory are not dependent simply on matching letter strings; knowledge of *code,* for example, will not help retrieve an unrelated word such as *cod.* Related words are activated in memory when they have meaningful connections and when they share structural elements at the morpheme level, especially when spelling reveals those connections.

Awareness of morphemes helps us understand and remember the differences among homophones (words that sound the same but mean different things). The spelling of a homophone can make sense if the word is known in relation to other words with a similar structure. *Site* is related to *situation* and means "place"; *cite* is related to *citation* and means "a reference in text." *Sight,* of course, is in that group of Anglo-Saxon words that refer to our senses. *Rite* and *ritual; wright, boatwright,* and *playwright; write, written,* and *writing;* and *right* and *righteous* are more likely to be remembered if their origin and meaning connections are understood.

Networks of semantically related morphemes are established in the memories of adults. How these networks become established is considerably relevant to the issue of language instruction. How children learn about morphological relationships and how much they know at certain developmental stages have been topics of limited investigation, primarily in studies involving either reading and spelling tasks or a combination of oral and written tasks.[12]

We know from cognitive experimental research that people with morphological awareness organize their mental dictionaries so that related words are associated and are more readily retrieved. In general, the mind is always seeking pattern recognition to reduce the load on memory and help retrieve linguistic information. When we see the word *postscript,* the whole network of familiar *script* words is activated. If we were to think quickly of all the words we know that have the morpheme *audi* in them, then we could easily call up *auditory, auditorium, audit, audition, audible,* and *audience* for starters. We would be able to retrieve this list more quickly than a series of morphologically unrelated words because they all share a root morpheme and use prefixes and suffixes that are familiar. Therefore, it should be productive to teach words in association with their morphological networks and to teach novice learners the derivatives of one root morpheme at a time.

Developing Morphological Awareness in Good and Poor Readers

Substantial individual variation has been the norm in studies that have attempted to map the development of morphological knowledge in typically progressing children. Rough developmental trends are established, but separating the effects of reading from the causes or characteristics of limited reading ability is challenging. Children do learn a great deal about word structure from reading and writing itself, so text exposure alone may account for substantial individual variation in word knowledge.

On both oral and written language tasks, good verbal learners are more sensitive to derivational relationships and use this knowledge more productively than poor verbal learners.[13] Phonological awareness facilitates morphological awareness in younger children[14] and both are associated with stronger reading skills. Better readers with excellent language abilities in fourth through eighth grade are able to talk about word structure and word meaning in a precise, decontextualized manner that reveals conscious knowledge of phonology and morphology.[15] Linguistically superior fifth-grade students do better than average eighth-grade students identifying and generating derivational morphemes.[16] Fifth-grade students with superior verbal learning ability are more able to detect and use word structure when deciphering word meanings than are typical, older students. Adults who read accurately and fluently have accumulated wide networks of word families for ready access and cross-referencing in the lexicon.[17] In contrast, adults who read poorly have less information in their mental dictionaries as well as less ability to organize and gain access to words using morphological relationships.[18]

When children who read poorly are tested orally with a morpheme-generation task, they find it difficult to apply morphological rules to unfamiliar base words.[19] These problems are attributable, in large part, to weaknesses in phonological processing.[20] Because morphemes are units of both sound and meaning, deficits in phonological processing contribute to confusion of similar-sounding words and word parts, failure to recognize similarities of structure, and failure to either remember or recall word form with precision.

Similarly, differences between good and poor spellers are associated with significant differences in sensitivity to word structure at the morphological level. Children with specific written language and spelling disorders have been shown to misuse, substitute, or omit inflected endings more than their typically developing peers, especially the past tense *ed*.[21] Insensitivity to morphological aspects of word structure also characterize adults who spell poorly.[22]

By sixth grade, average students have an understanding of *stem constancy*, which is reinforced by seeing words in print.[23] That is, they notice the parts of words that mean the same thing and the letters that spell those morphemes. Good spellers and people with larger vocabularies search for and notice letter sequences in new words that can give them a clue to meaning. That is why spelling and vocabulary programs for typical and challenged students should directly teach and focus their attention on morphemes—to make explicit the kind of understanding that good spellers tend to get on their own from seeing words in print.

Derivational Morphology: Principles of Instruction

Three basic principles should guide morphology instruction.

1. *Transparency*: Introduce morphemes in words in which the meaning of the morpheme is transparent. *Per* in *perfume* is more transparent than *per* in *perform* because the meaning of *fume* is straightforward, whereas the meaning of *form* in this verb is less so.

2. *Generativity*: Introduce morphemes that are used in the most words, such as *ject*, *tract*, and *form*.

3. *Complexity*: Introduce derived forms that do not change pronunciation or spelling first. Gradually introduce forms that involve orthographic and phonological changes in derivations. For example, the base word (help) in *helplessness* is not changed with the added suffixes, but the base word (discrete) in *indiscretion* undergoes both phonological and orthographic changes.

Sequence of Instruction

The general sequence outlined in Table 5.7 can be used to organize the presentation of morphemes in spelling and vocabulary instruction. It progresses from the most common or high-frequency constructions to less common

Table 5.7. Scope and sequence for morpheme instruction

Anglo-Saxon layer of language
Base words with single morphemes
Compounds: *doghouse, ballgame, blackbird, overplay, underreport*
High-frequency prefixes added to Anglo-Saxon base words:
> *un, re, dis, in, mis, a, fore, de, pre, en*
> *sub, inter, trans, super, semi, anti, mid*

Inflections and common derivational suffixes added to base words with no spelling change required in the base word:
> *ing, er, y, ly, s, es, ed* (feeding, teacher, squishy, sadly, hits, churches, missed, picked, wanted)

Other common suffixes that begin with a consonant: *ly, ful, ness, less, ment, hood*
Other common suffixes that begin with a vowel: *able/ible, en*
Inflections and common derivational suffixes with spelling changes required in the base word:
> final consonant doubling (shipping, robber)
> drop final *e* rule (hoping, likable, mover)
> change *y* to *i* (cried, happiness, sillier)
> double final consonant of accented syllable (occurrence, beginner)

Latin (Romance) layer of language
Prefixes (review of those listed previously)
> closed and vowel-*r* syllables: *non, ex, con, per, mal*
> open syllables: *bi, co, di, o, pro, tri, twi*
> two syllables: *super, circum, intra, contra, counter, extra, intro, multi, ultra*

Roots (see Table 5.2)
> *port, form, rupt, script, tract, cept*
> *spect, ject, struct, dict, mit, flex, fer*
> *cred, duc, pend, pel, fac, vert, tend*
> *curs, ped, vid, aud, vit/viv*
> *leg, greg, cap/cieve/cep, grad/gress*
> *voc/voke, leg/lect, lit/litera*
> *cede/cess, tain/ten/tin, fid/fide/feal*
> *sis/sta/stat, cad/cas/cid, pon/pose*
> *cern/cert, mob/mot/mov, gen/genus*
> *cid, cis*

Assimilated prefixes
> *in* (immigrate, illegal, irregular)
> *ad* (address, approach, aggressive)
> *ob* (obstruct, opportunity)
> *sub* (subtract, suppose, surround)
> *com* (commit, collide, corrode)
> *dis* (dissuade, difference)

Derivational suffixes
> *ion* (as in *tion* and *sion*)
> *most, ous, or, ess, ure/ture, dom, ent/ence, an, ant/ance, ist, ic, ty*
> *ar, ability, ible/ibility, ize, ary, ate, ward, age, al, ify, ity, ee, fy*
> *ism, ious, ory, ial, ian, cious, ation, ial, tious, ile, ade, ium*

Connectives that join the root and suffix
> *i* (menial, lenient, anxious) and *u* (superfluous, disingenuous, factual)

Greek morphemes and combining forms
Graphemes unique to Greek-based words
> *ch* = /k/ (chorus, monochrome)
> *y* = [ɪ] or [ɑj] (dyslexia, cytoplasm)
> *ph* = /f/ (phonology, grapheme)
> *x* = /z/ (xylophone)

Silent letter spellings
> *rh* (rheumatoid)
> *ps* (psychology)
> *pn* (pneumonia)
> *mn* (mnemonic)
> *pt* (pterodactyl)

Combining forms (see Table 5.5)
> *micro, scope, photo, graph*
> *tele, phon, geo, therm, bio*
> *meter, logy*

Sources: Henry (2003); Moats & Rosow (2003); White et al. (1989).

ones, and from less complex forms to more complex ones, such as nonneutral suffixes that produce phonologic and orthographic changes to the root. Direct Latin and Greek borrowings, including plurals, are included. These morphemes should be taught explicitly across oral (listening/speaking) and written (reading/writing) language.

Goals of Instruction

Knowing meaningful word parts, the ways in which they are combined, and how they are represented in spelling help children acquire vocabulary. Knowing roots and affixes facilitates rapid, efficient, and accurate reading of unfamiliar words as well as reading comprehension. Knowing that one word is derived from another helps children spell words, especially because written English is a system that preserves meaningful relationships in its orthography.[24] Awareness of word structure and the ability to use derivational relationships productively in turn is nourished by exposure to words in written text. Thus, developing an oral language competence is closely intertwined with developing reading and writing. This interaction is particularly important for learning derivational patterns and rules because many of the members of related word families may be encountered first in written text. Effective instruction at all levels will follow these principles.

- Students will pronounce the words orally.

- Students will attend to sound, spelling, meaning, and etymology.

- Words will be learned in lists and in the context of connected language.

- Lessons will contain varied practice routines—word construction (build it) and word dissection (break it apart).

- Words will be taught in relation to other words with the same morpheme(s) that include derived forms (*photo, photograph, photographer,* and *photographic*).

Primary Grade Instruction of Morphology

In first through third grade, we typically expect children to gain and use knowledge of inflectional and derivational morphology without explicit instruction or we teach them about word parts in a cursory way, perhaps in one or two circumscribed spelling lessons. Word structure at the morpheme level, however, should begin in the first grade. All children can benefit from understanding how their language works, but children who have deficits in linguistic awareness really need explicit, systematic, and direct instruction with ample practice opportunities.

Direct instruction about base words, inflections, and compounds can be started in first grade. Second- and third-grade students should continue to learn base words, prefixes, suffixes, and suffix ending rules. Word study lessons involving morphology can include activities such as the following.

1. Listen for suffixes, prefixes, or base words. Put your thumb up if the word I say means more than one of something: *bunches, windows, snack, parties, picture, sailing, coats.*

2. Combine single words into compounds and use them to label pictures.

fish	time	spoon	crawler	meat	owl
ball	tea	park	night	stand	hook

3. Remove inflections and simple suffixes from base words.

    fighting = fight + ing

    mighty = might + y

    sighted = sight + ed

    mightier = might + i(y) + er

    frightened = fright + en + ed

    frightening = fright + en + ing

4. Sort past tense and/or plural words by the sound of their ending.

/s/	/z/	/es/
soups	pegs	benches
pets	chums	kisses
socks	tables	fixes
baths	kebobs	bridges

5. Categorize inflected words by meaning.[25]

Words for things	*Words that describe*
money	funny
pies	wise
winter	better
wind	pinned

6. Categorize words by form.[26]

schoolbooks	weren't	newspaper	continue	aren't
suitable	we'll	grapefruit	calendar	weekend

Compound words	Contractions	Other

7. Identify, underline, and read words with inflections used in context.[27]

    We drift<u>ed</u> into the center of the grassland, which stretch<u>ed</u> as far as the eye could see. The dry land was crack<u>ed</u> and smell<u>ed</u> of dust.

8. Combine base words, prefixes, and suffixes and use the new words.

Prefix	Base word	Suffixes
un	teach	able
re	plant	ed
en	able	ing
pre	tend	er

Fourth Through Eighth Grade

According to one analysis, if students receive direct instruction in the meanings of the most commonly used prefixes, *un, re, dis,* and *in/im/ir,* the removal of the most common suffixes, *able/ible, ly,* and *ness,* and the spelling changes associated with adding inflections beginning with vowels, *es, ed,* and *ing,* they could successfully analyze 250 new printed words per year through morphological analysis.[28] Great differences among good and poor verbal learners' ability to use derivational relationships, however, might be expected.

Between third and seventh grade, children learn anywhere from several hundred new words per year to 5,000 new words per year, depending on their exposure to new vocabulary in and out of the classroom and their aptitude for verbal learning.[29] Most new words are encountered through reading; only a limited number can be taught directly because of limits on instructional time in the classroom. The greatest benefit from vocabulary and spelling instruction may be gained from exploring aspects of word structure that can be generalized or used independently when students encounter new words. Latin roots, prefixes, suffixes, and networks of related words are the best candidates for word study.[30]

Words with affixes outnumber single-morpheme words by a factor of 4 to 1 in English written text;[31] however, derived words with affixes are relatively more numerous among less common content words. For example, the word *demoralization* might be found infrequently in a history textbook about the Civil War, but it might be a key concept in understanding the consequences of a battle, and its meaning should be clear from morphological analysis. Listening, speaking, reading, and writing such words should be interwoven. Even older students with good verbal skills can benefit from direct instruction in derivational morphology.

Derivational relationships are complex and irregular; therefore, memorizing root and affix meanings may have little purpose unless the emphasis is on learning real words and connotations. Instruction should progress logically from the most transparent and common prefixes (see Table 5.3) to the more complex, nonneutral suffixes that cause phonological and orthographic changes in spoken and written words. The greater the phonological difference between the stem of the derived word and the base form (e.g., *anxious, anxiety; preside, president; philosophy, philosophical*), the more students may need direct explanation and practice to learn related word forms.

Instruction should begin with aural and visual recognition of meaningful word parts because this cognitive skill appears necessary for analyzing increasingly complex structural aspects of words in spoken and written form. Using the words in oral and written language is also important because word learning involves an understanding of language structure and knowledge of specific word forms, meanings, and uses. Students can engage in a variety of activities, including grouping related words, searching text for examples of words, generating definitions, using words in analogies, and creating maps of related words. Examples of productive activities follow.[32]

Classroom Activities

1. Teach about schwa.

    Read the first syllable. Then notice how the vowel sound gets muffled and emptied when you read it again in the second, unaccented syllable in the two-syllable word.

pen	happen	pet	trumpet	ton	carton
gel	angel	ban	turban	gus	fungus
est	slimmest	tom	custom	fort	effort

2. Establish awareness of the syllables and phonemes in the word.

    conclude   How many syllables? Where do you hear a schwa?

    stylish   If I take off the last syllable, then what is left? Is that a word you know?

    accomplished How many syllables? Where is the schwa? What is the last sound? What is left if you leave off the last sound?

3. Identify prefixes, roots, and suffixes.

    Circle prefixes, underline roots, and box suffixes.

    (in)/ tend / ed   (con)/ tend / er   (ex)/ tend / ed

    (com)/ plex   (per)/ plex / ed   (ex)/ pect

    (con)/ gest / ed   (sug)/ gest / ing   (in)/ gest / ed

    (col)/ lect / ed   (e)/ lect / ric   (se)/ lect

4. Define affixed words.

    The *age* suffix forms nouns (people, places, things, and ideas) and has many meanings, including the following.

    Amount of: *acreage, usage, postage*

    A result of an action: *slippage, anchorage, storage, outage*

    A condition: *shortage, vintage, courage*

    A collection of: *baggage, garbage, package*

A place: *hermitage, steerage*

Use the meanings of the suffix *age* to define the following words.

tonnage: an amount of tons.

luggage: a collection of bags.

shrinkage: the result of shrinking.

wreckage: the result of wrecking.

5. Proofread and correct misspellings.

Example: Correct this passage by supplying apostrophes where needed.

Its hard to overstate students low understanding about the apostrophes uses.

6. Practice word building with one root.

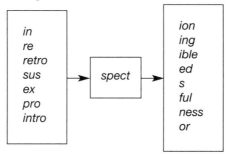

7. Build word webs or diagrams that show families of words built from a root.

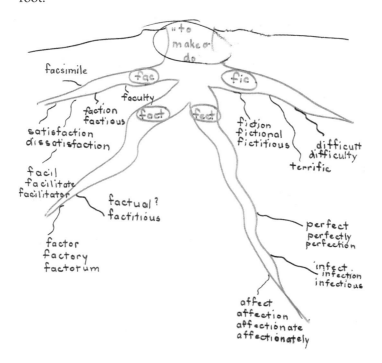

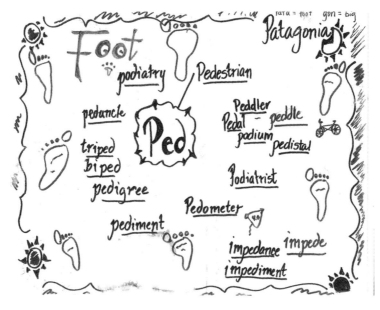

8. Complete words in a cloze passage.

    Fill in the missing blanks with either *able* or *ible.*

    It is poss____ and even prob___ that the dictionary saved Abel's
    deplor___ life. Abel spent innumer____ hours in front of his television
    watching reprehens____ reruns and question____ quiz shows.

To summarize, children use inflections and the simple derivational morphemes before they enter school. Complex derived forms and their alternation patterns are learned gradually over a period of years. Mastery of derivational morphemes is influenced by the frequency with which words are
encountered in text, the complexity of the derivational relationships that
characterize the words, and whether spelling itself is a clue to a word's structure, meaning, and origin. After children acquire phoneme awareness and
phonic knowledge, they can attend more easily to this additional layer of
language organization. In 1970, Carol Chomsky[33] observed that English
orthography is morphophonemic rather than a phonetic transcription of
speech and suggested that derivational word relationships should be taught
to school children. Her advice should, at last, be heeded.

Learning to Read and Spell: The Content Domain

To learn English orthography, the reader and speller must grasp a number of
different concepts about the relationship between print and speech, the
organization of the orthography, and the various levels on which words and
the writing system are structured. Whether students are taught explicitly,
acquiring reading and writing skills involves understanding the orthographic system on a number of dimensions, which are listed next in an outline form, to delineate the content knowledge appropriate for study of
orthography.

I.   Phoneme–Grapheme Correspondences (Grades K–1)
   A.   Predictable Spellings
      1.   Consonants *(him, napkin)*
      2.   Short vowels *(wet, picnic)*
      3.   Digraphs *(chin, fish)*
      4.   Blends *(dragon, scraps)*
   B.   Variant/Conditional Correspondences (Grades 1–3)
      1.   Single consonants *(dress, edge, result)*
      2.   Tense (long) vowels *(grown, light, explain)*
      3.   *R*-controlled vowels *(dear, port, bird)*
      4.   Diphthongs *(toil, boyfriend, tower, bout)*
      5.   Consonant blends *(blink, square, scary)*
      6.   Consonant digraphs *(which, kitchen)*
      7.   Silent letters and oddities *(knew, walk)*
II.   Irregular (Odd) Spellings of High-Frequency Words (Grades 1–3)
   A.   *of, one, enough, said*
III.   Compounds (Grades 2–4)
   A.   *breakfast, fifty-one*
IV.   Syllable Patterns (Grades 2–4)
   A.   Closed: short vowel ending with consonant *(sister, September)*
   B.   Open: long vowel, no consonant ending *(behind, nobody)*
   C.   Vowel team: vowel spelled with two or more letters *(great, weigh, bay)*
   D.   Consonant plus *le*: at the ends of words *(bugle, treatable)*
   E.   *R*-controlled vowel *(porter, hurdle)*
   F.   VCe *(compete, suppose)*
   G.   Idiosyncratic *(active, atomic, village)*
V.   Inflections (Grades 2–3)
   A.   Plural, past tense, and so forth *(walked, wanted, dogs, wishes)*
VI.   Orthographic Rules and Syllable Juncture (Grades 2–5)
   A.   *ve (have, give, love)*
   B.   *f, l, s* doubling rule *(hell, guess, off)*
   C.   doubling final consonant rule *(running, inferred)*
   D.   change *y* to *i* rule *(studious, beautiful)*
   E.   drop silent *e* rule *(baked, coming)*
VII.   Homophones (Grades 2–5)
   their, there; to, two, too
VIII.   Latin-Based Affixes and Schwa (Grades 4–8)
   predict, protection
   vision, enjoyment
   attend, appearance
IX.   Greek Combining Forms (Grades 6–8)
   microscope, psychobiology

X. Contractions (Grades 1–6)
you've, I'll, don't

XI. Possessives, Plurals (Grades 1–8)
night's, oxen, alumnae, crises

XII. Abbreviations (Grades 1–8)
etc., St., P.M.

XIII. Consonant Alternation (Grades 6–8)
mischief, mischievous
medic, medicine

XIV. Vowel Alternation (Grades 6–8)
hostile, hostility
explain, explanation
define, definition
serene, serenity

Supplementary Exercises

5.15 Divide these words into morphemes. Use a dictionary, if necessary.

misspell	stimulate	insanely
sensible	attached	forgettable
inoperable	beautifully	continuity
psychology	excitement	dismiss
preferring	inspiration	recommend
morphemic	pacify	television

5.16 The Greek combining form *psycho* means "mind." How many words can you generate that include that classical root? Make a list, and then organize the words into a web, picture, or map showing how they are related.

5.17 Divide the following words twice, once to show the syllables and again to show the morphemes. The two are not always in agreement because different language structures are involved at each layer of language organization.

competition	precision	scaling
tractor	invasive	gentle

5.18 Words such as *mother, finger,* and *hamburger* look as if they might have separate morphemes, but they do not. They cannot be divided into meaningful parts. Can you think of three more words that look as if they could be made of separate morphemes, but (at least in modern use) they are not?

5.19   Make up five new words composed of common prefixes, roots, and suffixes that could be real words but are not established in English, such as *uglification* and *unpudgable.*

5.20   Below is a list of correct and incorrect spellings of words. English spelling often retains the spellings of meaningful parts even when pronunciation changes, so the correct spellings of the words listed can be affirmed by knowing the pronunciation and spelling of another form of the word. Circle the correct spellings. Then, to the right of these lists, write a form of the word that can help you remember the correct spelling.

		Other word
practice	practise	*practical*
design	desine	*designation*
compitition	competition	_____
persperation	perspiration	_____
physician	physision	_____
restiration	restoration	_____
pleasure	plesure	_____
resign	resine	_____
publisity	publicity	_____
electrisity	electricity	_____
demacratic	democratic	_____
president	presedent	_____
comprable	comparable	_____
history	histry	_____
janiter	janitor	_____
managor	manager	_____
majer	major	_____
industry	indistry	_____

5.21   Match each of the terms in Column B to one of the words in Column A.

A		B
_____ incredible	1.	assimilated prefix (changed to match the root's beginning)
_____ credits	2.	derivational noun suffix
_____ accredit	3.	inflectional suffix
_____ cred	4.	bound root morpheme
_____ creditor	5.	derivational adjective suffix

5.22   Make observations about the orthographic and morphological structure of the following words that you could point out while teaching them to children.

messy

incredulous

solemn

Endnotes

1. Brown, 1973.
2. Berko, 1958; Brown, 1973; deVilliers & deVilliers, 1973.
3. Henry, 2003.
4. Tyler & Nagy, 1989.
5. Tyler & Nagy, 1989.
6. Carlisle, 1987, 1988.
7. Nagy & Anderson, 1984; White, Power, & White, 1989.
8. Derwing, Smith, & Wiebe, 1995.
9. Derwing & Baker, 1979; Derwing et al., 1995.
10. MacKay, 1978; Nagy, Anderson, Schommer, Scott, & Stallman, 1989.
11. Nagy et al., 1989.
12. Carlisle, 1987; Derwing & Baker, 1979; Freyd & Baron, 1982; Rubin, Patterson, & Kantor, 1991; Templeton & Scarborough-Franks, 1985.
13. Rubin, 1988; Shankweiler, Lundquist, Dreyer, & Dickinson, 1996; Stolz & Feldman, 1995.
14. Carlisle & Nomanbhoy, 1993.
15. Snow, 1990.
16. Freyd & Barron, 1982.
17. Nagy et al., 1989.
18. Cunningham & Stanovich, 1997; Leong, 1989; Shankweiler et al., 1996.
19. Carlisle, 2004.
20. Fowler & Liberman, 1995.
21. Bailet, 1990; Moats, 1996.
22. Fischer, Shankweiler, & Liberman, 1985; Liberman, Rubin, Duques, & Carlisle, 1985; Shankweiler et al., 1996.
23. Templeton, 1989.
24. Holmes & Brown, 1998.
25. Rubin, 1988; Rubin et al., 1991.
26. Hooper & Moats, 2010.
27. Hooper & Moats, 2010.
28. White, Power, et al., 1989.
29. Wysocki & Jenkins, 1987.
30. Henry, 2003.
31. Nagy & Anderson, 1984.
32. Moats & Rosow, 2003; Rosow, in press.
33. Chomsky, 1970.

Syntax
How Sentences Work

By the end of this chapter, you will understand:

- Influence of syntactic awareness on reading

- Different parts of sentences

- How to diagram sentence structure

- How sentences are made more complex

- Four basic types of sentences and allowable transformations

- How to teach sentence structure

Sentences are frames into which words can be slotted. Along with the meaning of each word, sentences carry the meaning of text. Sentence production requires both creativity and compliance with syntactic rules and conventions expected by other speakers of the language. Although every adult speaker knows—at least subconsciously—the rules and conventions of sentence production, writing and clearly expressing ideas depend in part on conscious sentence manipulation. Experts do not agree on the best ways to teach grammar, sentence comprehension, or sentence production,[1] but nevertheless, students must gain command of the sentence if they are to write effectively.

This chapter is not going to resolve the controversy surrounding traditional grammar instruction, sentence diagramming, or other methodologies. Researchers have demonstrated, however, that good readers process the structure of sentences (and thereby their meaning) quickly and accurately,[2] making inferences as they go. Poor readers benefit from instruction that builds syntactic awareness and attention to sentence form.[3] Furthermore, good writers know how to think about word order and its relationship with the underlying ideas or propositions in a text.[4] Deliberate practice with the conscious management of sentences, probably through a range of teaching techniques, leads to better writing. This chapter provides basic information about the operation of syntactic structures in language that may be useful in the classroom. With this conceptual foundation, teachers should have an easier time interpreting students' difficulties, demonstrating how sentences work, and selecting instructional strategies to foster growth in both comprehension and composition.

Correct or Incorrect Syntax?

To begin, the study of **syntax,** or sentence structure, in linguistics is not equivalent to the study of traditional grammar in English classrooms, which may focus on labeling parts of speech and learning conventions of standard, accepted usage. The study of syntax in linguistics describes the underlying architecture of phrases and sentences that reflect the mental representations of speakers of that language. Knowledge of this underlying linguistic architecture, which includes **phrase** structure trees and **syntactic categories,** allows speakers of a language to judge what word sequences are permissible, interpret the meaning of word sequences, and generate novel word sequences. Linguists[5] are interested in the nature of this underlying syntactic rule system and how people use it.

Linguists devise theories of syntactic rule systems to explain and describe actual patterns of speaking (**descriptive grammar**) but are not as concerned with upholding a particular standard of grammatical usage. The standards of correctness that are upheld by editors and writers of English and that are agreed on to promote consistent forms of expression are known as **prescriptive grammar.** Some countries formally assign the role of prescriptive grammarian to an individual or committee; for example, it is the duty of designated royalty in England to guard the integrity of the King's English and the duty of an appointed committee in France to guard the French language from destructive outside influences, such as the assimilation of American terms. Although most governmental attempts to regulate language fail to stem the tide of continual change, literate and educated societies usually do ascribe to standards of acceptable usage that are embodied in textbooks, writers' guides, editing manuals, and statements of academic standards.

Nevertheless, what is "correct" is often debated. Our education, home dialect, and current linguistic community may influence whether we judge a sentence to be grammatically correct. Even the most educated people will judge sentences acceptable that violate traditional rules of prescriptive grammar. Split infinitives, for example, have been frowned on in English class, but we can talk about *seeking to modify gradually* or *seeking to gradually modify* the way words are used, and our listeners are not likely to care which way we express the idea. The difference between *lie* and *lay* is being lost; although to lay something down pertains to putting an object down, it is common in American English to use the word *lay* for *lie,* as in *She went to lay down.* Acceptable grammatical usage is always in a state of flux.

Natural Knowledge of Syntax

Although it is beyond the scope of this book to explain syntactic structure in depth, to contemplate and become aware of some aspects of sentences is helpful. Consider the following sentences (an asterisk indicates a sentence that would not be spoken).

1a.   Addictions are overcome only with determination.

1b.   Only with determination are addictions overcome.

2a.   Flights are taken daily with instructors.

2b.   *Daily with instructors flights are taken.

In the case of sentences 1a and 1b, the meaning of the sentences is the same even though the order of the words is different. The word strings of the second set appear on the surface to be similar to those of 1a and 1b, respectively, but the change of word order that occurred between sentences 1a and 1b does not work to preserve the meaningful relationship between sentences 2a and 2b. Sentence 2b is awkward and would not be spoken. Something about it violates our natural sense of permissible syntax. Thus, we can recognize the relationship between word order and meaning and make judgments about sentences even though we may not be able to say why one sentence "sounds okay" and another does not. These examples, however, show that something beyond the surface arrangement of words is governing the structure of sentences. Meaning is not a simple function of the surface arrangement of words.

Other common linguistic phenomena must be explained by a theory of syntax. Consider the following sentence.

3.   Flying hang gliders can be hazardous.

Sentence 3 can have two different meanings: The act of flying hang gliders can be dangerous to the person who does the flying, or the hang gliders themselves, when they are being flown, can be hazardous to anything else that happens to be in the air. In this case, one sentence can have two different meanings. Such sentences are said to be ambiguous; the meaning is not clear without further clarification from context. Once again, something deeper than the surface order of the words governs our interpretation of meaning. We sense that there are two underlying meaning structures into which the same word sequence would fit.

There are, however, many instances in which meaning seems very dependent on word order. Consider the following sentences.

4a.   These are the times that try men's souls.

4b.   These times that are men's try the souls.

4c.   *Try times men's are souls the these.

The first sentence (quoted from Thomas Paine) is grammatical and well known to those who have studied the American Revolution. The second contains the same words in a possible order; however, not only is the meaning different from the first sentence, but it also would be lost on most of us. The last example is such an obvious transgression of word order possibilities that it has no meaning to any English speaker. In these cases, word order makes a great deal of difference to meaning.

Our knowledge of syntax also involves a sense of how words must be used in relation to one another. Consider the following sentences.

5a.   *The drunken man offended.

5b.   *Jerry laughed the joke.

Neither sentence is grammatical because the verbs are not behaving as they are designed. The first sentence is incomplete. Someone who offends must offend someone or something. The verb *offend* itself has grammatical properties that require it to be used in a specific slot within a structure and that require the sentence to contain something else known as an **object** (in this case, the person or entity that is offended). A parallel but different condition exists in Sentence 5b; the verb *laughed* cannot be followed by a noun phrase. We cannot laugh a joke, although we can tell a joke. Laughing is not something one does directly to someone or something else, although the verb often takes a prepositional phrase that tells at what, for what, when, or how the laughing occurred.

So, word order is related to meaning but in no simple way. Word order may change, but meaning may stay constant. Word order may be constant but may allow for different meanings. Changes in word order may drastically affect meaning. The properties of words themselves dictate some aspects of sentence structure because they only seem to fit in certain slots. A language user's ability to know what is permitted and to understand the relationship between word order and meaning is part of that speaker's **natural grammatical knowledge.** It is learned from exposure to language and requires little formal instruction. It does not depend on having heard any particular sentence before and does not depend on the speaker's knowledge of specific word meanings. The term *grammatical,* therefore, refers to the collective judgments of a group of language users, not to formal, testable knowledge of what is "proper" English usage.

Exercise 6.1

Which sentences are grammatical or acceptable and which are not, according to your knowledge of the English syntactic rule system? Can you explain why some of these sentences are ungrammatical to you?

Me and Harry went on a trip together.

I don't have no more gum to share.

If you breathe deep, you will be able to hold your breath longer.

Justina did real good on her examinations.

My friend was stressing over all she had to do before vacation.

Due to overbooking, Bart was not able to get on the flight.

Can I take my dog with me in the car, Mom?

Do you have enough to go around?

Molly slept the baby all night.

Evidence for Syntactic Structures

Clearly we do not learn to produce sentences by imitation or memorization because most of what we say is novel. The exact sequences of words in most of our sentences have not been spoken before. Other than stock phrases such as conversational niceties, routinized exchanges, or commands, we are more likely to produce a sentence that has not been produced before than we are likely to repeat a sentence that is already familiar or in some way practiced. In fact, in the world of publishing, there is a prohibition against using the exact words of another writer without explicit attribution; novelty is expected.

If we are a native speaker of English or any other language, then it is not necessary to have heard a sentence before to interpret its meaning or judge its grammaticality. Consider the following sentences.

6a. Paddington placed a purple azalea on the tiny tenderloin before serving it.

6b. Roman gladiators levitated before suddenly dematerializing.

These sentences most likely are novel; they do not refer to actual events, but they can be interpreted. They may not jive with either fictional or non-fictional reality—they may have no truth value—but they are grammatical forms that follow the requirements of English.

Likewise, groupings of words may sound like sentences, but the words may not mean anything. Consider the following sentences.

7a. Tawley blepped the righton so sormedly that it deniliated.

7b. If gyxes can squow the perfaction, then prinzes should remell the chobbifiddy.

Lewis Carroll's famous "Jabberwocky" poem from *Through the Looking Glass*[6] may be the best literary example of the delight that we can experience while reading syntactically correct nonsense. The existence of syntactically correct nonsense indicates that the syntactic rule structure exists apart from the meaning of the words it might contain. Sentences can have structure regardless of whether they mean anything true; conversely, truth can be expressed in sentences that are considered to be grammatically incorrect (*He weren't no good at caring for his family, no ways*). Syntax can be manipulated and analyzed in its own right, independent of meaning. We use the underlying forms to generate an infinite number of word combinations.

To summarize, so far, the following truths are evidence that syntactic rules and frameworks are part of what the speaker of a language knows.

- Words in a sentence do not have to make sense, even though we recognize that the word order fits into syntactic patterns.

- For sentences to make sense, speakers must follow certain word order constraints.

- The order and grouping of words allows us to understand relationships among the ideas, such as subject–object relationships.

- Some sentences are ambiguous—they can be interpreted in two or more ways.

- Sentences with different word sequences can mean the same thing.

- Words can be combined in an infinite number of ways within the syntactic frames or rules of a language.

Parts of Sentences

To understand how sentences work, we must take a closer look at their structure and their parts, including the slots or syntactic categories filled by words, phrase structures, and clauses.

Parts of Speech

Before we delve into the structure of sentences, a review of familiar grammatical terms is in order. Traditionally, English grammar books have categorized words according to their "part of speech," assigning them roles such as the following.

Part of speech	Meaning expressed	Example
Noun	Person, place, thing, idea; name for something concrete or abstract	*paradise, idealism, believing, nation, democracy*
Pronoun	A word or phrase that substitutes for a noun	*I, me, you, his, it*
Noun marker (article or determiner)	Word that precedes or marks a noun	*a, an, the*

Verb	Word for an action, state of being, or occurrence	*ride, toss, demonstrate*
Verb *to be* as the copula	Main verb linking the subject to the subject complement in the verb phrase.	*am, are, is, was, were, be, being, been*
Auxiliary verb or helping verb	A verb joined with the main verb to give more information about tense, mood, number, voice, or person	*be, have, do (are well, has gone, will go, does believe), should, would, could*
Adverb	Modifies (tells more about) a verb, adjective, or adverb	*well, poorly, persistently*
Adjective	Modifies a noun; a describing word	*bulbous, offensive, natural, green*
Preposition	Shows the relationship of one thing to another	*in, under, on, around, beside, over, of*
Conjunction	Joins words, phrases, or clauses to one another	*and, although, but, or*

These labels are often used to describe the properties of single words. Thus, these characteristics are sometimes called lexical properties. Although imperfect, these labels provide a way of talking about the role that a single word, or lexical entry in the mental dictionary, plays in a sentence. When we know a word, we know what slot it can fill in a grammatical structure.

Linguists prefer, however, to focus on the nature of the slots that words fill, or syntactic categories, in describing how words work in sentences. Linguists might talk about the category of nouns as those words that can fill the slots for nouns in basic sentence forms. Many words can fill several slots within a sentence, and their meaning can only be resolved with reference to how they are used in the whole sentence context. Consider the word *rock*, which is used as a verb, noun, or adjective: *Please don't rock the boat. White rocks surround the garden's edge. That candidate's résumé is rock solid.* Word meanings often depend on syntactic context, and many words fit into more than one syntactic category.

Syntactic categories, then, are groupings of expressions that have the same function within a sentence structure. Within a syntactic category, words or word groups can substitute for one another without affecting the structure of the sentence. Using this concept, we can then define a noun as any word or word combination that can fill the "noun" slot in a sentence frame. Before we go further, let's define and differentiate two other important syntactic categories—phrases and clauses.

Phrases

A phrase is a natural grouping of words that seem glued together as a functional unit. Words in a phrase may be slotted into an underlying syntactic frame when sentences are formed. Single words, or lexical items, are subsumed by phrasal categories. Phrases contain lexical items of the same type and function; noun phrases must contain a noun, verb phrases must contain a verb, and so forth.

Phrases clearly go together or work together within the architecture of a sentence. A standard simple sentence, such as, *The driver totaled the car*, has a natural break between the subject (the driver) and the predicate (totaled the car). The natural division between these two essential parts of a sentence can be depicted in a tree diagram as follows.

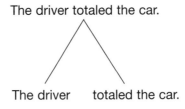

The natural groupings of words into two basic phrases in the simple sentence demonstrate the presence of underlying, functional phrase structure. The **subject** is composed of a **noun phrase** plus any modifiers that tell us more about the subject. A noun phrase is a syntactic category or slot into which other words can be placed in this sentence, such as *the child, the starlet*, or *the tornado*. The main noun in the noun phrase is called the **head noun.** Similarly, the **predicate** contains a **verb phrase** that describes the action or state attributable to the subject, plus any additional words that tell us more about that action or state of being. A verb phrase has a main verb. In the simple sentence, the slot for the verb phrase could contain the words *bought the car, polished the car*, or *totaled his taxes*. We can use symbolic shorthand to label the parts of a sentence. The symbols

$$S \longrightarrow NP + VP$$

mean that a sentence (S) may be composed of a noun phrase (NP) and a verb phrase (VP). Note that this is quite different from defining a sentence as "a complete thought" or as a "group of words with the first word capitalized and punctuation at the end." In a tree diagram, the symbols NP and VP are always noted as the first branches of the sentence tree.

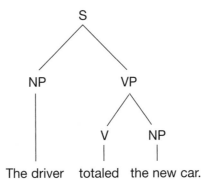

In our simple sentence, the VP includes the verb *totaled* and a noun phrase that functions as the **direct object,** *the car*. Our simple sentence, then, has two noun phrases—one is the subject and other the object of the verb. Some verbs take a direct object and a **prepositional phrase (PP),** a natural grouping of words in which a noun phrase is introduced by a **preposition**, as in, "The driver sent the car *to the junkyard,*" or "The officer put the report *on the seat.*" Prepositional phrases tend to answer the where, when, and how questions. Prepositional phrases almost always contain a noun phrase after the preposition, and that is why ending a sentence with a preposition (*Do you know where she went to?*) sounds awkward—sort of.

 ## Exercise 6.2

Next to each phrase note which of three syntactic categories the phrase belongs to: noun phrase (NP), verb phrase (VP), or prepositional phrase (PP).

in written material ____	consider the options ____	of a dialect ____
joined the opposition ____	played quietly ____	many students ____
with profound regret ____	a spectacular sunset ____	is a has been ____
was waiting ____	body weight ____	beside the stream ____

Adjective phrases and **adverbial phrases** also exist in English. An *adjective phrase* modifies or describes a noun, and an *adverbial phrase* modifies or tells more about the verb.

Clauses

A **clause** differs from a phrase in that it belongs to the syntactic category of a group of words containing a subject and a predicate. There are two kinds of clauses in English sentences: **independent** and **dependent.** An independent clause can stand alone as a sentence. A **simple sentence** is one independent clause. Examples of independent clauses include:

Harry threw the pizza dough up in the air.

He twirled it around with his fist.

Then, he popped the crust into the oven.

A dependent clause also contains a subject and predicate, but it cannot stand alone as a sentence. It depends on, is attached to, or is subordinate within the structure of an independent clause. Examples of dependent clauses include:

When I was frightened

Although he made a good argument

Believing that the world would end

Until he learned how to do it

Clauses may have **compound subjects,** or more than one head noun in the subject:

Harry and Jake threw pizza dough up in the air.

Pizza dough and bread have similar ingredients.

Clauses may also have **compound predicates,** or verb phrases with more than one main verb:

Harry *threw* the pizza dough in the air, *twirled* it with his fist, and *fit* it into the pan.

We *ate* salad, *drank* lemonade, and *munched* on a large pizza until dark.

Clauses may also have compound objects within the verb phrase:

Harry cooked *the pizza dough and the sauce* simultaneously.

Simple, Compound, and Complex Sentences

A simple sentence is a single independent clause. A **compound sentence,** however, is one in which two or more independent clauses have been joined by a coordinating **conjunction.** For example, these are compound sentences:

Harry molded the dough, *and* Hanna baked the bread.

Jeff drove off the road, *for* he was in a blinding snowstorm.

Beatrice sold the clunker, *but* she still had to pay off the loan.

Linda wrote well, *yet* she was unable to publish her book.

We were unable to get seats behind home plate, *so* we sat in the bleachers.

A **complex sentence** is one in which one or more dependent clauses are attached to or embedded in an independent clause. Complex sentences may introduce a dependent clause with a subordinating conjunction, as in the following:

When I was frightened, I hid under the bed.

Although she made a good argument, Nancy lost the vote.

Believing that the world would end, Paul stashed supplies in his basement.

Until she learned how to bid, Melanie refused invitations to play bridge.

Complex sentences may also embed relative clauses, introduced by a relative pronoun *that, who,* or *what:*

Columbus believed *that* the earth was flat.

He thought *that* he would find India.

She knew *who* she wanted to invite to the wedding.

The accident was exactly *what* I was trying to avoid.

Complex sentences may also include dependent clauses introduced by a **participle.** A participle is a word formed from a verb that can function as part of a verb phrase. Two kinds of participles are used in English—a present tense, formed by adding *ing* to a base verb, and a past tense, formed by adding *ed* to a verb or by using an irregular form of the past tense. Past tense participles can be used as adjectives (an *exhilarated* fan; previously *bought* tickets), as adjectives within passive voice constructions (the car was *totaled*), or with the verb *have* to make the perfect past tense (he *had shouted* his lungs out). Present tense participles are found in the progressive or continuous form of a verb (he *was shouting* at the top of his lungs); are used as adjectives in noun phrases (the *giving* tree); and can be **gerunds,** which are nouns created from verbs (*flying* can be stressful). The following sentences are examples of dependent clauses introduced by participles:

> *Knowing that the weather would be poor,* she canceled her trip.

> *Wondering where they were embarking,* Craig called the tour company's office.

Finally, infinitive clauses can be embedded in complex sentences. An *infinitive* is a verb preceded by the word *to*; it has no tense. Examples of infinitive clauses are as follows:

> *To believe that extraterrestrials visit Nevada* is strange.

> *To keep on doing the same thing* is counterproductive.

> The publisher believes *the author to be truthful.*

More About Conjunctions

A *conjunction* is a word that links words, phrases, or clauses. We have already mentioned two types of conjunctions—coordinating and subordinating. The coordinating conjunctions always join syntactic elements from the same category. For example, they may join nouns to nouns, verbs to verbs, noun phrases to noun phrases, verb phrases to verb phrases, or one sentence to another sentence. The term *compound element* is used for the joined elements. The mnemonic acronym "fanboys" refers to all seven coordinating conjunctions: *for, and, nor, but, or, yet,* and *so.*

There are many more subordinating conjunctions—words that connect subordinate clauses to a main clause. Subordinating conjunctions are adverbs that appear at the beginning of the subordinate, adverbial clause. Some subordinators are two or three words, such as *only if, even if, whether or not,* and *in case.* Conjunctions can be categorized by the relationships between the words, phrases, or clauses that they join (see Table 6.1).

Correlative conjunctions are pairs of words used together to join similar elements. They include *both, and; not only, but also; either, or; neither, nor;* and *whether, or.*

> *Either* she *or* I would be chosen for the team.

> *Neither* George *nor* Jennifer could understand the tax code.

> *Not only* were the costumes brilliant, *but also* the acting was superb.

Table 6.1.   Examples of conjunctions, classified by meaning relationships

Time sequence	Causation	Reversal or contradiction	Conditionality
then	because	but	if
when	since	yet	unless
while	now that	although	only if
since	as	though	whether or not
after	in order that	even though	even if
until	so	whereas	in case (that)
		while	

Conjunctive adverbs are both adverbs and conjunctions; they can join two independent clauses. When these adverbs are part of an independent clause, they are set off by commas (*The panel, meanwhile, did its work in private,* or *Meanwhile, the panel did its work*). When two independent clauses are connected with a conjunctive adverb, they must be separated by a semicolon, not just a comma, as in the following.

The bear heard us approach; *fortunately,* he turned and ran.

The cyclist did his best; *still,* he could not beat the time of the leader.

Dyslexia is a lifelong condition; *nevertheless,* it can be overcome.

Other conjunctive adverbs include *also, anyway, besides, therefore, certainly, finally, furthermore, thus, however, incidentally, indeed, still, instead, likewise, similarly, meanwhile, moreover, namely, nevertheless, undoubtedly, next, now, otherwise,* and *then.*[7]

 Exercise 6.3

Identify whether each word group is a phrase (P), a dependent clause (DC), or an independent clause (IC).

while the baby slept _____

seeing is believing _____

all the pretty horses _____

unrelenting school pressures _____

Mary spent her fortune _____

over the hill _____

who voted in the affirmative _____

wrapped corn is baking _____

which he helped accomplish _____

until the play was done _____

into thin air _____

although the evidence accumulates _____

pound dogs need homes _____

How Sentences Grow

Three kinds of syntactic categories have been discussed so far: words, phrases, and sentences, which are composed of one or more clauses. Single words can function as noun phrases, as long as they fit into the slot in the sentence frame where the noun phrase goes. In the sentence, *Harry and Martha ate pizza*, we can substitute the word *they* for *Harry and Martha*. Each one is a subject noun phrase. Thus, a pronoun substitutes for a noun phrase. We could also substitute any number of words, phrases, or clauses for the object noun phrase, as in *They ate <u>fattening food</u>* or *They ate <u>the pizza that came out of the oven that Martha preferred</u>*. Again, phrase structures of sentences contain groups of words that fit the slots for allowable syntactic categories and are organized in hierarchical trees.

Elaborating sentences works systematically within the subject noun phrase and/or the main verb phrase and the basic hierarchy of sentence organization. For example, we can elaborate the subject and the predicate by adding adjectives (Adj.) before the nouns. In our tree diagram, we can also label the article (Art.) and noun (N) within each noun phrase, and mark the verb (V) and any noun phrase that acts as a direct object within the verb phrase.

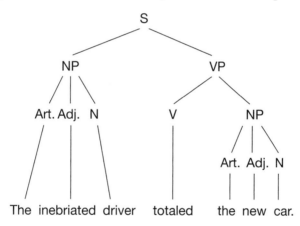

We can also elaborate the subject and/or the predicate by adding a prepositional phrase (PP), consisting of a preposition (Prep.) and a noun phrase, to either a noun or a verb phrase.

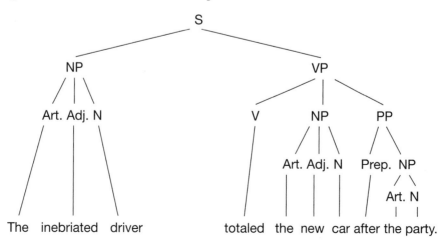

The phrase structure tree shows the words that naturally are grouped together and shows the nested or hierarchical nature of sentence organization.

A similar array of words, however, could represent a different underlying phrase structure. If the sentence were, *The inebriated driver totaled the new car with the sunroof,* the hierarchical structure of the sentence would be somewhat altered. *With the new sunroof* would be nested under the direct object noun phrase because the sunroof belongs to the car. In the previous sentence, *The inebriated driver totaled the new car after the party,* the prepositional phrase modified the verb: It told when the car was totaled, not what kind of a car it was.

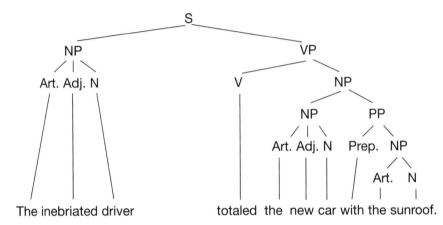

Clearly, a sentence is more than a string of words. Sentence meaning is governed by underlying, hierarchical structures that allow us to interpret the clusters of words (phrases) that convey sense. Postulating underlying syntactic structures also helps to explain phrase ambiguity. A phrase such as *modern fashion designer* can have two possible meanings, as shown in the following diagrams.

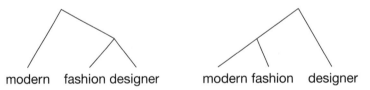

Either the designer creates modern fashions, or the fashion designer is modern, depending on what the context demands. Without a theory of underlying syntactic structure, linguists would not be able to explain why the phrase *modern fashion designer* is ambiguous at all. No other explanation at the level of word order or word meaning suffices to explain the fact that one simple phrase can have more than one sense.

The underlying syntactic scaffolding has slots. Each slot in a syntactic structure can hold any word that fits into the category. Some of the slots are obligatory (NP + VP), but others are optional. The categorical slots or categories also come with specifications. For example, the category of words that are allowed right before a noun (also known as *adjectives*) in a noun phrase are not always found in a sentence, as in *The teacher lowered her voice.* Conversely, syntactic rules allow us to add as many adjectives as we want before a noun:

The *dedicated, knowledgeable, tireless, saintly, brilliant, fabulous* teacher lowered her voice to gain her students' attention. Words in the adjective category also have comparative and superlative forms, as in *the most talented teacher* or *the wisest teacher.* No other words besides adjectives can be modified in such a manner.

Categories of words can only be used in certain places in a sentence structure. In addition, they have other constraints and properties governing their use. The category of nouns has words that can be plural, and no other category of words can be plural. Thus, a test for whether a word is a noun is whether it can be plural. In English, plurals are formed in several ways—not only by adding the morpheme *s* or *es,* but also by using irregular plural forms (*deer, sheep*) or by using plurals borrowed from Latin or Greek (*alumni, crises, criteria, vertebrae*).

Transformations

Sentences can be classified into these four basic types: statements (marked with periods), questions (marked with question marks), imperatives (often marked with exclamation points), and exclamations (marked with exclamation points).

Sally got moving when the bell rang.

When did Sally get moving?

Sally, get moving!

Geepers! Sally is slow.

To further explain the structure of sentences, linguists must uncover the underlying rules of syntax that govern how statements are transformed into questions, imperatives (commands), and exclamations. Students are constantly required to transform questions into statements, such as on tests. If students lack transformational skill, then they make errors similar to a seventh-grade student who answered a question about ionic bonds on a science test: *Why ionic bonds are capable of conducting electricity is that ionic bonds...*

A **transformation** is an operation that moves phrases around within a given sentence structure. Our syntactic knowledge tells us that we can move some phrases and not others; we can move phrases to certain positions but not others; and certain rules must be followed to change a simple sentence from a positive statement to a negative statement, a passive voice statement, or an interrogative, or our meaning will not be understood by the listener. Consider the following sentences.

9a.   Becket murdered the prince in the castle.

9b.   The prince was murdered by Becket in the castle.

9c.   In the castle, Becket murdered the prince.

9d.   Becket murdered the ruler of the nation.

9e.   The ruler of the nation was murdered by Becket.

9f.* Of the nation, Becket murdered the ruler.

Sentences 9a and 9d appear on the surface to be very much alike. Simple diagrams, however, demonstrate that their underlying structures are different.

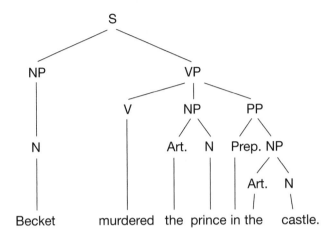

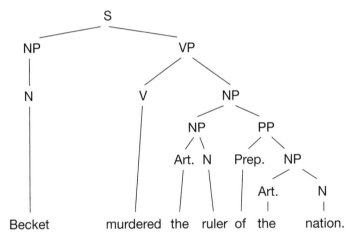

The prepositional phrase in 9a acts differently from the prepositional phrase in 9d. In 9a, the prepositional phrase *in the castle* modifies the verb or is directly subsumed under the verb phrase. In 9d, the prepositional phrase *of the nation* modifies the noun in the noun phrase that makes up the object. These differences become important when a transformation from the active to the passive voice is constructed. In the passive voice (Sentences 9b and 9e), the prepositional phrase occupies a different place. In Sentence 9b, it stays with the verb phrase. In Sentence 9e, it is moved with the noun phrase. Sentences 9c and 9f also show that the prepositional phrase behaves differently according to underlying syntactic structure. If the prepositional phrase *of the nation* is separated from the noun that it modifies (*ruler*), then the sentence no longer has integrity (9f). When the phrase *in the castle*, however, is moved to precede *Becket murdered the prince* as in 9c, no meaning is lost and the sentence is permissible.

Differences in the underlying structure also determine what kind of interrogative (question) transformations are allowed. Consider the following sentences.

10a.   Becket murdered the prince in the castle.

10b.   Whom did Becket murder in the castle?

10c.   Becket murdered the ruler of the nation.

10d.   Whom did Becket murder?

The first question transformation (10b) uses the interrogative pronoun *whom* to replace the object noun phrase *the prince,* inserts the auxiliary *did,* and preserves the verb and prepositional phrase that modifies it. The second question transformation (10d) replaces the entire object noun phrase *the ruler of the nation* with *whom.* We could not transform 10c into *Whom did Becket murder of the nation?* because the prepositional phrase is part of the noun phrase in that sentence structure.

Teaching Sentence Structure

The goal of sentence instruction for writing is to build students' awareness of incomplete sentences, run-on sentences, awkward expressions, ambiguity, unclear or poorly expressed meaning, and conventions of grammar so that strong sentences can be composed. The goal for reading comprehension purposes is to aid students' grasp of meanings expressed in longer, complex, or more difficult sentence forms[8] because not all sentences are equally easy to understand. Consider the following examples.

Passive voice
Mazzie was the last cheerleader to be designated by Matilda for the team.

Double negative
We had no reason to think she was unqualified.

Ellipsis (omission of words) in compounds
A polar bear is well adapted to the arctic, and a tortoise to equatorial conditions.

Interruption of main subject and verb
Marco Polo, whose trade routes extended from China to central Europe and who established cultural interdependencies still viable today, grew up in Italy.

Sentence awareness, for both reading and writing, can be developed—just as phonological awareness can be developed—with various sentence manipulation exercises. These can be used as warm-ups for reading and writing. Skills practice works best if it is done in tandem with meaningful application. Exercises can be practiced orally or in writing. It is best to connect the activities to a theme or topic relevant to what the students are learning in other subject matter instruction. The following techniques are among the many suggested by Hochman[9] in her handbook on teaching basic writing skills.

1.   Scrambled sentences (sentence anagrams)

Rearrange words on cards: *Tom where did live*

2. Complete the subject or predicate

    Finish the sentence: The frisky dog _____.

    _____bought a toy car.

3. Generate questions from statements

    The war ended with a truce and a compromise.

    How did the war end?

4. Combine sentences

    The quarterback threw the ball.

    The quarterback was helped by great blocking.

    The quarterback threw the ball to the wide receiver.

    The wide receiver leapt high.

    The wide receiver caught the ball for a touchdown.

    Helped by great blocking, the quarterback threw the ball to the wide receiver, who leapt high and caught the ball for the touchdown.

5. Begin a sentence with a subordinate clause

    After the storm passed, _____.

    While we were sleeping, _____.

    When I was frightened, _____.

6. Expand a simple sentence by adding information about who, what, when, where, why, or how.

    Whales migrate.

    Humpback whales, traveling with their young, migrate to northern feeding grounds in summer in order to fatten up for the winter.

7. Join two independent clauses with a coordinating conjunction.

    Dennis likes pancakes, so _____.

    Dennis likes pancakes, but _____.

8. Identify the subject and predicate, underlining the subject with one line and the predicate with two. Circle the head noun and box the main verb.

    Our founding fathers, stung by the experiences of British domination and mindful of the states' desire for autonomy, provided, after much debate, a good balance of federal and states' rights in the Constitution.

Traditional sentence diagramming still has many strong advocates[10] who follow the Reed-Kellogg system. Basics of this system can be downloaded from the Internet.[11]

Summary

As speakers of a language system, we have syntactic knowledge that includes tacit awareness of phrases and grammatical categories for words, the underlying phrase structures on which sentences are built, and the ways in which various transformations can be produced. The "sentence sense" we would like to cultivate in students should enable them to control or choose how they express ideas in writing and should improve their ability to understand complex or unusual syntax when they read. In addition, awareness of syntax improves spelling and enables students to rely on themselves as they are proofreading or editing. In our schools today, many students speak nonstandard dialects, have limited access to models of standard English usage, and are dependent on direct teaching to master language at this level. Others may have subtle problems with syntax comprehension and production that are most obvious under the stringent demands of complex text reading and academic writing. It is for these reasons that academic language arts instruction should focus on the sentence, along with higher levels of discourse.

The theoretical constructs discussed in this chapter do not explain in detail what type of practice or instruction is most likely to improve students' ability to formulate, interpret, or manipulate the parts of sentences for comprehension or writing. Direct practice with sentence manipulation, however, can build students' facility with language analysis and production. The exercises that conclude this chapter represent a variety of strategies for sentence expansion, transformation, combination, and analysis that can be adapted for any age group.

 ## Supplementary Exercises

6.4   Form several groups of students. Each person should write a 6- to 12-word sentence on a strip of paper and then cut it apart into words. (Long sentences are not necessarily more difficult than short sentences.) Each group member gives his or her sentence anagram to another person as a puzzle—the object is to reconstruct the original sentence. Observe whether the person clusters words in phrases as he or she begins to work. As a group, discuss strategies that people used to solve the sentence puzzles.

6.5   Combine the following sets of simple sentences into elaborated single sentences that preserve the main idea of each simple sentence.

Set 1

The team won the game.

They won in overtime.

The team was determined.

The game was for the championship of the league.

Set 2

The Coast Guard undertook a mission.

They searched immediately after the plane crash.

They searched for debris.

They looked for survivors.

They were not optimistic.

Describe the operations you carried out on the simple sentences to combine each of the sentence sets into one complete, elaborated sentence.

6.6   Following are some kernel sentences. Elaborate each kernel sentence by first asking questions of the subject and predicate, such as "How many?" "What kind?" "Where?" "How?" "When?" or "How long?" and then add these answers to the kernels.

Presidents lie.

Fans swoon.

Hawaii calls.

6.7   The following sentences are uninteresting because they are both unelaborated and formed with "1 dollar" words. Change the sentences to make them more interesting; use some "10 dollar" words that preserve the part of speech of the originals, and elaborate each sentence by adding phrases to the subject and predicate. Complex and compound sentences are allowed.

The fish swam around the boat.

The boy caught the fish.

He threw it back.

6.8   Identify the subject and predicate of each sentence.[12] Then, identify the grammatical category (part of speech) that each of the italicized words is likely to be.

'Twas *brillig* and the *slithy toves* did *gyre* and *gimble* in the *wabe;*

All *mimsy* were the *borogoves* and the *mome raths outgrabe.*

6.9   In one nonstandard English dialect, speakers say, "I is going with you," and "You is going with me;" the past tense becomes, "I were going" and

"He were going." In addition to observing that this is nonstandard grammar, can you find any reason that this verb form might be a systematic change in a grammatical category? Consider all of the forms of the verb *to be*, and speculate on the nature of the change to the verb in the nonstandard dialect.

I am	we are	I was	we were
you are	you are	you were	you were
he is	they are	he was	they were

6.10   The following phrases are ambiguous. Draw simple tree diagrams to show the phrase structures underlying the ambiguities of each phrase. Explain the different meanings of each.

negative film developer

older women's doctor

English language translator

white Audi driver

red maple cabinets

6.11   These ungrammatical sentences occurred in the writing of fourth-grade students. What kind of error does each sentence represent? How could each sentence be fixed or corrected?

a)   When I was frightened.

b)   When I was frightened, it was because I was alone.

c)   Things that are frightenly, can scare you that you will not know what happen to you.

d)   Very bad frightened by the scary monster.

e)   A game that never ended.

Endnotes

1. Graham & Perin, 2007.
2. Cain & Oakhill, 2007.
3. Singer & Bashir, 2004.
4. Scott, 2004, 2009.
5. See, for example, Chomsky, 1965; Fromkin et al., 2003; Pinker, 1999.
6. Carroll, 1865/1960.
7. Hochman, 2009.
8. Scott, 2004.
9. Hochman, 2009.
10. Florey, 2008.
11. See Basics of Reed-Kellogg Diagrams at http://www.utexas.edu/courses/langling/e360k/handouts/diagrams/diagram_basics/basics.html
12. Carroll, 1865/1960, p. 134.

Recommended Resources for Sentence Comprehension and Writing Instruction

Carreker, S. (1993). *Multisensory grammar and written composition.* Bellaire, TX: Neuhaus Education Center.

Florey, K.B. (2008). A picture of language: A diagrammed sentence is a bit like art. *American Educator, 32*(2), 40–42.

Greene, J. (2009). *Language!* (4th ed.). Longmont, CO: Sopris West Educational Services.

Greene, T., & Enfield, M.L. (1993). *Framing your thoughts.* Bloomington, MN: Language Circle Enterprises.

Hochman, J. (2009). *Teaching basic writing skills: Strategies for effective expository writing instruction.* Longmont, CO: Sopris West Educational Services.

University of Texas. (n.d.). *Basics of Reed-Kellogg diagrams.* Retrieved August 16, 2009, from http://www.utexas.edu/courses/langling/e360k/handouts/diagrams

Semantics
Word and Phrase Meanings

By the end of this chapter, you will understand:

- Denotative and connotative meanings of words

- Word synonyms and antonyms

- Noun and verb phrases

- Idioms and metaphors

- How students make sense of words in situational and linguistic contexts

- How to teach vocabulary and word meaning

Semantics
+Lexical Semantics
  • word meanings

+Sentential
  • sentence

+Pragmatics
  social context

Reading is typically defined as the act of deriving meaning from print. Ironically, however, the nature of meaning is the least understood and most abstract area of linguistics. We know when words make sense to us; yet, the challenge of unraveling the nature of meaning itself has occupied philosophers for several thousand years. Meaning in language resides in several places simultaneously—in words and their morphemes, in sentence structure, and in the context of the communication. **Lexical semantics** is the study of word meanings, **sentential semantics** is the study of sentence meanings, and **pragmatics** is the study of social context and its effect on meaning interpretation. This chapter has more to say about lexical semantics than about the other topics, but these other topics are touched on as well.

Meaning construction is also individual and personal. You and I might say we comprehended a newspaper editorial we both just read. Yet, if asked to summarize it, we might give significantly different responses depending on our backgrounds, expectations, prior knowledge, and verbal reasoning skills. The sense we have of our own understanding or misunderstanding drives the process of **comprehension monitoring.** An important aspect of comprehension is knowing when and what we have not comprehended. If we are adaptive, then we reread, rethink, search for more information, ask for an explanation, or engage in other strategies until we do understand. No two people are exactly alike in the way they go about deriving meaning from a text.

The basic organization of lexical (word) and sentential (sentence) knowledge still can be explicated and should constantly inform our instruction. This chapter discusses the meaningful relationships among words, phrases, and sentence structure and ties information about language to recommendations for teaching vocabulary. This chapter's theme is that verbal knowledge is organized in networks of associations that have definable structures. Words and concepts are known in relation to one another, not as isolated units. New verbal information is learned in accordance with prior knowledge. Effective teaching of vocabulary involves listening, speaking, reading, and writing. Effective teaching also elaborates various connections among better-known and lesser-known words, deepens and enriches existing knowledge, and seeks to build a network of ideas around key concepts that are well elaborated.

Aspects of Word Meaning

Word meanings are, for the most part, completely arbitrary verbal signals for things and ideas. There is no particular reason that the word *scar* means one thing and *scare* means another. Norton Juster portrayed the arbitrary nature of word meaning in *The Phantom Tollbooth* when the main character, Milo, found himself wandering in a strange land called Dictionopolis and noticed that letters were hanging off the tree branches:

> "I didn't know that words grew on trees," said Milo timidly.
> "Where did you think they grew?" shouted the earl irritably. A small crowd began to gather to see the little boy who didn't know that letters grew on trees.

"I didn't know they grew at all," admitted Milo even more timidly. Several
people shook their heads sadly.

"Well, money doesn't grow on trees, does it?" demanded the count.

"I've heard not," said Milo.

"Then, something must. Why not words?" exclaimed the undersecretary tri-
umphantly.[1]

Words have meanings that are agreed on by speakers of a language.
Although word meanings are constantly evolving, individual speakers are
not free to use words in any way they like or to make up words at will
because others may not understand the words. Meanings are shared and
meanings evolve by agreement. Each of us has a lexicon, a mental dictionary
residing in the brain that contains more information about words than a
published dictionary would be able to print.

Denotative and Connotative Meanings

Words have a **denotative** meaning and a **connotative** meaning. Denotative
meaning is embodied in formal definitions and describes the theory, quality,
action, or relationship denoted by the word. Connotative meaning triggers the
network of associations to other words and ideas. For example, the denotative
meaning of the word *prejudice* is "judgment before the truth is known" (*pre*
and *judi* are the Latin prefix and root meaning "before" and "to judge," respectively), usually resulting in unfair treatment of the person or group being
judged. This denotative meaning, however, does not include the instanta-
neous reaction most of us have to the mention of the word *prejudice,* which in
our society has become associated with injustice to social and racial groups,
political movements, and legal actions. Those associations, learned from reading or hearing a word in context repeatedly, are connotative. Connotative
meanings may be rich and are tempered by individual experience. They comprise many other concepts and experiences that together compose a semantic
field (see Figure 7.1). Semantic fields are constructed gradually over time on
the basis of many encounters with words in context. As we read or hear new
words, we constantly add to the information in our semantic fields.

Definitions and Semantic Features

Denotative meaning is concisely stated in dictionary definitions. Definitions
may include an alternate phrase or **synonym**, the category to which the idea
or thing belongs, and the characteristics or features of meaning that distinguish the word from others similar to it. For example, a *train is a transport
vehicle that travels on a rail system.*

Content words, which are nouns, verbs, adverbs, and adjectives, are
defined by or embody two important features: 1) the category to which the
object, action, or idea belongs and 2) the properties of the object, action, or
idea, including its grammatical class. Content words have essential and
peripheral attributes—<u>semantic features</u>—that define them and cause them
to be distinct from or to overlap with other words. The essential attribute of
the word *knee* is that it is a joint; the essential attribute of the verb *to race* is

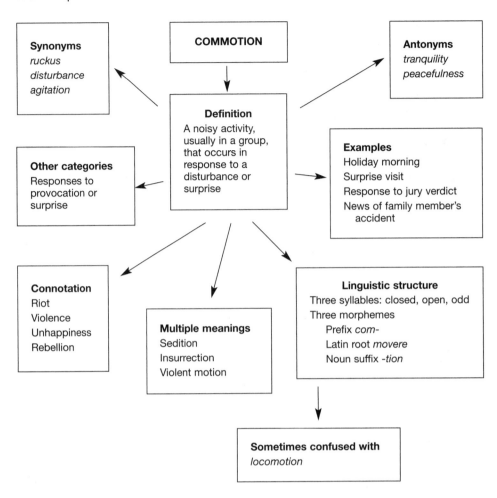

Figure 7.1.   Semantic field for the word commotion.

that of competition involving speed; the essential attribute of *red* is that of primary color; and so forth.

Exercise 7.1

Practice defining these content words by providing both parts of a definition. First, state a synonym or category for each word. Second, state its most important properties, distinguishing characteristics, or semantic features. For example, to *saunter* means to *walk slowly, without any visible sense of direction or purpose or to meander.* Then, list a few connotations that each word has for you.

gut organ/intestines/stomach to cut out vital organs, to feel deeply *or intuitively*
family loved ones
princess daughter of king, Cinderella
impeach find guilty/but not hold responsible.
powder dust, fine powder

An essential attribute of a content word is the **superordinate category** to which it belongs. *Superordinate* means "above" or "inclusive of the concept we are talking about"; thus, the superordinate category is the umbrella under which specific words or concepts fit. The superordinate category *joints* includes *knees, elbows, ankles, knuckles,* and *shoulders* as category members or examples. Additional attributes differentiate each item from others in the same category. For example, the category *joints* can be further subdivided into *hinge joints* and *ball joints*. Within the **subordinate category** of *hinge joints*, the peripheral attributes of *knee* that differentiate it from *elbow* are the direction in which the joint moves, the location in the body, and the presence of a kneecap.

Word/meaning back

Meaning becomes refined and elaborated in our lexicons as more attributes are learned and associated with a word. As more refinements and distinctions between members of a category are understood, a **hierarchical** set of ideas evolves in our understanding, in which some ideas are superordinate and some are subordinate or subsumed within others.

What is the superordinate category and what are the major subcategories in Exercise 7.2? Are any words more difficult to classify than others? How deep and thorough does one's knowledge and experience with the subject matter have to be before this kind of exercise can be undertaken productively?

Exercise 7.2

Arrange the following words into categories as quickly as you can. Do not add any words or leave out any words (Time limit: 10 minutes).

paper	maple	rope	bark
softwood	beams	pine	axe
hardwood	mulch	oak	chainsaw
paneling	birch	root	kindling
parts	branch	truck	needle
guitar	skidder	products	trees
spruce	mahogany	leaf	trunk
tools			

In the Landmark College program (in Putney, Vermont) for students with language learning difficulties, an exercise similar to Exercise 7.2 is used to assess how well incoming students can impose organization on material that belongs to a semantic network. The ability to manage the structure of meaning by identifying superordinate and subordinate categories to which words and concepts belong is a critical skill both for reading comprehension and for written composition. Success with outlining and categorizing depends on classifying ideas, which in turn is supported by background knowledge and experience with the content.

Content words (nouns, verbs, adverbs, and adjectives) have many attributes known as *semantic properties*. The better a word is known, the more of its properties or features are known. Deep or rich vocabulary knowledge involves knowing many facets of a word. For example, you probably recognize that *sumptuous* is an adjective that means "luxurious" or "opulent," which often is used to refer to feasts, which usually connotes decadent overindulgence and is probably related to *presumption* by the same root. Sacred celebrations in many tribal cultures often include sumptuous banquets that are prepared with great effort. The word *costly* shares some meaning with sumptuous, although it is not a synonym. The words *sumptuous* and *costly* are often used in the same context to describe lavish events, but the two words do not refer to exactly the same qualities. The meaning of the words *sumptuous* and *costly* overlap partially; they share some semantic properties but not enough for the words to be used interchangeably as synonyms.

Synonyms

Semantic properties of words may overlap to any degree, from a few shared elements of meaning to many, so the condition of synonymy (sameness of meaning) exists on a continuum. Some words are tentative or possible synonyms, whereas others are near-perfect substitutes for each other. *Car* and *automobile* are near-perfect synonyms; *van* and *truck* are further apart in meaning but are often used to refer to the same type of vehicle. *Picture* and *photograph* are partial synonyms; they are used interchangeably in some instances but not when the word picture refers to a framed painting. Absolutely perfect synonyms do not exist because each word has connotative and denotative meanings that distinguish that word from every other word. Even *couch* and *sofa* convey slight differences of formality and function within a house, depending on the speaker's frame of reference.

Class Membership

When words share semantic properties, they are said to be in a semantic class or network. *Tense, relaxed, explosive, laconic, hostile,* and *cautious* are adjectives that belong to the class of words that have to do with temperament. *Bright, capable, brilliant, dull, average,* and *slow* are terms that are used (some more kindly than others) to describe intellectual ability. *Multiply, divide, add, subtract, square,* and *factor* are words in the semantic class having to do with mathematical operations. When we use words or hear words that we know, we mentally activate all of the words we have learned within that semantic network. A context that activates what we know will make it easier for us to recognize known or partially known words. If we are already thinking about math, for example, and we expect to read a word that belongs in our semantic field for math, then we will recognize mathematical terms and read them a little bit faster than we would if there were no context.[2] This phenomenon is known as a **priming effect** in psychological experiments designed to unravel how we read words. The priming effect results from prior activation of a semantic network in memory.

 Exercise 7.3

What essential shared attribute or semantic feature of the following groups of words causes them to belong to a semantic network?

1. elephant, ostrich, giraffe, hippopotamus, rhinoceros
2. nephew, son, mother, daughter, cousin, aunt, grandfather
3. lamp, flashlight, candle, lantern
4. bob, crop, shave, plait, braid, curl
5. rice, barley, wheat, millet, oats

Formal Marking of Semantic Features

Semantic feature analysis is the process of identifying the meaning elements that words share or do not share. Semantic feature analysis is a way of objectifying, or describing formally, how meanings overlap and how they differ. By marking the presence or absence of a meaning element in a word with a plus (+) or minus (–), we can represent the ways in which words share meaning. *Home* and *house* are words that share a great deal of semantic overlap, to the point that they are often used as synonyms. We could represent some of their features as follows (a +/– symbol indicates that the feature is optional).

home   + dwelling   + human   + familial   + occupied   +/– structure
house   + dwelling   + human   +/– familial   +/– occupied   + structure

The featural overlap of common words in our vocabularies can be illustrated with a semantic feature chart that delineates the attributes shared by two or more words.

 ## Exercise 7.4

Mark the semantic features of the words *wood* and *timber* with a plus or a minus sign. Your answers may be different from those of another person.

	trees	processed	grows	large	burns	rots	breathes
wood							
timber							

The difference between the terms is slight and is likely to be known better by people who work in construction, logging, milling, or hardware supply. Knowing a word well means knowing its shades of meaning, when to use it, and how it is different from other words with overlapping features. A major use of the word *timber* is its reference to the raw material in trees, standing and cut, before they have undergone milling or processing. Lumberjacks might use these terms more selectively than ordinary individuals because their knowledge of connotative meanings is much deeper than that of other people. The words *timber* and *wood* have several other meanings that overlap much less with each other. For example, *timber* also refers to a support beam in a house, an object that is not usually referred to as *wood*.

Words also have other properties or features that determine how they can be used in sentences and what words we combine with them or substitute for them. For example, nouns may be subdivided into those that are countable and those that are not. **Countable nouns** can take the quantifier adjectives *many* and *few;* **noncountable,** or mass, nouns can take the adjectives *much* and *less.* You can eat too many carrots but not too much carrots; or you can have too much rice but not too many rice. You can, however, have too few dollars or less money than you would like. The word *more* can modify either countable or noncountable nouns.

Antonyms

Antonyms are words of opposite meaning, but they fall into three subordinate categories—gradable, complementary, or relational—that differ in several ways. **Gradable antonyms** take meaning from the context in which they are used. Their meaning is relative and expresses the degree to which an attribute characterizes a person, action, or object. The attribute exists on a hypothetical scale, and the word conveys a point on that scale. For example, *virtuoso* and *mediocre* may be used to describe opposing views of a musical performance, but in between are the adjectives *inspired, gifted, exceptional, accomplished, competent, acceptable,* and *fair.*

Gray area (handwritten margin note)

Exercise 7.5

Consider these terms, and insert as many words as you can between the qualitative poles that each of these antonyms represents.

elated ——————————————————————————— depressed

scalding ——————————————————————————— freezing

expensive ——————————————————————————— cheap

Interpreting a gradable antonym depends on one's frame of reference. For example, cheapness is a quality that exists primarily in relation to the resources of the buyer and the norm of the context. A cheap ring at Tiffany & Co. is an expensive ring most everywhere else. Objects can also be affordable or inexpensive, two points between sets of gradable antonyms.

Variable relationships exist within gradable antonym pairs. In some cases, one of the pair is **marked** and the other unmarked. The unmarked feature is the one that we use to ask questions about the attribute. For example, with *tall* and *short,* we ask, "How tall is the athlete?" even if someone tells us that he or she is short. If an object is described as small, then we are likely to ask how big it is. *Tall* and *big* are the unmarked partners in the antonym pairs. If we are adjusting the volume on a stereo between loud and soft, we can ask if the music is loud enough or soft enough to please the listener. *Loud* and *soft* are members of a gradable antonym pair that are not marked.

Complementary pairs of opposites are dichotomous and do not represent points on a scale. The qualities exist in a complementary relationship; if one condition exists, then the other cannot, and vice versa. There are no gradations between the opposite conditions. One can be married or single, dead or alive, male or female. The expression "to see things in black and white"

Black or White (handwritten margin note)

means to think that if something is one thing it cannot be the other. A person who thinks this way thinks of all opposites as complementary when in fact some are gradable and fit into a continuum of qualities that has points referred to as "gray areas."

Antonym pairs may also be relational or symmetrical. Although they do not represent mutually exclusive qualities, relational antonyms represent qualities that exist in reciprocal relationship to one another, such as coach–team, parent–child, supervisor–supervisee, doctor–patient, and cause–effect. That is, if you refer to one member of the relational pair, then the existence of the other member of the pair is assumed.

A common way of forming antonyms in the language is to add prefixes, including *un, in, non, mis,* or *dis,* to words as permitted: *happy, unhappy; hospitable, inhospitable; conformist, nonconformist; identify, misidentify;* and *allow, disallow.*

 ## Exercise 7.6

Determine whether these antonym pairs are gradable (g) or complementary (c).

light, heavy _g_
left, right _c_
pretty, ugly _g_
awake, asleep _c_
open, shut _c_
buy, sell _c_

introvert, extrovert _g_
terrestrial, celestial _c_
present, absent _c_
empty, full _g_
indoors, outdoors _c_
civilized, barbaric _g_

Multiple Meanings

Many English words have more than one meaning, especially the ones that derive from Anglo-Saxon. Some of our most common words can refer to dozens of different concepts or objects. This property of words is called polysemy; **polysemous** words have multiple meanings, and many words are polysemous. Even the words that children encounter early in their reading experience, such as *pan, block, green,* and *pitch,* have multiple meanings. For example, think of the meanings of *run* that come to mind without looking them up in a dictionary. They would include the following and many more.

- Move the legs in a fast gait
- A fast gallop of a horse
- The first leg of a race
- A flaw in a stocking
- A path for skiers
- The path of a small creek
- The flow of sap in trees
- To print a story in a newspaper

Exercise 7.7

List as many meanings as you know for the following words.

stand

cap

pot

jam

fit

Now, consult a dictionary to compare its listings with your meanings (an unabridged dictionary is best because it will show many meanings for each word). How many meanings did you know compared with how many are listed?

Phrase and Sentence Meaning

Phrase meaning depends on both individual word meanings and the structural combination of the words. Structural combination includes the order of the words and their grammatical role in the phrase or sentence. For example, *reading to learn* means something different from *learning to read, I mean what I say* is different from *I say what I mean,* and so forth.

A **paraphrase** preserves the meaning of a phrase but may change the order of the words or use different words that refer to the same ideas. Paraphrasing is one device by which writers vary their mode of expression and keep the interest of the reader.

Exercise 7.8

Paraphrase the following items; express the same thought or idea in different words. Preserve the meaning as you substitute words or, if allowed, change the order of words.

lying over and over

a curious fantasy

stuff and nonsense

guests at the execution

ignore the petty details

blazing away brightly

mind the master's words

these melancholy little sighs

Children must be able to draw on an extensive vocabulary to write paraphrases or substitute words for each other with the intention of preserving meaning. Once again, a critical skill that we expect of children when they write depends on breadth and depth of word knowledge, including knowledge of the grammatical roles that words can play.

Noun Phrases

Phrasal meaning is organized around nouns and verbs—the two kinds of content words found in a kernel sentence (a minimal sentence with a head noun and a main verb). A noun phrase includes the head noun and various modifiers, including articles, adjectives, appositives, and relative clauses, as in the noun phrase *the antique desk, a barrister's table, that my father gave to me,* which is organized around the head noun, *desk.* *Kernel sentence*

The meaning of a noun phrase depends on how its adjectives, articles, and clauses are combined. In English, word order in the noun phrase influences meaning. The head of the phrase follows the preceding modifier(s). For example, *tile floors* are different from *floor tiles.* When a noun phrase includes a prepositional phrase, the preposition conveys the relationship between the head noun and the noun that follows the preposition, as in *the antique desk with the brass handles* or *the full moon over the mountain.*

The term **reference** is used to denote the relationship between a noun phrase and the object or idea to which it points. The object or idea to which a noun points is called a **referent.** **Co-referents** are two or more terms that refer to the same thing. For example, the words *White Fang* (proper noun), *wolf* (noun), *he* (pronoun), and *snarling brute* (noun phrase) all may refer to the same animal and therefore are co-referential. Reference is so embedded in our use of language that we may have little conscious awareness of our dependence on it for making sense of what we read. A good writer, however, is constantly aware of the need to make reference explicit and unambiguous to the reader.

 ## Exercise 7.9

With lines and arrows, mark the referential relationships that exist among the nouns, pronouns, and noun phrases in this passage from the *Wizard of Oz* (the first few are done for you):

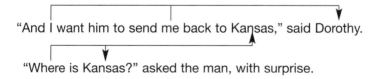

"And I want him to send me back to Kansas," said Dorothy.

"Where is Kansas?" asked the man, with surprise.

"I don't know," replied Dorothy sorrowfully, "but it is my home, and

I'm sure it's somewhere."

"Very likely. Well, Oz can do anything; so I suppose he will find

Kansas for you. But first you must get to see him, and that will be a

hard task; for the Great Wizard does not like to see anyone, and he

usually has his own way. But what do you want?" he continued,

speaking to Toto. Toto only wagged his tail, for, strange to say, he

could not speak.[3]

Interpreting a noun reference can be problematic for students who read slowly, are inattentive, or have trouble understanding the structure of written language. We must rely on linguistic cues while reading to a much greater extent than while conversing. Face-to-face communication supports messages in a number of ways that written communication does not. When we read, no other person is present who will, through gesture, phrasing, repetition, or emphasis, clarify what a word or phrase refers to. The reader must figure it out as he or she proceeds.

Verb Phrases

Verbs play the central role in the meaning and structure of sentences. The verb phrase is the one grammatical entity that is a requirement in any written English statement or question. Even one-word imperative sentences have a verb: *Halt!*

Thematic Roles   In traditional grammar, verbs may be classified into three groups: those that can stand alone without an object, those that must take a direct object, and those that must take a direct and an indirect object. This is called the **transitive property** of a verb or valence of a verb. For example, I can subject someone to something, but I cannot subject (with no object). I can reject something, but I cannot just reject. I can, however, procrastinate all by myself, without doing anything to anyone but me. Other intransitive verbs are *sleep, think,* and *hesitate. Sleep* and *think* can be followed by prepositional phrases (*I will sleep until 9:30; I thought about what you said*). But the word *hesitate* must be followed by an infinitive (*I hesitated to call you*).

Speakers of a language know whether verbs must be or can be followed by direct objects, indirect objects, infinitives, or prepositional phrases. Properties of verbs also determine the semantic properties of those objects in the phrases. For example, the verb *give* requires a giver, a recipient of the gift, and an entity that is given, as in *Molly gave water to the soldier.*

The verb of a sentence has semantic properties that affect the selection and role of the noun phrases and prepositional phrases. In formal linguistic terminology, these are called **thematic roles** of the verb. In the sentence,

Molly gave water to the soldier on the battlefield, Molly is the doer of the action and is assigned the role of **agent.** Water is what she gave and is called the **theme.** The battlefield describes the **location** of the action. The soldier is the person to which the action is directed and is called the **goal.** The verb *to give* requires an agent, a theme, and a goal. Some of the thematic roles of verbs can be summed up as follows.[4]

Thematic role	Description	Example
Agent	The doer; the one who performs the action	*Molly* ran.
Theme	The one thing that undergoes the action	He found *the gold watch.*
Location	Where the action occurs	Wolves roamed *in the valley.*
Goal	The place or person to which an action is directed	Put the water *in the dish.*
Source	The place from which an action originates	They trekked *from base camp.*
Instrument	Object used to accomplish the action or the means by which it was performed	Pound the tent peg *with the mallet.*
Experiencer	One who receives sensory input or who perceives something	*Mark* felt the rain drops.
Causitive	A natural force that brings about change	*Global warming* is causing glacial melting.
Possessor	One who owns or who has something	The mood *of her sister* lightened.

Thus, knowing a verb includes knowing how the verb must be used in relation to the semantic properties of the noun phrases. For example, as speakers of English, we know that the verb *to take* requires, at a minimum, an animate subject who will perform this action (agent) and a thing that will be the object of this action (theme). *The farmer takes,* thus, would not be a grammatical sentence because the verb lacks its required theme or object. We know that verbs such as *put* need an agent, a theme, and a goal and that *sleep* only needs an agent.

Paraphrases of sentences keep the same thematic roles of the constituent phrases even though the word order changes. Thus, the active and passive voices in these sentences are equivalent in meaning.

The red van was hit by the white truck.

The white truck hit the red van.

Truth Value   Sentence meaning depends on the meaning of the constituent noun and verb phrases. The facts, events, or states of being to which the sentence refers may be true or false, depending on what we know about the world. *Mark McGwire hit 30 home runs in the 1998 baseball season* is a false sentence (he hit 70) even though it is made of meaningful words in a grammatical order because the factual reality of the world does not match the sense of the sentence.

Sentences that mean the same thing have the same truth conditions. The active and passive constructions *Princeton defeated North Carolina* and *North Carolina was defeated by Princeton* refer to the same conditions of truth. The statements *Roger is taller than Barrett* and *Barrett is shorter than Roger* also refer to the same truth or extension of meaning. The existence of truth conditions allows us to know when ideas expressed in different ways mean the same thing. In a sense, truth conditions are the referents for sentences, just as objects, events, and ideas are the referents for single words.

truth conditions (handwritten margin note)

One sentence **entails** another if the truth of one sentence includes or implies the truth of another. For example, the sentence *Paula has lived with her husband for 20 years* entails the sentence *Paula is married*. The sentence *We buried the cat yesterday* entails the sentence *The cat died*. If the first sentence is true, then the entailed sentence must be true.

Nonsense

For various reasons, some sentences may make no sense. A grouping of words may sound like a sentence because word order follows the rules of syntax, but the sentence may include logical, lexical, and/or grammatical impossibilities. For example, the sentence *The Tower of Pisa leans straight up* contains a logical impossibility—towers that lean are not straight up. *Silent clanging wishes believe in magic* sounds poetic but makes no sense because the verb *believe* must have an animate subject (agent) and nothing can clang and be silent simultaneously. Poetic imagery, even in common children's rhymes, often exploits logical impossibilities to stir the imagination or please the ear, such as in this nursery rhyme.

> Hey! diddle, diddle,
> The cat and the fiddle,
> The cow jumped over the moon;
> The little dog laughed to see such a sport,
> And the dish ran away with the spoon.

The sentence *So frelled was she with her dumboggery that she zappled a shraveport right there* obeys the rules of word order and word structure. The words are even pronounceable and spelled according to standard syllable structure; they just have no referents. Therefore, they cannot be understood and are uninterpretable. Children's poems and stories, fortunately, often delight in nonsense, such as this New England lullaby.

> Winky, Blinky, niddy, nod!
> Father is fishing off Cape Cod.
> Winky, Blinky, sleepy eyes,
> Mother is making apple pies.

Winky, Blinky, cannot rise
What's the matter with baby's eyes?
Winky, Blinky, cre, cri, creep,
Baby has gone away to sleep.

Special Phrases: Idioms

All languages use word combinations or phrases that do not mean literally the sum of what their individual words mean. **Idioms** are phrases used as a unit to convey meanings and tend to resist any kind of evolutionary modification of form. Idioms must be known by the reader or interpreted from context just the way a new word meaning must be deciphered from context. Learning the meaning and use of idioms such as *get off your high horse, he took me to the cleaners,* and *my goose is cooked* is often a challenge for those who are learning a language because the whole idiomatic phrase has denotative and connotative meanings. Idiomatic usages must be learned separately from those of the individual words that compose them.

Exercise 7.10

What does each of these idioms mean?

mark my words   *truth*
hit me up   *ask*
tread on his toes   *offend*
blow the whistle   *tell/tattle*
leave her high and dry   *unexpected leaving —abandon*
bite your tongue   *stop talk*
'til the cows come home   *ongoing or refusal*
get out of my hair -   *leave me alone*
line your pockets   *have finances*

Many idiomatic expressions can, of course, be interpreted literally to mean something quite different from their figurative sense. *Look me up, size up, pony up,* and *write up* do not use the concrete meaning of *up*. When students misunderstand an idiom, they are usually hung up (so to speak) on its literal meaning. If one thinks that emotional baggage has something to do with suitcases, then one might miss the point of a discussion about character dynamics. Likewise, if you tell someone, "Eat my hat," then they should know you are not telling them to eat anything.

Metaphor

Metaphor is ubiquitous in written language, especially in descriptive or poetic text, and is probably the most common figure of speech. A *metaphor* is an implied or indirectly stated comparison between an idea and an unusual referent. A metaphor invokes the qualities of an unusual referent to describe or characterize the target word. For example, if someone is *blinded by love*, it means that the person's ability to make good decisions is impaired, that he or she has lost his or her way, and that he or she behaves like someone needing guidance—like a person who cannot see. The sense is clear, whereas the meaning is figurative.

Metaphor is an efficient and pleasing way to convey sense. Expressions can be spare but rich in associations, as in this elegant poem about autumn by Emily Dickinson.

The morns are meeker than they were,
The berry's cheek is plumper,
The nuts are getting brown;
The rose is out of town.
The maple wears a gayer scarf
The field a scarlet gown.
Lest I should be old-fashioned
I'll put a trinket on.

Pragmatics: Making Sense in Context

Usually, meaning is conveyed and understood within a context. Context, or the conditions that surround the use of language, may be either situational or linguistic. Situational context includes all of the real-life circumstances in which verbal communication takes place and the relationships among those who are communicating. **Linguistic context** comprises the words that precede and follow a given phrase or sentence—the **discourse** in which the language is embedded. Discourse consists of combinations of sentences that are woven together to convey complex ideas and may include a few sentences or 1,000 pages of a novel.

Situational context includes what we know about the sensitivities and needs of our listener or the person who is reading what we write. We adjust how we say things according to what we think the listener (or reader) needs or wants to hear (or read). In conversation, we take turns; we give as much information as the listener wants; we attempt to inform clearly; we maintain a topic; we fill in gaps of silence when people are unfamiliar to us; we avoid asking intrusive questions; and so forth, or other people view us as socially insensitive. Such pragmatic skills of verbal communication have parallels in producing written language. Writers should be considerate of their readers' needs. For example, the author of a textbook provides more or less information about a topic depending on the anticipated background knowledge and interests of readers. Just as we would adjust our tone of voice and manner in saying, "Would you mind if I borrowed your car?" in accordance with who owned the car we wanted to borrow, so we adjust for our audience when we write. **Considerate text** is written so that the reader's need for clarity, topic maintenance, background, explicitness, and so forth is respected.

All of us speak a form of English that is a *dialect*, a regional or cultural variation of Standard English. For some speakers, dialectical variation from Standard English is minor; for others, home language patterns vary so extensively from the standard that "academic" language, the language of books, must be learned almost as a second language. Learning Standard English does not require giving up a home dialect. It does, however, require awareness of which dialect to use in which situation. Individuals who shift easily between a home dialect and Standard English engage in "code switching" on cue. For example, many members of the African-American community who use both African-American English Vernacular and Standard English will speak one dialect with community members in informal, home situations and another in formal, academic, or multicultural situations.[5] Most important, they know which situation calls for which linguistic behavior. Similarly, all of us use one tone of voice with children and another with elders; we use one choice of words with old friends and another with new acquaintances. Interpreting dialogue, understanding an author's tone and intent, or composing a formal letter are pragmatic aspects of reading and writing.

As we formulate expressive language, both oral and written, we choose words and construct sentences according to the social demands of the situation and the context in which the communication exchange is occurring. Social communication entails adjusting our words to accommodate our own beliefs in relation to known or assumed beliefs of the hearer or reader, as well as our beliefs about what the hearer or reader believes about our beliefs. Accommodations of expression are also shaped by a myriad of factors, including the series of events that have preceded or that will follow a communicative act. For example, profanity might be highly offensive and inappropriate in a school context; within street gangs, it may be a norm or necessity. Expressing a strong political opinion during an election may be considered confrontational and offensive at a dinner party given by a friend who supports a different candidate, but may be called for at a town meeting.

People who are viewed as socially insensitive seem to disregard such constraints. They cannot adjust their mode of expression according to the requirements of a situation, and they may be inclined to misinterpret the words of others as well. Students with language learning disabilities are sometimes viewed as socially awkward or inappropriate because of pragmatic communication problems. They often must be taught to pay attention to context and the nonverbal and verbal cues coming from their listener, to take turns in conversation, to monitor how much they are saying, to be clear, and to initiate and end contact appropriately.

Reference in Discourse

Many topics in the domain of discourse analysis are beyond the scope of this book, but several are relevant to our discussion of meaning. Groups of sentences, arranged as paragraphs within larger organizational structures, are tied together thematically with a number of devices. **Anaphora** is the replacement of a whole noun phrase, thought unit, or sentence with a pronoun, as in *Teaching spelling with the new program is so effective that I make time for it every day.* In this sentence, the neutral pronoun *it* refers to more than spelling; the pronoun refers to *teaching spelling with the new program,* an elaborated noun phrase.

In written discourse it is not uncommon to find the anaphoric referent for a pronoun some distance away from the pronoun in the text. Obviously, the ability to hold the beginning of a sentence in phonological memory is important for making sense of an anaphoric reference that is distant from its source, as in this passage from *Alice's Adventures in Wonderland*.

> There was a table set out under a tree in front of the house, and the March Hare and the Hatter were having tea at it: A Dormouse was sitting between them, fast asleep, and the other two were using it as a cushion, resting their elbows on it, and talking over its head. "Very uncomfortable for the Dormouse," thought Alice, "only, as it's asleep, I suppose it doesn't mind."[6]

In contrast to anaphora, **deixis** is the relationship of a word to its referent that relies exclusively on situational context. The pronouns of the first and second person, including *I, you, we, yours, ours,* and *mine,* always depend on the specific context of the speaker and those whom the speaker addresses. The demonstrative articles *this* and *that* are always deictic; to know what they refer to, one must know the context in which they are used. Time expressions such as *yesterday, today,* and *tomorrow* are deictic; their referents change daily. *Here, there, this park, that mountain,* and similar terms of place are deictic; what they mean depends on where you are. These terms, along with anaphoric reference, present another challenge of language interpretation to young readers. If the referents are misunderstood, then comprehension suffers.

Teaching Vocabulary and Other Aspects of Meaning

Reading researchers know that a substantial amount of the variance in reading comprehension is attributable to knowing the meanings of individual words. That is why the most valid and reliable reading tests usually include a direct measure of vocabulary knowledge. Good readers know more words and are better at deciphering the meanings of new words as they read. Likewise, they comprehend better because they know more words. Knowledge of a word, however, may be superficial or deep, sparse or elaborated, and abstract or deeply personal. Even if we knew little about the systematic comparison of methods in reading research, we might surmise from the earlier sections of this chapter that instruction should respect and complement the way in which semantic knowledge is organized in our verbal memories. In fact, research on vocabulary instruction has upheld teaching principles that are logical extensions of the language processes presented here.[7]

1. Choose words for direct teaching that are central in a semantic field. Of the 1,000–3,000 new words that fourth- through eighth-grade students encounter in the texts they read each year, teachers have time to teach directly only a few per day. Even if 10–15 new word meanings were taught to a class each week, there would be time to teach fewer than 400 all year long. Many more words are learned from context, usually during reading. How should the words for instruction be chosen?

    Words important to the theme of a passage read in the classroom are the most appropriate to study. Words presented in lists dissociated from a meaningful context are less desirable. Words are most likely to be learned thoroughly within a network of related ideas pertinent to a topic, theme, or text whose meanings are the primary focus of instruction. Words are learned more deeply when many aspects of their meaning have been explored, when they have been read and used in context, and when the entire knowledge structure to which they belong has been activated and developed.

2. Teach word meanings in relation to other words that are known. Vocabulary instruction should aim to teach students the relationships that exist among words so that they are learned as part of a network of ideas. The conceptual network should be presented as a structure that encompasses the superordinate, subordinate, and coordinate relationships between terms. Synonym and antonym relationships, analogies, and categorization should be staples of vocabulary development as well because they highlight the connections between ideas.

   Graphic techniques for depicting semantic networks and word relationships are helpful to children. Semantic maps are visual depictions of the relationships among words and concepts and are drawn as branches emanating from a central idea. When categories are labeled, examples of the categories and properties of category members are given. A map of the relationships among ideas in the semantic network *friends* might look like the following.

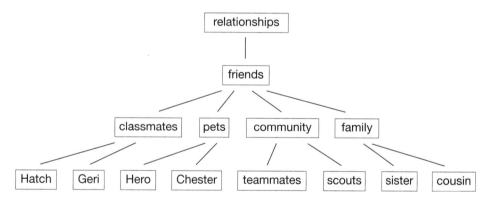

   The web of interconnected ideas can be expanded as widely as one wishes. Traditional outlines are also extremely useful for depicting superordinate, subordinate, and coordinate relationships among concepts.

3. Use linguistic and situational context to develop word knowledge. The majority of words children learn are learned from reading itself.[8] Many more words are encountered in fiction and nonfiction text than are ever learned from television, conversation, or language spoken by adults.[9] We may have to read and hear words many times in context before we attempt to use or "own" a new word. There is no substitute for wide and varied reading to gain that exposure. Context supplies implicit information not only about word definition but also about the pragmatic constraints of appropriate word use. Reading itself also supplies a network of experiential associations to which a new word's meaning can be anchored.

4. Teach both denotative and connotative meaning. Students should be taught that complete definitions include a synonym and/or category to which the word belongs and some information about the word's distinguishing features. Connotative meaning should be discussed as well. When is this word used? What associations does it bring to mind? Connotative meaning will be learned when the word is encountered repeatedly in situational context.

5. Teach multiple meanings for the same word. Learning more than one meaning for a word deepens and broadens students' vocabulary knowledge and may facilitate word recognition, word retrieval, and comprehension. Even a simple word such as *lot* can be explored by young children from the early stages of reading instruction.[10] Children may generalize an expectation for diversity and variation in language use when they discover that words have multiple meanings. Children might be less concerned with memorizing a "right" definition and more interested in learning and using several meanings for words.

6. Teach idioms, metaphors, and other figures of speech. Many students, such as those who are learning English as a second language, those who are concrete or literal in their interpretation of language, or those who simply have not been exposed to a wide range of uses of words and phrases, need to be taught to interpret and use idiomatic language. In lieu of memorizing meanings, students usually enjoy locating figurative uses of language in fables, poetry, songs, and tall tales. Using these terms in songs, poems, descriptions, and students' own stories should be encouraged.

7. Identify the referents for nouns, pronouns, and phrases. During discussions of text, awareness of anaphoric and deictic reference should be heightened through simple questioning techniques. Can the students say to whom or what a word, phrase, or pronoun refers? Can they draw arrows from one word to its referent or actually replace words with others? Can they rewrite sentences in which proper nouns are replaced by pronouns? Can they list all of the words in a passage that refer to the same person, place, or thing?

Summary

Understanding what we read depends on the ability not only to decode the words in print, but also to know the words' meanings in relation to real world truths and in relation to other words. Effective vocabulary instruction will target words most important in a semantic field and teach not only their individual meanings, but also how they are connected to other words. Connections among words can be portrayed as synonyms, antonyms, overlapping meanings, thematic associations, analogies, class and example relationships, and figures of speech.

Meanings themselves are both definable and context dependent. Knowing a dictionary definition (denotative meaning) is important but is not sufficient for being able to use a word appropriately. We also must know how to use the word, with whom, when, and for what shade of meaning. We must use it many times over to use it well. Thus, memorizing a dictionary of all of the words in a language would not enable someone to communicate with other speakers of that language. Deep, rich knowledge of words and varied experiences with their use are necessary for proficient reading and writing; paradoxically, children will learn words most readily from reading itself.

 Supplementary Exercises

7.11   On a separate sheet of paper, make an outline or visual categorization using the following words. Use all of the words and no others. Take about 10 minutes.

creep	adult	cockroaches	legs
burrow	body parts	blood	egg
homes	locusts	cocoon	antennae
invertebrates	algae	soil	larva
food	grasshoppers	wings	abdomen
ants	pupa	sac	mosquitoes
crawl	locomotion	thorax	
nest	web	species	
hop	head	leaves	
flies	microbes	phases	

7.12   Choose an important abstract word used in science teaching, such as *symmetry, evolution,* or *microscopic.* Make up several sentences that use the word. Then, leave the word out of the sentences and give the "cloze" sentences you have created to someone else. Did he or she identify the word? Now ask your subject if he or she could define the word based on the contextual uses you gave. What are the advantages and limitations of context use in word definition?

7.13   In what way are the following groups of nouns the same and different?

a)   daughter, sister, niece *versus* nun, waitress, actress
b)   rooster, bull, ram *versus* hen, ewe, cow
c)   table, chair, pencil *versus* water, cream, sand
d)   table, chair, pencil *versus* faith, hope, charity
e)   husband, brother, son *versus* clerk, preacher, judge
f)   grandfather, mother, niece *versus* brother, sister, cousin

7.14   Indicate whether antonym pairs are gradable (opposite ends of a continuous scale) or complementary (either/or).

dead, alive _____

hot, cold _____

above, below _____

married, single _____

bland, spicy _____

hostile, welcoming _____

hideous, gorgeous _____

straight, curved _____

introvert, extrovert _____

winner, loser _____

Now take one of the gradable antonym pairs and fill out the scale from one extreme to the other with words that show degrees of meaning.

7.15   Use a plus (+) or a minus sign (-) to mark the semantic features that do or do not describe the following four objects.

	cup	glass	mug	bowl
handle				
ceramic				
round				
tall				
holds hot liquid				
holds cold liquid				
paper				
transparent				

7.16   Use the following format to make a definition for each of these words: *web, tornado,* and *poem.*

A/An _____ is a/an _____ (synonym)

that _____ (is, does, has) _____ (critical feature).

7.17   Without using a dictionary, list on a separate sheet of paper all of the meanings you can think of for the following words: *walk, mouth, star,* and *book.*

7.18   List all of the descriptive words that come to mind when you think of the word *palace.*

Compare notes with another person. How many of the same words or associations did the other person have?

Endnotes

1. From THE PHANTOM TOLLBOOTH by Norton Juster. Copyright © 1961 by Norton Juster. Copyright renewed 1989 by Norton Juster. Reprinted by permission of HarperCollins Publishers Ltd.
2. Adams, 1990, 1998; Becker, 1985.
3. Baum, 1956, p. 84.
4. Fromkin et al., 2003.
5. Perry & Delpit, 1998.
6. Carroll, 1865/1960.
7. Beck, McKeown, Hamilton, & Kucan, 1998; Beck, McKeown, & Omanson, 1990; Irvin, 1990; Nagy, 1988; Stahl & Shiel, 1992.
8. Cunningham & Stanovich, 1997, 1998; Nagy et al., 1987.
9. Hayes & Ahrens, 1988.
10. Wolf, Gottwald, & Orkin, 2009.

Additional Resource

Pinker, S. (1999). *Words and rules: The ingredients of language.* New York: Basic Books.

Language and Reading Instruction

By the end of this chapter, you will understand:

- The content, methods, and sequence of structured language teaching

- Instruction needs of prealphabetic, early alphabetic, and later alphabetic learners

- Spelling–decoding continuum for teaching students in elementary school

- How the information in this book guides analysis of students' writing samples and instructional needs

Language can be the theme that unites varying perspectives on literacy acquisition and instruction. Chapter 1 argued that students' progress in reading and writing is closely related to both verbal proficiency and metalinguistic skill. How well students use language determines, at least at the whole-class level, how well they learn to read and write.[1] Both lower-level and higher-level language skills are important components of proficient reading and writing. At the word level, awareness of phonology, orthography, morphology, and semantic relationships must be developed and woven together like strands in a rope (see Figure 8.1).

At the text comprehension level, knowledge of syntax, discourse organization, and the social context of language must be deepened and refined. Language learning at each level involves perceiving, assimilating, and **retrieving** structural patterns and rules; developing the ability to discern when those patterns and rules apply; and memorizing specific linguistic units and linguistic forms, which are then used to comprehend and communicate ideas. As students gain skill, they must learn to pay close attention to language form and use; it is the gateway to the meanings that lie beneath the words.

Proficiency within each strand of the reading rope is gained gradually and in parallel. Phases of learning, as described in Chapter 1, and the tasks that characterize each of them, provide conceptual guideposts for what to emphasize as students progress.

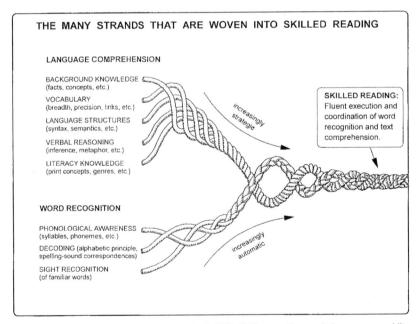

Figure 8.1.   Reading rope. (From Scarborough, H. [2001]. Connecting early language and literacy to later reading (dis)abilities: Evidence, theory, and practice. In S.B. Neuman & D.K. Dickinson [Eds.], Handbook of early literacy research [p. 98]. New York: Guilford Press; reprinted by permission.)

The Prealphabetic Learner

Establishing the Alphabetic Principle

The child who comes to reading and writing with some exposure to books and stories may or may not understand the alphabetic principle, that alphabet letters are used to represent the segments of speech. Gaining this understanding is critical for early reading success. Prealphabetic learners in kindergarten must be helped to gain this insight. As intervention studies have shown, children who do not grasp what the alphabet is for or how the alphabet works are likely to need help developing phoneme awareness as well as knowledge of letter names and the sounds they represent.[2] These are the most critical skills to teach directly and systematically in kindergarten if reading failure is to be prevented.

Phonological skills, however, should not be taught in isolation. Phonological skills develop in reciprocal relationship with vocabulary. Students who know the names of more words and what they refer to have more points of reference when speech sounds are the focus of a task. In the other direction, vocabulary learning is supported when students develop an ear for the structure of spoken words. Growth of vocabulary, background information, language comprehension, and language production in kindergarten sets the stage for later reading comprehension.

If students have limited English vocabularies, should direct teaching of phonological skills be delayed until oral language proficiency and knowledge of the world improve? Research suggests that by kindergarten, there is no advantage to waiting; direct teaching about speech sounds and letters still lowers the risk of reading delays, as long as it is part of a rich curriculum and robust language development.[3]

Exposure to language in books, which have far ranging and unusual vocabulary and more demanding syntax, is particularly helpful in fostering language development. Children expand their vocabularies when they are read to and engaged in talking about their experiences and about the information and ideas embodied in books.[4] Vocabulary is learned from books more than from normal conversation with adults or children or from television exposure. Children who are less familiar with books may need to be taught what to expect from print. Table 8.1 aligns the child's learning behaviors with appropriate instruction goals and strategies.

Phoneme Awareness

Several validated instructional approaches for kindergarten phoneme awareness, letter knowledge, and phoneme–grapheme correspondence development are now published.[5] About 15–20 minutes of class time per day over a period of 15–20 weeks during the last half of kindergarten are sufficient to develop phoneme awareness and to connect phonemes with their most common spellings. Well-designed programs follow the sequence of phoneme

Table 8.1.   Prealphabetic reading and writing (typically ages 4–5): Teaching strategies

Child knows	Goals of instruction	Teaching strategies
A few alphabet letters	All alphabet letters; uppercase, then lowercase	Movable letters: matching to templates, naming, ordering
Rhyming, clapping syllables	Consonant and vowel phonemes; two- and three-phoneme words	Segmentation in sound boxes; say-it-and-move-it; touch-and-say blending
How to write letters in own name	Make letters with manipulatives; write all letters, group by basic strokes; write on rough surface or large chalkboard	Trace letters; follow directional arrows; use clearly lined paper
How to "read" a book: left to right, top to bottom, front to back	Match words to voice; finger-point reading	Share reading of familiar text; follow text with fingers
A few (or no) letter–sound connections	A high-frequency phoneme–grapheme correspondence for each consonant and short vowel	Sound-spelling cue cards; beginning reading and spelling of short vowel; regular pattern words; use letter tiles to add beginning and ending sounds when given a vowel
A few, context-dependent "sight" words	20–40 high-frequency words recognized as wholes (some irregular)	Trace and say letters; build words with letter tiles; match words to pictures
No "real" reading	Preprimer books: few words, repetitious, decodable with consonant-vowel-consonant words	Support reading; rehearse words prior to reading; preview text; look carefully at print for accurate reading of words
That a narrative progresses in time	Basic elements of a narrative: setting, character, problem, events, resolution	Read aloud; storyboard or framework; retell
More than 2,000 word meanings (oral)	Theme or topic-focused readings, experiences, class projects	Dialogic reading; querying; classroom conversations; scaling words; antonym charts; categories
How to speak in phrases, unelaborated sentences	Comprehend and produce complete sentences; elaborate with prompting	Use question words to prompt expansion of verbal responses; recite rhymes, poems, predictable books; discuss shared experiences

awareness development typical of most young learners (see Table 3.2 in Chapter 3) and give children ample practice with each activity over several days. Activities are aimed at progressive differentiation of sounds in words. A number of research studies[6] have suggested that powerful phoneme awareness development programs have the following characteristics.

- A gradual, systematic progression through a developmentally and linguistically appropriate sequence of activities

- Brief, fun, active manipulation of oral language

- Minimal or carefully chosen use of print in beginning lessons

- Gradual introduction of print as children become aware of sounds

- Instruction in how to blend sounds together as well as how to take them apart or substitute them for one another

- Use of modeling, demonstration, and application rather than lengthy explanations

- Use of active responses from children, such as moving counters into boxes, showing syllables or sounds with blocks, matching objects, moving cards in a pocket chart, clapping, speaking, and singing (worksheets are seldom effective during lessons)

Early Alphabetic to Later Alphabetic Phases (Ages 5–7)

The ability to decode words fluently using letter–sound correspondences is the cornerstone for early reading success (see Table 8.2 for more on **early alphabetic** reader characteristics and needs). Accurate association of phonemes with graphemes permits and fosters a child's **automatic** recognition of whole words as **reading fluency** is acquired.[7] Some words, such as *said*, must be memorized as "memory," "tricky," or "heart" words from the beginning because they are both irregular and frequent in written text. Phoneme awareness training should continue in first-grade reading instruction, with an emphasis on **phoneme–grapheme mapping** and transferring blending skills to reading. Many students need to read **decodable text** that is written with a high proportion of phonetically regular words whose patterns have been taught.

Decodable text provides concentrated practice with application of sound–symbol associations in word reading. It also includes a few learned **sight words** that have been previously taught. Decodable text provides a bridge between phonics instruction and the reading of trade books or less controlled text. Interspersing text for an adult to read with lines that the beginning reader can read is one strategy for making decodable text more appealing in content and storyline than is usually achieved with a limited vocabulary.[8]

Even though the focus of beginning reading instruction must be learning how to read, daily lessons must also include vocabulary development, exposure to information and ideas in books, listening and speaking, and familiarity with language patterns in written text. Language instruction at these levels may occur in conjunction with reading aloud to children or helping them memorize repetitive language patterns in books designed for shared reading.

At the first-grade level, the teacher must ensure that the student can employ a strategy of sound–symbol association and sound blending so that independent reading of unknown words is possible. At the second-grade level, fluency and consolidation of skills in the service of accurate reading for meaning is the goal (see Table 8.3 for first- to second-grade reader characteristics and needs). During this stage, rapid recognition of whole words develops in tandem with phonic word recognition; one supports the other. Most of the regular one-syllable correspondence patterns should be introduced for word recognition in the first half of first grade, although the introduction of these patterns for spelling should be more slowly paced.

Table 8.2.   Early alphabetic reader characteristics and instructional needs

Child knows	Goals of instruction	Teaching strategies
All alphabet letters, uppercase and lowercase	Alphabetical sequence	Writing whole alphabet from dictation, then from memory; alphabetizing by first letter
How to identify consonant and vowel phonemes in two- and three-phoneme words	Phoneme blending, segmentation; substituting and manipulating words with three to four sounds	Word chains; compare similar sounding words; segment words with blends
A high-frequency phoneme–grapheme correspondence for each consonant and short vowel	Apply phoneme–grapheme correspondence in regular word reading	Sound-by-sound blending, graphemes to phonemes, in regular one-syllable words
40 words by sight	Recognize 100 words by sight, including regular and irregular spellings	Vary practice to build automatic recognition
Phonetically accurate spelling using preconventional strategies, salient sounds represented	Position-based graphemes, such as *ck* and doubled letters after short vowels; beginning long vowel spellings	Sound-spelling cue cards; beginning spelling of short vowel, regular pattern words; use letter tiles for spelling; word family (rime) patterns
How to read preprimer books with few words, repetition, decodable with consonant-vowel-consonant words	Apply decoding skills to word reading in context	Practice with decodable text, including patterns that have been taught
How to write captions and a few words; using letter-name strategies	Write complete sentences with initial word capitalized and end punctuation	Prompt writing with given words; sentence frames; sentence completion
How to read some words and short sentences	Read a decodable book by browsing, predicting, and summarizing the main idea	Guide oral reading of books with previewing, querying, and retelling
How to retell a sequence of events	Identify problem/solution structure of stories; sort important from less important details	Restate the gist or main ideas of what was read; prediction; reenactment
3,000 word meanings	Learn 10–15 new words per week, related to themes or topics	Dialogic reading; querying; classroom conversations; scaling words; antonym charts; categories
How to comprehend and produce complete sentences; elaborates with prompting	Organized retelling or sequencing of ideas; staying on topic; main idea/detail differentiation	Locate and paraphrase main ideas and key information; verbal production of this information

Principles for Systematic, Explicit, Code-Emphasis Instruction

Instruction in decoding (phonics) has not been executed effectively at times because it is a complex and technical undertaking. If the following principles are adhered to, however, it can be efficient, fun, and successful.

Teach the System of Phoneme–Grapheme Correspondences in Logical Order   Some traditional "phonics" programs teach sound–symbol correspondences based on the alphabet sequence and the sounds of 26 letters. If beginning instruction in decoding is limited to the alphabet letter

Table 8.3. Later alphabetic reader characteristics and needs

Child knows	Goals of instruction	Teaching strategies
Short vowel patterns; silent e; blends and digraphs	Vowel teams; diphthongs; vowel-r patterns; basic syllable division and combination	Identify the vowel sound(s) before analyzing and blending the whole word
How to read/spell words with inflections (grammatical endings) inconsistently	Analyze, synthesize, and spell base words with grammatical suffixes	Decompose, sort, and combine base words with endings
No strategy for multi-syllable words	Six syllable types and combinations; compounds	Identify vowel; divide syllables; say and blend syllables
How to read 40–60 words correct per minute	Increase fluency to 90 words correct per minute	Phrase-cued reading; repeated reading of passages; self-graphing
More than 100 high-frequency "sight" words	200–300 high-frequency sight words	One-minute fluency drills on high-frequency words
Primer level reading	Sustain reading of text with several short chapters	Partner reading; alternate oral reading; teacher-guided small-group shared reading
How to read without attention to detail, location of information in text	Locate source of information used to answer questions	Close reading of text; state inferences; relate details in text to students' own background information
How to read with teacher and group support	Independent reading with self-monitoring	Take-home books; incentive programs for independent reading; reading logs
How to write incomplete, run-on, or unelaborated sentences	Simple sentences; compound subjects and predicates; compound sentences; adverbial clauses	Sentence combining; sentence building; complete or elaborate subject or predicate
How to write narratives and journal entries with no plan	Plan an outline before writing	Use graphic organizers or simple planning devices; talk through ideas before writing
Only disorganized or incomplete communication of ideas	Give complete and coherent explanations of ideas and events	Oral reports on topics, with visual prompts available

sounds, however, then the identities of consonants [ŋ], [θ](voiceless), [ð] (voiced), [š], [č], and [ž] and vowels [ɔj], [æw], [ɔ], [ʊ], and [ə] (schwa) are obscured because no single letters of the alphabet represent these phonemes. Twelve phonemes of approximately forty remain "hidden" when the alphabet is the organizing basis of instruction. A few letters also have no defined job. The letter *c* is redundant for [k] and [s]. The letter *q* is redundant for the sound of [k], and the letter *x* is redundant for the combination [ks] or the phoneme [z].

The alphabet–sound approach in phonics instruction also overlooks the fact that some letter names bear little relationship to the sounds that the letters represent and are much harder to learn than the sounds themselves. If a child learns letter names without a clear conceptual and associative emphasis on the sounds the letters symbolize, then confusion in reading and spelling will occur (see Table 8.4, which shows the letters that typically are confused in reading and in spelling).

Children who confuse *will* and *yell* need more practice differentiating letter sounds from letter names. Teachers should carefully and correctly use the labels "name" and "sound" during teaching when referring to letters and phonemes, respectively. Some experts argue that teaching letter names

Table 8.4.   Letters often confused in reading and spelling

Letter	Name	Sound	Typical reading errors	Typical spelling errors
y	/waɪ/	/y/	*will = yell*	YL for *will*, BOU for *boy*
u	/yu/	/u/	*use = us*	UESTRDA for *yesterday*
w	/dʌbl yu/	/w/	*then = when*	UEN for *when*
x	/ɛks/	/ks/ or /gz/		ECKSAM for *exam*
h	/eč/	/h/		WOH for *watch*

is unnecessary,[9] but letter names are so much a part of daily classroom life that clarity and practice are probably the most important factors in helping children learn them.

   Well-designed instruction will anchor the learning of print to awareness of speech. Good key-word associations on manipulative sound-spelling cards will help students remember graphemes. Key words should be carefully chosen. Commercially prepared alphabets often have confusing and inaccurate information, so they should be used cautiously. For example, the letter *e* should not have the word *eye* associated with it. The "word wall" idea that has proliferated in primary classrooms must be used with care as to how sounds are represented. Alphabet letters often are posted along a colorful bulletin board; under each are high-frequency words for which children are to develop automatic recognition. The resulting array typically includes confusing lists of words under the vowel letters, such as the following.

Aa	*Ee*	*Ii*	*Oo*	*Uu*
apple	egg	it	orange	under
and	eight	is	of	use
away	eat	in	on	us
all	end	I'm	once	united
are			open	
			off	
			out	

   If children notice that words starting with the letter *o* begin with as many as six different sounds, including the [w] in *once*, they may surmise that letters are irrelevant to sound and that words must be learned by a visual memory process. Sight words do need to be learned, gradually and cumulatively, but they should not be used to teach the regular correspondences. At the first-grade level, word walls—which can be organized by postings of sound-spelling cards—should emphasize the most reliable phoneme–grapheme correspondences (see Tables 8.5 and 8.6 for traditional and alternative ways of teaching consonant spellings).

   Teaching children each sound, then anchoring the sound to a grapheme (letter, letter group, or letter sequence) with a key-word mnemonic, mimics the way alphabetic writing was invented. The sound [s] is associated first with *snake* and the letter *s* and later with *ce, ci,* and *cy* combinations, as in *city, race,* and *bicycle*. With an instructional goal of teaching 80–120 spellings for the approximately 40 phonemes and then moving to syllables and mor-

Table 8.5. Typical sequence for teaching consonant spellings in traditional basal reading series

Categories	Examples
Single consonants (one sound)	*b, d, f, h, j, k, l, m, n, p, r, t, v, w*
Variant or odd consonants	*c, g, s, qu, x, z*
Digraphs	*th, sh, ch, wh, ph, gh, ng*
Blends	*cr, dr, br, fr, tr, gr, pr, sc, sw, sk, sl, sn, tw, fl, cl, pl, gl, sl, spr, spl, squ, str, scr, shr, thr, chr, -nd, -nk, -nt, -lt, st, sk, sp*
Silent consonants	*wr, kn, ps, mn, gn, -mb, -ck, -lk*

phemes, educators can teach the whole system in a comprehensive, clear, logical sequence over several years. Instruction can begin with high-utility, low-complexity consonant and vowel units and move gradually to less common, conditional, and more complex graphemes. Graphemes of several letters (*tch, igh, mb, ce, ough*) are treated as the blocks from which words are built, rather than as mysterious combinations of "sounded" and "unsounded" letters.

With the sound-to-spelling approach, children are taught that spelling units (graphemes) represent the approximately 40 sounds and often are more than one letter. For example, *eight* has two phonemes and two graphemes—the vowel "long a" [e] spelled *eigh* (also in *weigh, weight, sleigh*) and the consonant [t]. Teachers are less likely to try to "blend" [t] and [h] to make [θ] or [s] and [h] to make [š] if the letter combinations are understood as digraph units. In addition, words that begin with [s] will not be grouped with those that begin with [š].

From the beginning of a decoding program, children are also shown that there is often more than one way to spell a phoneme. This approach has been called establishing a set for diversity, or helping students expect that there will be variation in the representational system.

Teach Pattern Recognition, Not Rule Memorization   Most individuals learn to decode words in print because they accumulate explicit and tacit knowledge of linguistic patterns—phonological, orthographic, and morphological. Any audience of literate adults can be cajoled into displaying their unconscious knowledge of orthographic constraints. Ask a group to spell [θrɔǰ]. The majority will use *oi* instead of *oy*, although many will have trouble explaining that *oi* is used internally for /ɔj/ and that *oy* is used at the ends of words. Most will also use *ge* instead of *dge* because a diphthong is never followed by *dge*.[10] If a group is asked to read a nonword such as *pertollic*, the middle syllable will be stressed and the vowel written as *o* will be identified as a "short o." Readers of English know intrinsically that in the Latin layer of the language, the root, not the prefix or suffix, is usually stressed and a doubled consonant following a vowel causes the root to be short.

Awareness and use of such organizational patterns, not memorization of rules, facilitates learning; the goal of gaining insight is to read more fluently, not to recite orthographic trivia. Some critics of phonics instruction lament that there are too many rules to teach, that the rules do not always apply, or that the rules are too complicated to be taught. This criticism is most apt when the correspondence system is represented in long lists of

Table 8.6. Nontraditional, alternative presentation of consonant spellings (sound–symbol organization)

/p/	/b/	/t/	/d/	/k/	/g/
pot	bat	tent	dime	cup	go
		walked	stayed	kettle	ghost
				deck	fatigue
				school	
				oblique	
/f/	/v/	/θ/, /ð/	/s/	/z/	/š/
fish	very	thin	see	zoo	shop
phone		then	fuss	jazz	sure
stiff			city	Xerox	Chicago
tough			science	rose	-tion, -sion
/č/	/ǰ/	/m/	/n/	/ŋ/	/h/
cheer	judge	man	net	king	hair
batch	wage	tomb	knight	lanky	who
	gent	autumn	sign		
	gym				
	gist				
/l/	/r/	/j/	/w/	/ʍ/	
lake	run	yes	want	whistle	
tell	wrist	use	one		

statements about orthographic patterns without using the speech–sound system as the reference point, such as the following.

- If a vowel letter is at the end of the word, then the letter usually stands for the long sound.

- The letter *w* is sometimes a vowel and follows the vowel digraph rule.

- The letter *a* has the same sound when followed by *l*, *w*, and *u*.

These observations, among many others, obscure what is at work in speech–print correspondence, and children should not be asked to learn them. To demonstrate the language patterns embodied in these "rules," we should show children groups of words that share a single-letter, long-vowel spelling: *me, he, she, we, be; go, so, no,* and *yo-yo*. We should explain that the letter *w* never represents a vowel alone, although it is used in vowel digraphs to show the feature of lip rounding on the back vowels *aw, ow,* and *ew*. Finally, we should demonstrate that *aw* and *au* are two spellings for [ɔ]; *au* is used internally in a syllable, as in *applaud, laundry,* and *taut,* and *aw* is used in word-final position and before word-final *n* and *l,* as in *saw, thaw; brawn, brawl;* and *drawn, drawl*. Part of teaching decoding well is to select what is useful, understandable, and applicable and to represent it as directly and logically as possible.

What does worthwhile practice entail, beyond phoneme awareness, initial sound–symbol linkage, and sound blending? Many teaching strategies apply. Words can be analyzed in a student–teacher dialogue so that students discover their structures and then **generalize** them to new words; patterns may be sorted so that groups of words are compared and classified;[11] phonic concepts may be applied to reading "foreign" words, names, low-frequency words, or nonwords; and cloze exercises can require students to make fine discriminations of words that look or sound alike in text reading. Writing words after reading them reinforces pattern knowledge. Some children with significant reading impairments need to be taught every phoneme–grapheme association explicitly, but others will begin to generalize independently if they have a solid basis from which to proceed.[12] Thus, we teach the major spellings for [k] as a beginning decoding skill (*c, k, ck*) but wait to highlight the Greek *ch* and the French *que* until entries from those languages are considered as an etymological group, as in *chorus, orchestra, school, chloroform, pachyderm;* and *antique, pique, mystique.*

Use Active, Engaging, "Hands-on" Methods   Workbooks are great for independent practice when concepts have been taught well. They are not categorically despicable but, unfortunately, they are often used as a substitute for teacher-directed learning. Concepts, however, should be developed in the context of student–teacher interaction and activities designed to encourage reflection about language form. The brain responds to novelty and to tasks that ask us to respond actively and strategically,[13] which is why we usually learn better by doing than by listening. Some powerful approaches to phonological awareness, for example, emphasize mouth position and the ability to compare how words feel when they are spoken.[14] Some decoding programs ask children to stand at the chalkboard and write words as the words are analyzed, sounded out, and explained. Other programs use manipulative letters and trays. Still others give children small lap slates to write words as they are dictated and illustrated on an overhead projector. Letter cards can be manipulated in personal pocket charts that are made with manila folders. Hand gestures are employed for sweeping through sounds and blending them into words. All of these active techniques require the learner to select, classify, and consciously manipulate sounds and letters so that more thorough word learning occurs.

A Spelling–Decoding Continuum for Elementary Instruction

As Marcia Henry suggested, every layer of language organization merits attention in the elementary curriculum.[15] A coherent progression for reading and spelling begins with phoneme awareness training and concludes with study of the Greek combining forms that are so prevalent in math and science vocabulary. Grade by grade, a typical emphasis would be as follows.

K	Phoneme awareness, letter names, and letter sounds
1	Anglo-Saxon consonant and vowel sound–spelling correspondences
2	More complex Anglo-Saxon spelling patterns, inflections, and compounds

3   Syllabication and word endings (inflections) that require a change in the base

4   Latin-based prefixes, roots, and suffixes

5–6   More complex and unusual Latin-based forms

7–8   Greek combining forms

Decoding Beyond Second Grade

Understanding word structure for reading, vocabulary, and spelling necessitates knowing syllable patterns and morphology. Some aspects of morphology, in turn, are governed by syntax. Good readers will learn to break longer words into segments if necessary, supply accent, and relate familiar word parts to meaning when possible. Each level of orthography—sounds, syllables, and morphemes—has its own organization, and each of those levels differs according to the language from which a word is derived. As word analysis skills are developing, words must also be read and written in sentence contexts.

At each level of word knowledge, there is an order of difficulty inherent in the material itself and a general progression by which children master the domain. For example, children learn the past tense *ed* for speaking, reading, and spelling over several years. At first, children become aware that the past-tense form means that the event happened already. Then they read and spell *ed* as a phonetic element, as in WAKT for *walked*. As they develop a category for word endings, children may confuse *ed* with other endings, such as *ing* and *s*. Next, children over-generalize the spelling *ed* to any base word that has a /t/ or /d/ on the end (MOSTED). Finally, they learn when and why to use the spelling *ed* and notice the presence of the construction in print. All of this takes 3 or 4 years.

Instruction that follows a systematic progression to help children learn the past tense might proceed like this. First, children would focus on the concept of past-tense actions in spoken language. Next, they might be asked to notice the presence of the ending on written words and identify the sounds the endings make (/t/, /d/, /əd/). In late first and early second grade, they might begin to spell some words with *ed* but would not necessarily have to learn the rules for dropping *e* and changing *y* when an ending is added (see Table 8.7 for more on second-grade reader characteristics and needs). At about mid-second grade, children would be expected to read accurately all of the major inflections (*ed, ing, est, er, es, s*). Not until third grade would they delve into rules for changing spellings when *ed* is added. An advanced skill (fourth grade, perhaps) would involve discovering the pattern that determines how to pronounce *ed* and realizing that it is not pronounced as a separate syllable in words such as *attached, raced,* or *used.*[16]

The following lesson scripts were developed by Mike Minsky of the Greenwood School in Putney, Vermont, to illustrate the nature of good instruction. Notice that the teacher is explicit—leaving little to guesswork or chance—and that each aspect of the lesson builds on what has been taught before.

Table 8.7.   Orthographic stage reader characteristics and needs (approximately second grade)

Child knows	Child needs to learn	Teaching strategies
How to read with some fluency (60–80 words per minute)	Fluency of more than 80 words per minute	Have child reread familiar books, alternate oral reading with partner, or audiotape reading.
How to write more than one sentence but uses no logical structure	Use of connecting words and paragraph sequence	Supply connecting words to unlinked sentences.
Most one-syllable word patterns	Recognition of closed, open, r-controlled, vowel team, consonant-le, and silent-e syllables in longer words	Provide practice in syllable identification and classification, syllable combining, and syllable division.
Spelling of regular, one-syllable words and 50–100 basic sight words	Spellings of compounds, words with endings, vowel team words, and more variant patterns	Ask child to sort words, test-study-test in organized program, and use in writing and proofreading.
Common vocabulary (overuses it)	More variety in speaking, writing, and reading	Teach antonyms, synonyms, classification, definition, and context use.
Only period and question mark; is unfamiliar with other punctuation	Use of comma, capitals, and exclamation and quotation marks	Offer dictations, proofreading, and group composition.
How to write about own experiences in "train of thought" style	More control over flow of ideas, and use a plan	Encourage and model individually stages of writing process.
How to retell without summarizing or extracting main idea	Paraphrasing, summarizing, questioning, and connecting	Provide guided discussion, reader response, and modeling of strategies.

Example Lesson 1: Introducing Letter–Sound Correspondence to a Novice Reader

The student already knows that the letter *a* represents the "short *a*" sound, as in *lamb*, and knows the sound–symbol correspondences for consonants *d*, *f*, *g*, *n*, *p*, *s*, and *t*. The student's reading is restricted to consonant-vowel-consonant words involving those letters and a few sight words. The goal of the lesson is to introduce the "short *i*" sound, as in *itch*.

The lesson begins with the teacher writing a list of one-syllable words with short *i* on the board. These may have some letters and combinations the student does not know, so the teacher reads the list first. (What the teacher might say is in quotation marks.)

"I am going to write some words on the board and read them aloud." The teacher writes and reads the list.

bit	mitt	sit	fit	knit	lit
sip	flip	grip	ship	nip	

"What sound do you hear in the middle of all of these words?" If the student cannot say the sound, then the teacher explains that the first sound of *itch, in,* and *if* is the sound in the middle of all of the words.

"Say the sound [ɪ] by itself. Is it an open sound or a closed sound? If it is an open sound, then it is a vowel. What kind of sound is [ɪ]?"

The teacher points to the list of words. "What is the letter (shape) in the middle of these words?"

"Can you think of any other words that have [ɪ]?" Note that vowels followed by /n/ and /m/ are nasalized and may be problematic for some children to identify; examples containing these patterns are to be avoided initially. Words with [ɪg] are also to be avoided because the vowel before [g] sounds like "long *e*." The teacher gives the student sentences that will cue recall of a target word.

Another word for lie is (fib).

The small sail on the front of the sailboat is a (jib).

A word for a child is a (kid).

The witch has wart on her (lip).

My brother takes his fishing pole to the river to catch (fish).

Tag. You are (it).

Sometimes you just have to scratch an (itch).

The letter we use to show this sound is *i*. This letter is called *i*. When we spell a word with [ɪ], we use the letter *i* to show the sound." The teacher writes the letter *i* on the chalkboard. "This letter is *i*. The key word is *it*. The sound *it* makes is [ɪ]. Now copy the letter *i* while you look at the example. Make it big so that you can feel your arm move. Start at the top, go down to the line, and dot the *i*. Name the letter. Say the key word. Say the sound." The teacher repeats several times if necessary.

"When we see the letter *i* at the beginning or inside of a word, it can tell us to make the [ɪ] sound with our mouths. The [ɪ] sound is a vowel, an open sound, like the one you already know, [æ]. For which vowel is your jaw lower, [ɪ] or [æ]?" The teacher shows the chart that shows vowel spellings by mouth position (see Figure 2.5) and locates the two vowels in their positions.

"Now I'll say a word. You say the vowel you hear in the word, [ɪ] or [æ]."

"Now we'll use letter cards to read some words and make new words." The teacher gives letter cards for *g, t, p, n, f, s, d, a,* and *i*. "This word says *tip*."

"What word do I get if I take away [t] and put [s] in its place? What happens if I take the [s] and make it a [d]?"

"Spell it with your cards. Good, you changed *sip* to *dip*. Now change *dip* to *nip*. Now, I will write some letters. Give me the sound for each letter I write." As each letter is written, the teacher points to the letter, waits for the student to make the sound, and then sweeps under the sounds to indicate that the student is to blend them.

The teacher guides the student to use the letter cards to build as many words as possible. Sentence cues and other meaningful cues can help a student identify what word is to be spelled. The teacher always has the student say the word aloud and repeat the sound sequence. Words can be built by changing one sound at a time in a chain of words, such as *pat, pit, pin, pan, Dan, din, fin, fit, fat,* and *fan.*

"I am first going to tell you a word: *pit.* Repeat it after me: *pit.* Say the sounds. Spell it aloud as you write it. Read the word you have written." The teacher then gives phrases for dictation that use the most common sight words already studied, such as *the, is, a, not,* and *has.*

The teacher discusses with the student that *pit* has several meanings, illustrating each with a picture or phrase.

Example Lesson 2: Working with Suffixes

This lesson introduces a group of suffixes. Students have previously studied the concept of a suffix and the spelling and meanings of suffixes, such as *ed, ing, less, ness,* and *ly.* This lesson is essentially a dialogue between teacher and students moving from previously learned to new material.

"The word *happiness* has a suffix. Can anyone tell me what a suffix is?" The teacher waits for a response. "Yes, a suffix is a part of a word that is added to the end of another word and that changes the meaning in some way. Can you give me an example of some suffixes?" The teacher waits for responses.

"Good. Now we are going to learn a new one. I'll give you a root and then say a sentence that needs a new word made out of the root and a suffix. Tell me what word I need to add to finish the sentence." After the students say each word, the teacher writes it on the board.

Play. My puppy likes to play. He is very _____.

Care. You have to take a lot of care when crossing a street. You have to be _____.

Thank. My cousin thanked me a lot when I cleaned his garage. He was _____.

Fear. I was full of fear in the deserted building. I was _____.

"What does the suffix *ful* mean? Yes, it means full of. A cheerful person is full of cheer. A joyful person is full of joy. But be careful when you spell the suffix—it has only one *l.* It is not spelled like the word *full.*" The teacher makes new words by putting a card with the suffix *ful* next to roots. Then the teacher reviews these words to see how many of those words can take the additional suffix *ly.* Students are asked to write new words with the two suffixes: *carefully, thankfully, joyfully, playfully, fearfully,* and so forth.

The teacher makes a word web with all of the forms of the word *help* that can be created by adding the suffixes and prefixes the students have studied: *helpful, unhelpful, unhelpfully, helping, helped, helps, helpless, helplessness, helpers, helplessly,* and so forth. The teacher picks several words to use in creating written sentences with the students and emphasizes the construction of strong, detailed sentences with elaborated ideas. Sentences should tell enough about who is doing what, as in this sentence: *The cheerful boy ran up the stairs excited that he had won a puppy.*

Example Lesson 3: Oral Reading for Fluency

This lesson follows a sequence called Standard Oral Reading Procedure (SORP) in the Orton-Gillingham approach.[17] The teacher supports students to achieve fluency and accuracy in text reading. Daily practice with both oral and silent reading in text at the students' independent reading level or at the instructional reading level is recommended for developing readers.

"We are going to read some passages aloud from Chapter 8 in *Hatchet* by Gary Paulsen.[18] First let's go over the words that might be new but that you can probably read. Look at these words." The teacher prints the words on the chalkboard, cards, or chart paper.

"First, divide the words into syllables before trying to pronounce them. In the word *gesture,* pay attention to the letter that comes after the *g*. The two last words have suffixes, and a final *y* has been changed to an *i*. So, you might want to cover the suffix with a card and read the root word first." The students read the words. If necessary, the teacher corrects syllable division and has the students read the individual syllables correctly before they are blended into a word.

"Here are two more words that I am going to divide into syllables and read for you." The teacher writes me/di/um and in/i/tial on the chalkboard, cards, or chart paper.

"Now can you read these words? We will be studying words such as *medium* and *initial* next week. I want you to skim pages 79–81 first, and underline any words you think you might need help with." After the students have browsed the selection, the teacher says, "Are there any words you want me to go over with you? Spell them aloud for me from the book, and I will write them on the board for you to divide into syllables and figure out." The teacher keeps track of these words for later review. As much as possible, the teacher enables students to analyze the words, read them by making analogies to known words, or use the sentence context as an aid to figure them out.

"Now we'll start reading aloud from page 79. Who would like to begin? Remember to read the outlaw (sight) words correctly." The teacher can vary the strategies for oral reading. Exchanging paragraphs, reading simultaneously, or having students raise a hand when they are ready to take over are effective. Students who are afraid to read aloud should never be forced into an embarrassing confrontation and can read aloud for the teacher in private. The teacher keeps a running record of errors on a list and selects some for later instruction in word analysis and phrase reading. New vocabulary can also be placed into sentence anagrams—sentences broken apart and written word by word on cards for rebuilding. Every oral reading lesson should include comprehension activities such as summarizing the main points, predicting what is coming next, interpreting passages that entail both literal and figurative meanings, explaining the use of words in context, and questioning what the author intended.

Case Studies

In the following cases, concepts presented in the previous chapters can be applied to analyzing students' writing samples and determining basic instructional needs.

Jeremy

A spontaneous journal entry (see Figure 8.2) was written during the first week of November by Jeremy, a first-grade student who had just experienced an introductory lesson on the [č] phoneme and its spelling with *ch*. His spelling shows good knowledge of basic sound–symbol correspondences and orthographic patterns. He is beginning to spell morphemically, keeping the parts of *coming* intact (come + ing) and spelling *learned* as lurn + ed. Jeremy is ready to study the spelling of words with inflections and should be encouraged to write personal **narratives,** descriptions, and paragraphs that explain observations about the real world.

Figure 8.2.   Jeremy's journal entry.

Robbie

Robbie is in the same first-grade class as Jeremy, and his journal entry was produced on the same day (see Figure 8.3). After the lesson on spelling /č/ with *ch*, Robbie writes *Chuck likes to eat some chili and some chocolate.* He demonstrates confusion of the voiced and voiceless consonant pair /ǰ/ and /č/ when he uses the letter *j* as the initial letter of the words *chili* and *chocolate.* He does not spell morphemically: He spells the speech sounds in *likes* with a sound-by-sound approach. He inserts a nasal after a vowel where it does not belong in *eat.* These may be the initial signs of a problem with phoneme identity that merit focused practice with minimal pairs of words that contrast the target sounds. Robbie may have a mild problem with phoneme awareness that needs additional screening and assessment.

Bruce

Bruce, a first-grade student in a class taught with a reading program that included systematic phoneme awareness and phonics instruction, wrote a journal entry after 2 months in the first grade (see Figure 8.4). Bruce's teacher has written correct spellings underneath the misspelled words. Note the

Figure 8.3.   Robbie's journal entry.

omission of the nasals /n/ and /m/ in the child's spelling of *haunted* and *gramp,* respectively. The omission of nasals occurs only when the nasal consonant comes between a vowel and a following consonant within a syllable. Bruce has learned the words *went* and *and* as wholes by this time, along with other sight words such as *my* and *the.* The unknown vowel /ɔ/ in *haunted* is spelled with the vowel that is closest in articulation: /ɑ/ ("short *o*"). Syllabic [r] in *birthday* is spelled logically with one letter, as there is no separate vowel segment in that syllable. Sentence structure is developing well for Bruce. He is ready to learn words with nasal blends at the end (*mp, nd, nt*) and the spellings for some *r*-controlled vowels.

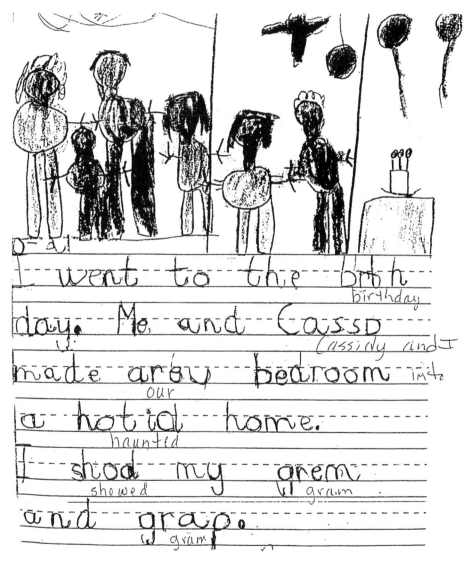

Figure 8.4.   Bruce's journal entry.

goo	go
ann	and
yel	will
hme	him
coc	cook
lot	light
jrs	dress
reh	reach
ntr	enter

Figure 8.5. Spellings given by Janet, a second grader (actual spellings on right).

Janet

Janet is a second-grade student who has fallen behind in reading and has scored below grade level in spelling accuracy. She is a very slow reader, reading at less than 40 correct words per minute in spite of solid average intellectual ability. Janet's spelling, however, is phonetically accurate (see Figure 8.5). The speech sounds are represented faithfully, although Janet's knowledge of the actual symbols used in conventional spelling is limited. The spellings are generated with letter names and sequential spelling strategies typical of later phonetic spelling. The spellings are typical of a child about a year behind second-grade level.

Note the use of the letter name *h* to spell [č] in *reach*, the representation of affrication of the initial [d] in *dress* (spelled with a *j*), the choice of the mid low vowel /ɑ/ for /ɑj/ in *light*, and the use of the letter name *y* to spell /w/ in *will*. The syllabic spellings of *enter*, the doubling of the /n/ in *and* in place of the final /d/, and the doubling of /o/ in *go* all are typical for phonetic spellers. Janet seems to assume that all words have three letters. Her phoneme awareness is quite well developed; instruction must emphasize remembering the graphemes used to represent phonemes, being aware of spelling patterns, and obtaining fluency in word recognition. Writing regular words to dictation, practicing sight words through multisensory tracing techniques, learning graphemes for phonemes, and sorting words by spelling pattern would be appropriate for her. These exercises should be supplemented with brief, 1-minute timed drills on recognizing high-frequency words, reading in phrases, and repeating readings of texts at her instructional level.

Harry

Harry, a second-grade student, wrote sentences on the Test of Achievement in the Woodcock-Johnson Psychoeducational Test Battery–Revised (see Figure 8.6).[19] The spelling is typical of late phonetic and early orthographic

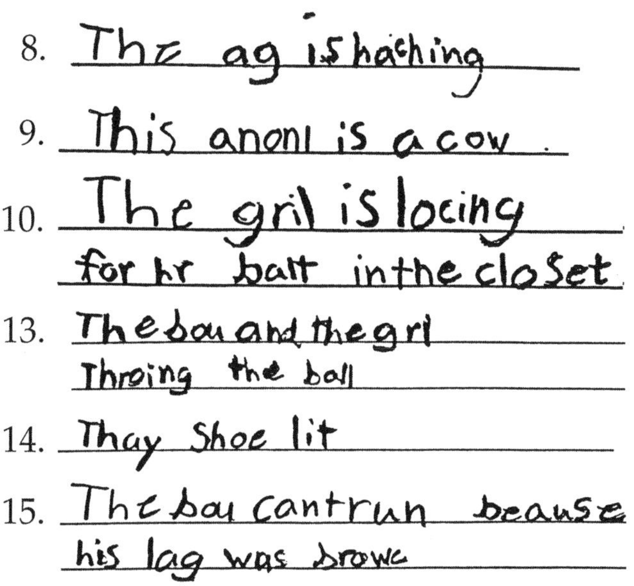

8. The ag is haching

9. This anoni is a cov .

10. The gril is locing
    for hr bait in the closet

13. The bai and the grl
    Throing the ball

14. Thay shoe lit

15. The bai cantrun beause
    his lag was browe

Figure 8.6. Harry's sentences from the Test of Achievement in the Woodcock-Johnson Psychoeducational Test Battery–Revised.

stages (see Chapters 1 and 8, respectively, for descriptions of these stages). Note that the words *egg* (Item 8) and *leg* (Item 15) are spelled as they sound, with the [ɛ] raised up to an [e] when the tongue anticipates rising in the back of the throat to make the velar consonant [g]. Note the confusion of the nasal consonants in *animal* (Item 9). In *girl* (Item 10), the inseparable combination [ɛr] is spelled with the logical letter choice, *r*, and the *i* is inserted as an afterthought because it is unnecessary for portraying the sounds in the word. In *throwing* (Item 13) and *light* (Item 14), the long vowels are spelled with single letters that contain the vowel sounds in their names. Orthographic awareness is evident when the child spells the diphthong [ɔj] in *boy* (Item 15) with a vowel–letter combination *ou*. Harry seems to understand that the vowel is a diphthong but is unsure of the correct spelling. Harry would benefit from the instructional activities and goals described in Table 8.3.

Cynthia

Cynthia is a 9-year-old third-grade student with an above-average verbal IQ score. Figure 8.7 presents her written expression subtest of the Wechsler Individual Achievement Test,[20] on which she was asked to describe her ideal place to live. She has rather prominent difficulties identifying and transcribing the speech sounds in words in spite of her high verbal reasoning ability. She did poorly on diagnostic tests of phonological awareness.

Cynthia's spelling of the word *items* contains an alveolar nasal [n] in place of a stop consonant [t]. Her spellings of the words *bay* and *bathrooms* begin with a reversed *b* (*d*) that is clearly an orthographic substitution. In addition to orthographic errors, however, Cynthia's writing contains phonologically based errors. Her spelling of the word *garage* ends with a voiceless sound [č] in place of the voiced [ž] or [ǰ]. She seems to use the letter *a* as a default vowel in words such as *with, slide, real,* and *dining.* Her spelling of the word *kitchen* includes a nasal after the vowel that does not belong there, and her spellings of the words *point, basement,* and *front* in the last three lines all are missing a nasal after a vowel and before a consonant. Diffuse problems with placement of /r/ and /l/ within a syllable are evident in *apple, tree,* and *garage.* Substituting /w/ for /r/ in *real* is common in children with lingering phonological production problems. The *p* at the beginning of *basement* is evidence of a voicing confusion. The many phonological confusions suggest that Cynthia's fundamental problem with phoneme awareness must be addressed directly if she is to improve. Instruction for her should emphasize **phoneme identification,** phoneme contrasts, and phoneme sequencing during the decoding and spelling components of lessons.

Cynthia uses a listing strategy for her ideas, and there are no capital letters. Her vocabulary and descriptive detail are good for her age, but she cannot simultaneously generate complete sentences and transcribe her thoughts. Her verbal ability as measured by IQ tests appears to be considerably higher than the level of her written language output. She needs a structured approach to sentence expansion and sentence construction as well as emphasis on planning her writing before she makes a draft.

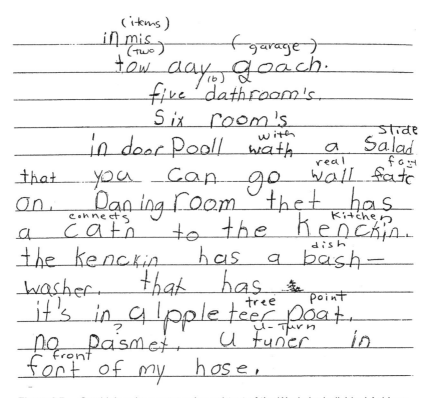

Figure 8.7. Cynthia's written expression subtest of the Wechsler Individual Achievement Test.

Britt

Britt, a third-grade student, has fallen behind grade level in reading. She has scored about one standard deviation below her expected level on a test of word recognition and relies heavily on context to decode new words. She attempts to spell phonetically, although she uses a letter-name strategy typical of much younger children: spelling long vowels with one letter as in words such as *slide, alpine,* and *near.* She omits the liquid /r/ in *warm* but spells the middle syllable of *Saturday* with a syllabic /r/. She substitutes voiceless for voiced consonants in *over* (/f/ for /v/) and *lunch* (/ǰ/ for /č/). She omits the nasal consonant after the vowel and before the final consonant in *plans.* On another spelling test given at the same time, she made several other voicing substitutions, including UNGL for *uncle,* HOSPIDAL for *hospital,* and EFRY for *every.* She also has little mastery over sentence structure, as the composition contains one long, run-on sentence (see Figure 8.8): *Dear Emily, Want to go to the Alpine Slide with me on Sunday? If you can come, call me on Saturday near lunch time and then we can make the plans over the telephone and it will be a sleepover, so bring your sleeping bag and warm clothes because we are going to camp out. From B.*

Britt's inability to keep up with her classmates in reading and spelling appears to have its origin in a phonological processing weakness, evident in persistent confusions of consonant phonemes that share some features but

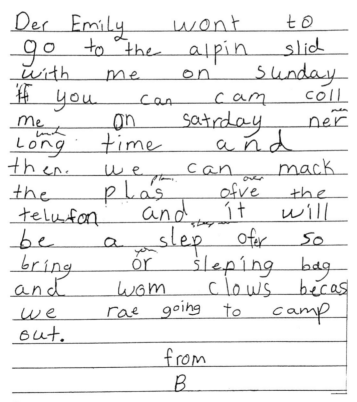

Figure 8.8. Britt's composition.

not others. Her reading and spelling lessons should begin with phoneme awareness exercises designed to contrast the speech sounds she confuses. As part of a comprehensive language arts program, Britt's writing instruction should build sentence-level writing skills, including sentence combining, sentence expansion, and transformations from one type of sentence to another.

Summary: The Power of Instruction

Word recognition, reading fluency, knowledge of word meanings, and familiarity with complex syntax enhance reading comprehension; likewise, exposure to text enhances familiarity with words and linguistic structures. Achieving balance in reading instruction does not mean dabbling superficially in a variety of skill domains but means teaching each component thoroughly, systematically, and well. Maintaining a balance also means covering a range of components daily and weekly, along with a steady supply of great literature and purposeful writing projects. Considerable expertise is required to teach everyone to read, but well-informed classroom teachers using valid instructional programs are up to the job. There is no more important task for educators to undertake.

Endnotes

1. Mehta et al., 2005.
2. Blachman, Tangel, Ball, Black, & McGraw, 1999; Brady, 1997; Foorman et al., 1998; Torgesen, 2004.
3. Roberts, 2009.
4. Dickinson, McCabe, & Clark-Chiarelli, 2004; Hart & Risley, 1995.
5. Adams, Foorman, Lundberg, & Beeler, 1998; Blachman et al., 1999; Gillon, 2004.
6. Ehri, 2004.
7. Ehri & Snowling, 2004.
8. An example of this strategy is the "duet" reading embedded in the instructional program ReadWell (Sprick, Dunn, Jones, & Gunn, 2003).
9. McGuinness, 1997.
10. Hanna et al., 1966.
11. Bear, Invernizzi, Templeton, & Johnston, 2000.
12. Share & Stanovich, 1995.
13. Bransford, Brown, & Cocking, 1999.
14. Lindamood & Lindamood, 1998.
15. Henry, 2003.
16. The pronunciation of the past-tense ending in English is governed by the speech sound that precedes it. If the preceding sound is a voiced consonant or vowel, then the past-tense ending is pronounced /d/. If the preceding sound is a voiceless consonant, then the past-tense ending is pronounced /t/. If the word ends in a /d/ or a /t/, then the full syllable /əd/ is used.
17. Gillingham & Stillman, 1997.
18. Paulsen, 1988.
19. Woodcock & Johnson, 1989.
20. Wechsler, 1992.

References

Aaron, P.G., Joshi, R.M., & Quatroche, D. (2008). *Becoming a professional reading teacher.* Baltimore: Paul H. Brookes Publishing Co.

Adams, M.J. (1990). *Beginning to read: Learning and thinking about print.* Cambridge, MA: MIT Press.

Adams, M. (1998). The three-cueing system. In J. Osborn & F. Lehr (Eds.), *Literacy for all: Issues in teaching and learning* (pp. 79–99). New York: Guilford Press.

Adams, M.J., Foorman, B.R., Lundberg, I., & Beeler, T. (1998). *Phonemic awareness in young children: A classroom curriculum.* Baltimore: Paul H. Brookes Publishing Co.

Akmajian, A., Demers, R.A., Farmer, A.K., & Harnish, R.M. (1998). *Linguistics: An introduction to linguistics and communication* (6th ed.). Cambridge, MA: MIT Press.

Archer, A., Gleason, M., Vachon, V., & Isaacson, S. (2000). *The REWARDS Program.* Longmon, CO: Sopris West.

Ashby, J., Sanders, L.D., & Kingston, J. (2009). Skilled readers begin processing subphonemic features by 80 ms during visual word recognition: Evidence from ERPs. *Biological Psychology, 80*(1), 84–94.

Bailet, L.L. (1990). Spelling rule usage among students with learning disabilities and normally achieving students. *Journal of Learning Disabilities, 18,* 162–165.

Balmuth, M. (2009). *The roots of phonics: A historical introduction* (Rev. ed.). Baltimore: Paul H. Brookes Publishing Co.

Baum, L.F. (1956). *The wizard of Oz.* New York: Grosset & Dunlap.

Bear, D.R., Invernizzi, M., Templeton, S., & Johnston, F. (1996). *Words their way: Word study for phonics, vocabulary, and spelling instruction* (1st ed.). Upper Saddle River, NJ: Prentice Hall.

Bear, D., Invernizzi, M., Templeton, S., & Johnston, F. (2000). *Words their way* (2nd ed.). Upper Saddle River, NJ: Prentice Hall.

Beck, I.L., McKeown, M.G., Hamilton, R.L., & Kucan, L. (1998). Getting at the meaning: How to help students unpack difficult text. *American Educator, 22*, 66–71, 85.

Beck, I., McKeown, M.G., & Omanson, R.C. (1990). The effects and uses of diverse vocabulary instructional techniques. In M.G. McKeown & M.E. Curtis (Eds.), *The nature of vocabulary acquisition* (pp. 462–481). Mahwah, NJ: Lawrence Erlbaum Associates.

Becker, C.A. (1985). What do we really know about semantic context effects during reading? In D. Besner, T. Waller, & G. MacKinnon (Eds.), *Reading research: Advances in theory and practice* (Vol. 5, pp. 125–166). New York: Academic Press.

Berko, J. (1958). The child's learning of English morphology. *Word, 14*, 150–177.

Berninger, V.W., & Wolf, B. (2009). *Teaching students with dyslexia and dysgraphia: Lessons from teaching and science.* Baltimore: Paul H. Brookes Publishing Co.

Birsh, J.R. (Ed.). (2005). *Multisensory teaching of basic language skills* (2nd ed.). Baltimore: Paul H. Brookes Publishing Co.

Blachman, B.A., Ball, E.W., Black, R., Tangel, D.M. (2000). *Road to the code: A phonological awareness program for young children.* Baltimore: Paul H. Brookes Publishing Co.

Blachman, B.A., Schatschneider, C., Fletcher, J.M., & Clonan, S.M. (2003). Early reading intervention: A classroom prevention study and a remediation study. In B.R. Foorman (Ed.), *Preventing and remediating reading difficulties: Bringing science to scale* (pp. 253–271). Timonium, MD: York Press.

Blachman, B.A., Tangel, D.M., Ball, E.W., Black, R., & McGraw, C.K. (1999). Developing phonological awareness and word recognition skills: A two-year intervention with low-income, inner-city children. *Reading and Writing: An Interdisciplinary Journal, 11*, 239–273.

Bolinger, D.L., & Sears, D.A. (1981). *Aspects of language* (3rd ed.). Orlando, FL: Harcourt Brace & Co.

Bos, C., Mather, N., Dickson, S., Podhajski, B., & Chard, D. (2001). Perceptions and knowledge of preservice and inservice educators about early reading instruction. *Annals of Dyslexia, 51*, 97–120.

Brady, S. (1997). Ability to encode phonological representations: An underlying difficulty of poor readers. In B. Blachman (Ed.), *Foundations of reading acquisition and dyslexia: Implications for early intervention* (pp. 21–47). Mahwah, NJ: Lawrence Erlbaum Associates.

Brady, S., Gillis, M., Smith, T., Lavalette, M., Liss-Bronstein, L., Lowe, E., et al. (2009). First grade teachers' knowledge of phonological awareness and code concepts: Examining gains from an intensive form of professional development and corresponding teacher attitudes. *Reading and Writing: An Interdisciplinary Journal, 22*, 425–455.

Brady, S., & Moats, L.C. (1997, Spring). *Informed instruction for reading success: Foundations for teacher preparation. A position paper of The International Dyslexia Association.* Baltimore: International Dyslexia Association.

Bransford, J., Brown, A., & Cocking, R. (Eds.). (1999). *How people learn: Mind, brain and experience in school.* Washington, DC: National Academy Press.

Brown, R. (1973). *A first language: The early stages.* Cambridge, MA: Harvard University Press.

Cain, K., & Oakhill, J. (2007). Reading comprehension difficulties: Correlates, causes, and consequences. In K. Cain & J. Oakhill (Eds.), *Children's comprehension problems in oral and written language: A cognitive perspective* (pp. 41–75). New York: Guilford Press.

Calhoon, M.B. (2005). Effects of a peer-mediated phonological skill and reading comprehension program on reading skill acquisition for middle school students with reading disabilities. *Journal of Learning Disabilities, 38*(5), 424–433.

Carlisle, J.F. (1987). The use of morphological knowledge in spelling derived forms by learning disabled and normal students. *Annals of Dyslexia, 37*, 90–108.

Carlisle, J.F. (1988). Knowledge of derivational morphology and spelling ability in fourth, sixth, and eighth graders. *Applied Psycholinguistics, 9*, 247–266.

Carlisle, J. (2004). Morphological processes that influence learning to read. In C.A. Stone, E.R. Silliman, B.J. Ehren, & K. Apel (Eds.), *Handbook of language and literacy: Development and disorders* (pp. 318–339). New York: Guilford.

Carlisle, J.F., & Nomanbhoy, D.M. (1993). Phonological and morphological awareness in first graders. *Applied Psycholinguistics, 14*, 177–195.

Carroll, L. (1960). *Alice's adventures in wonderland and through the looking glass: A Signet classic.* New York: The New American Library. (Original work published 1865)

Cassar, M., Treiman, R., Moats, L., Pollo, T.C., & Kessler, B. (2005). How do the spellings of children with dyslexia compare with those of nondyslexic children? *Reading and Writing, 18*, 27–49.

Catone, W.V., & Brady, S. (2005). The inadequacy of individual educational program goals for high school students with word-level reading difficulties. *Annals of Dyslexia, 55*(1), 53–78.

Catts, H.W., & Kamhi, A.G. (2005). *Language and reading disabilities.* Boston: Allyn & Bacon.

Chall, J. (1983). *Stages of reading development.* New York: McGraw-Hill.

Chomsky, C. (1970). Reading, spelling, and phonology. *Harvard Educational Review, 40*, 287–309.

Chomsky, N. (1965). *Aspects of the theory of syntax.* Cambridge, MA: MIT Press.

Chomsky, N., & Halle, M. (1968). *The sound pattern of English.* New York: Harper-Collins.

Comrie, B., Matthews, S., & Polinsky, M. (Eds.). (1996). *The atlas of languages: The origin and development of languages throughout the world.* London: Quarto Publishing.

Connor, C.M., Morrison, F.J., & Katch, E.L. (2004). Beyond the reading wars: The effect of classroom instruction by child interactions on early reading. *Scientific Studies of Reading, 8*(4), 305–336.

Cunningham, A.E., Perry, K.E., Stanovich, K.E., & Stanovich, P.J. (2004). Disciplinary knowledge of K–3 teachers and their knowledge calibration in the domain of early literacy. *Annals of Dyslexia, 54*, 139–172.

Cunningham, A.E., & Stanovich, K.E. (1991). Tracking the unique effects of print exposure in children: Associations with vocabulary, general knowledge, and spelling. *Journal of Educational Psychology, 83*, 264–274.

Cunningham, A.E., & Stanovich, K.E. (1997). Early reading acquisition and its relation to reading experience and ability 10 years later. *Developmental Psychology, 33*(6), 934–945.

Cunningham, A., & Stanovich, K. (1998, Spring/Summer). What reading does for the mind. *American Educator, 22*, 8–15.

Cunningham, A.E., Zibulsky, J., Stanovich, Z.E., & Stanovich, P.J. (2009). How teachers would spend their time teaching language arts: The mismatch between self-reported and best practices. *Journal of Learning Disabilities, 42*(5), 418–430.

Derwing, B., & Baker, W. (1979). Recent research on the acquisition of English morphology. In P. Fletcher & M. Garman (Eds.), *Language acquisition* (pp. 209–223). Cambridge, England: Cambridge University Press.

Derwing, B.L., Smith, M.L., & Wiebe, G.E. (1995). On the role of spelling in morpheme recognition: Experimental studies with children and adults. In L.B. Feldman (Ed.), *Morphological aspects of language processing* (pp. 3–27). Mahwah, NJ: Lawrence Erlbaum Associates.

deVilliers, J., & deVilliers, P. (1973). A cross-sectional study of the acquisition of grammatical morphemes. *Journal of Psycholinguistic Research, 2*, 267–278.

Dickinson, D.K., McCabe, A., & Clark-Chiarelli, N. (2004). Preschool-based prevention of reading disability. In CA. Stone, E.R. Silliman, B.J. Ehren, & K. Apel (Eds.), *Handbook of language and literacy: Development and disorders* (pp. 209–227). New York: Guilford.

Edwards, H.T. (1992). *Applied phonetics: The sounds of American English.* San Diego: Singular Publishing Group.

Ehri, L. (1994). Development of the ability to read words: Update. In R. Ruddell, M. Ruddell, & H. Singer (Eds.), *Theoretical models and processes of reading* (pp. 323–358). Newark, DE: International Reading Association.

Ehri, L.C. (2002). Phases of acquisition in learning to read words and implications for teaching. *British Journal of Education Psychology: Monograph Series, 1*, 7–28.

Ehri, L.C. (2004). Teaching phonemic awareness and phonics: An explanation of the national reading panel meta-analyses. In P. McCardle & V. Chhabra (Eds.), *The voice of evidence in reading research* (pp. 153–186). Baltimore: Paul H. Brookes Publishing Co.

Ehri, L.C., & McCormick, S. (1998). Phases of word learning: Implications for instruction with delayed and disabled readers. *Reading and Writing Quarterly: Overcoming Learning Difficulties, 14,* 153–163.

Ehri, L., & Snowling, M. (2004). Developmental variation in word recognition. In A.C. Stone, E.R. Silliman, B.J. Ehren, & K. Apel (Eds.), *Handbook of language and literacy: Development and disorders* (pp. 443–460). New York: Guilford Press.

Farrell, L., & Hunter, M. (2007). *Phonics blitz.* Cabin John, MD: Really Great Reading Company.

Fischer, F.W., Shankweiler, D., & Liberman, I.Y. (1985). Spelling proficiency and sensitivity to word structure. *Journal of Memory and Language, 24,* 423–441.

Fletcher, J.M., Lyon, G.R., Fuchs, L., & Barnes, M. (2007). *Learning disabilities: From identification to intervention.* New York: Guilford Press.

Fletcher, J.M., Shaywitz, S.E., Shankweiler, D.P., Katz, L., Liberman, I.Y., Steubing, K.K., et al. (1994). Cognitive profiles of reading disability: Comparisons of discrepancy and low achievement definitions. *Journal of Educational Psychology, 86,* 6–23.

Florey, K.B. (2008). A picture of language: A diagrammed sentence is a bit like art. *American Educator, 32*(2), 40–42.

Foorman, B.R., Francis, D.J., Fletcher, J.M., Schatschneider, C., & Mehta, P. (1998). The role of instruction in learning to read: Preventing reading failure in at-risk children. *Journal of Educational Psychology, 90,* 37–55.

Foorman, B.R., & Moats, L.C. (2004). Conditions for sustaining research-based practices in early reading instruction. *Remedial and Special Education, 25,* 51–60.

Fowler, A., & Liberman, I.Y. (1995). The role of phonology and orthography in morphological awareness. In L.B. Feldman (Ed.), *Morphological aspects of language processing* (pp. 157–188). Mahwah, NJ: Lawrence Erlbaum Associates.

Francis, D.J., Shaywitz, S.E., Stuebing, K.K., Shaywitz, B.A., & Fletcher, J.M. (1996). Developmental lag versus deficit models of reading disability: A longitudinal, individual growth curves study. *Journal of Educational Psychology, 88,* 3–17.

Freyd, P., & Baron, J. (1982). Individual differences in acquisition of derivational morphology. *Journal of Verbal Learning and Verbal Behavior, 21,* 282–295.

Fromkin, V.A., & Rodman, R. (1993). *An introduction to language* (4th ed.). Orlando, FL: Harcourt Brace & Co.

Fromkin, V.A., & Rodman, R. (1998). *An introduction to language* (6th ed.). Orlando, FL: Harcourt Brace & Co.

Fromkin, V., Rodman, R., & Hyams, N. (2003). *An introduction to language* (7th ed.). Boston: Heinle.

Gillingham, A., & Stillman, B.W. (1997). *The Gillingham manual: Remedial training for children with specific disability in reading, spelling, and penmanship* (8th ed.). Cambridge, MA: Educators Publishing Service.

Gillon, G. (2004). *Phonological awareness: From research to practice.* New York: Guilford Press.

Glaser, D., & Moats, L.C. (2008). LETRS *foundations: An introduction to language and literacy.* Longmont, CO: Sopris West Educational Services.

Good, R.H., Simmons, D.C., & Kameenui, E.J. (2001). The importance and decision-making utility of a continuum of fluency-based indicators of foundational reading skills for third-grade high-stakes outcomes. *Scientific Studies of Reading, 5,* 257–288.

Goswami, U. (2000). Phonological and lexical processes. In M.L. Kamil, P.B. Mosenthal, P.D. Pearson, & R. Barr (Eds.), *Handbook of reading research* (Vol. 3, pp. 251–267). Mahwah, NJ: Lawrence Erlbaum Associates.

Grace, K. (2007). *Phonics and spelling through phoneme-grapheme mapping.* Longmont, CO: Sopris West Educational Services.

Graham, S., & Perin, D. (2007). *Writing next: Effective strategies to improve writing of adolescents in middle and high schools: A report to the Carnegie Corporation of New York.* New York: Alliance for Excellence in Education.

Greene, J. (2009). *LANGUAGE!* (4th ed.). Longmont, CO: Sopris West Educational Services.

Haager, D., Heimbichner, C., Dhar, R., Moulton, M., & McMillan, S. (2008). *The California Reading First year 6 evaluation report: December 2008.* Retrieved March 1, 2009, from http://www.eddata.com/resources/publications/RF_Evaluation_2007-2008

Hanna, P.R., Hanna, S., Hodges, R.E., & Rudorf, E.H. (1966). *Phoneme-grapheme corre-spondences as cues to spelling improvement.* Washington, DC: Department of Health, Education, and Welfare.

Hart, B., & Risley, T.R. (1995). *Meaningful differences in the everyday experience of young American children.* Baltimore: Paul H. Brookes Publishing Co.

Hatcher, P.J., Hulme, C., & Snowling, M.J. (2004). Explicit phoneme training com-bined with phonic reading instruction helps young children at risk of reading fail-ure. *Journal of Child Psychology and Psychiatry, 45,* 338–358.

Hayes, D.P., & Ahrens, M.G. (1988). Vocabulary simplification for children: A special case of "motherese?" *Journal of Child Language, 15,* 395–410.

Henderson, E. (1990). *Teaching spelling.* Boston: Houghton Mifflin.

Henry, M.K. (2003). *Unlocking literacy: Effective decoding and spelling instruction.* Balti-more: Paul H. Brookes Publishing Co.

Hochman, J. (2009). *Teaching basic writing skills: Strategies for effective expository writing instruction.* Longmont, CO: Sopris West Educational Services.

Holmes, V.M., & Brown, N.F. (1998, April 18). *Effective strategies in skilled spellers.* Paper presented at the Society for the Scientific Study of Reading, San Diego.

Hooper, B., & Moats, L. (2010). *Spelling by pattern: Level 2.* Longmont, CO: Sopris West Educational Services.

Irvin, J. (1990). *Vocabulary instruction: Guidelines for instruction.* Washington, DC: National Education Association.

Joshi, R.M., Binks, E., Graham, L., Dean, E., Smith, D., & Boulware-Gooden, R. (2009). Do textbooks used in university reading education courses conform to the instruc-tional recommendations of the national reading panel? *Journal of Learning Disabil-ities, 42*(5), 458–463.

Joshi, R.M., Binks, E., Hougen, M., Dahlgren, M., Dean, E., & Smith, D. (2009). Why elementary teachers might be inadequately prepared to teach reading. *Journal of Learning Disabilities, 42*(5), 392–402.

Juster, N. (1989). *The phantom tollbooth.* New York: Alfred A. Knopf. (Original work published 1961)

Kibel, M., & Miles, T.R. (1994). Phonological errors in the spelling of taught dyslexic children. In C. Hulme & M. Snowling (Eds.), *Reading development and dyslexia* (pp. 105–127). London: Whurr.

Kroese, J.M., Mather, N., & Sammons, J. (2006). The relationship between nonword spelling abilities of K–3 teachers and student spelling outcomes. *Learning Disabil-ities: A Multidisciplinary Journal, 14,* 85–89.

Leong, C.K. (1989). Productive knowledge of derivational rules in poor readers. *Annals of Dyslexia, 39,* 94–115.

Liberman, I.Y., Rubin, H., Duques, S., & Carlisle, J. (1985). Linguistic abilities and spelling proficiency in kindergartners and adult poor spellers. In D. Gray & J. Kavanaugh (Eds.), *Biobehavioral measures of dyslexia* (pp. 163–175). Timonium, MD: York Press.

Liberman, I.Y., Shankweiler, D., & Liberman, A.M. (1989). The alphabetic principle and learning to read. In D. Shankweiler & I.Y. Liberman (Eds.), *Phonology and read-ing disability: Solving the reading puzzle* (pp. 2–33). Ann Arbor: University of Michi-gan Press.

Librarious. (n.d.). *Geoffrey Chaucer (1342–1400)—"The Canterbury tales" from general prologue, II. 413–446.* Retrieved January 28, 2010 from http://www.librarius.com/canttran/genpro/genpro413-446.htm

Lindamood, P., & Lindamood, P. (1998). *The Lindamood sequencing program for reading, spelling, and speech: Teacher's manual for the classroom and clinic.* Austin, TX: PRO-ED.

MacKay, D.G. (1978). Derivational rules and the internal lexicon. *Journal of Verbal Learning and Verbal Behavior, 17,* 61–71.

Mathes, P.G., Denton, C.A., Fletcher, J.M., Anthony, J.L., Francis, D.J., & Schatschnei-der, C. (2005). The effects of theoretically different instruction and student charac-teristics on the skills of struggling readers. *Reading Research Quarterly, 40,* 148–182.

McAdam, E.L., & Milne, G. (Eds.). (2005). *Johnson's dictionary: A modern selection.* Mineola, NY: Dover Publications.

McCutchen, D., Abbott, R.D., Green, L.B., Beretvas, S.N., Cox, S., Potter, N.S., et al. (2002). Beginning literacy: Links among teacher knowledge, teacher practice, and student learning. *Journal of Learning Disabilities, 35,* 69–86.

McCutchen, D., Green, L., Abbott, R.D., & Sanders, E.A. (2009). Further evidence for teacher knowledge: Supporting struggling readers in grades three through five. *Reading and Writing: An Interdisciplinary Journal, 22,* 401–423.

McCutchen, D., Harry, D.R., Cunningham, A.E., Cox, S., Sidman, S., & Covill, A.E. (2002). Reading teachers' content knowledge of children's literature and phonology. *Annals of Dyslexia, 52,* 207–228.

McGuinness, D. (1997). *Why our children can't read and what we can do about it.* New York: Free Press.

Mehta, P.D., Foorman, B.R., Branum-Martin, L., & Taylor, W.P. (2005). Literacy as a unidimensional multilevel construct: Validation, sources of influence, and implications in a longitudinal study in grades 1 to 4. *Scientific Studies of Reading, 9*(2), 85–116.

Moats, L.C. (1994). The missing foundation in teacher education: Knowledge of the structure of spoken and written language. *Annals of Dyslexia, 44,* 81–102.

Moats, L.C. (1995). The missing foundation in teacher education. *American Educator, 19*(2), 9, 43–51.

Moats, L.C. (1996). Phonological spelling errors in the writing of dyslexic adolescents. *Reading and Writing: An Interdisciplinary Journal, 8,* 105–119.

Moats, L.C. (1999). *Teaching reading is rocket science: What expert teachers of reading should know and be able to do.* Washington, DC: American Federation of Teachers. (Item No. 39-0372)

Moats, L.C. (2009). *Language essentials for teachers of reading and spelling: Module 2. The speech sounds of English: Phonetics, phonology, and phoneme awareness* (2nd ed.). Longmont, CO: Sopris West Educational Services.

Moats, L.C., & Foorman, B.R. (2003). Measuring teachers' content knowledge of language and reading. *Annals of Dyslexia, 53,* 23–45.

Moats, L.C., & Foorman, B.R. (2008). Literacy achievement in the primary grades in high-poverty schools. In S.B. Neuman (Ed.), *Educating the other America: Top experts tackle poverty, literacy, and achievement in our schools* (pp. 91–111). Baltimore: Paul H. Brookes Publishing Co.

Moats, L.C., & Lyon, G.R. (1996). Wanted: Teachers with knowledge of language. *Topics in Language Disorders, 16*(2), 73–86.

Moats, L., & Rosow, B. (2003). *Spellography.* Longmont, CO: Sopris West Educational Services.

Nagy, W.E. (1988). *Teaching vocabulary to improve reading comprehension.* Urbana, IL: National Council of Teachers of English.

Nagy, W.E., & Anderson, R.C. (1984). How many words are there in printed English? *Reading Research Quarterly, 24,* 262–282.

Nagy, W.E., Anderson, R.C., & Herman, P.A. (1987). Learning word meanings from context during normal reading. *American Educational Research Journal, 24,* 237–270.

Nagy, W.E., Anderson, R.C., Schommer, M., Scott, J.A., & Stallman, A.C. (1989). Morphological families in the internal lexicon. *Reading Research Quarterly, 24,* 262–282.

National Adult Literacy Survey. (2003). Washington, DC: National Center for Education Statistics.

National Center for Education Statistics. (2006). *National assessment of educational progress: The nation's report card.* Washington, DC: U.S. Department of Education.

National Institute of Child Health and Human Development. (2000). *Report of the National Reading Panel. Teaching children to read: An evidence-based assessment of the scientific research literature on reading and its implications for reading instruction.* Washington, DC: Author. Retrieved December 5, 2007, from http://www.nationalreadingpanel.org/Publications/summary.htm

Owens, R. (1992). *Language development: An introduction.* New York: Merrill.

Paulsen, G. (1988). *Hatchet.* New York: Viking Penguin.

Paulson, L.H. (2004). *The development of phonological awareness skills in preschool children: From syllables to phonemes.* Ed.D. dissertation, University of Montana. Retrieved January 28, 2010, from Dissertations & Theses: Full Text. (Pub. No. AAT 3166292)

Paulson, L., & Moats, L.C. (2009). *LETRS for early childhood educators.* Longmont, CO: Sopris West Educational Services.

Pedersen, H. (1959). *Linguistic science in the 19th century.* Cambridge, MA: Harvard University Press.

Pennington, B.F. (2009). *Diagnosing learning disorders: A neuropsychological framework* (2nd ed.). New York: Guilford Press.

Perfetti, C.A. (1999). Comprehending written language: A blueprint of the reader. In C.M. Brown & P. Hagoort (Eds.), *The neurocognition of language* (pp. 167–210). New York: Oxford University Press.

Perry, T., & Delpit, L. (Eds.). (1998). *The real Ebonics debate: Power, language, and the education of African American children.* Boston: Beacon Press.

Piasta, S.B., Connor, C.M., Fishman, B.J., & Morrison, F.J. (2009). Teachers' knowledge of literacy concepts, classroom practices, and student reading growth. *Scientific Studies of Reading, 13*(3), 224–248.

Pinker, S. (1999). *Words and rules: The ingredients of language.* New York: Basic Books.

Rayner, K. (1998). Eye movements in reading and information processing. *Psychological Review, 124*(3), 372–422.

Rayner, K., Foorman, B.R., Perfetti, C., Pesetsky, D., & Seidenberg, M.S. (2001). How psychological science informs the teaching of reading. *Psychological Science in the Public Interest, 2,* 31–74.

Roberts, T.A. (2009). *No limits to literacy: For preschool English learners.* Thousand Oaks, CA: Corwin.

Rosow, B. (in press). *Spelling by pattern: Levels 5 and 6: Advanced spellography.* Longmont, CO: Sopris West Educational Services.

Rubin, H. (1988). Morphological knowledge and early writing ability. *Language and Speech, 31,* 337–355.

Rubin, H., Patterson, P.A., & Kantor, M. (1991). Morphological development and writing ability in children and adults. *Language, Speech, and Hearing Services in the Schools, 22,* 228–235.

Scarborough, H.S. (2001). Connecting early language and literacy to later reading (dis)abilities: Evidence, theory, and practice. In S. Neuman & D. Dickinson (Eds.), *Handbook for research in early literacy* (pp. 97–110). New York: Guilford Press.

Scarborough, H.S., & Brady, S.A. (2002). Toward a common terminology for talking about speech and reading: A glossary of the "phon" words and some related terms. *Journal of Literacy Research, 34,* 299–334.

Schatschneider, C., Fletcher, J.M., Francis, D.J., Carlson, C.D., & Foorman, B.R. (2004). Kindergarten prediction of reading skills: A longitudinal comparative analysis. *Journal of Educational Psychology, 96,* 265–282.

Scott, C. (2004). Syntactic contributions to literacy development. In C. Stone, E. Stillman, B. Ehren, & K. Apel (Eds.), *Handbook of language and literacy* (pp. 340–362). New York: Guilford Press.

Scott, C. (2009). Language-based assessment of written expression. In G. Troia (Ed.), *Writing instruction and assessment for struggling writers: From theory to evidence-based practice* (pp. 358–385). New York: Guilford Press.

Seymour, P.H.K. (1992). Cognitive theories of spelling and implications for education. In C. Sterling & C. Robson (Eds.), *Psychology, spelling, and education* (p. 53). Clevedon, England: Multilingual Matters.

Shankweiler, D., Lundquist, E., Dreyer, L., & Dickinson, C. (1996). Reading and spelling difficulties in high school students: Causes and consequences. *Reading and Writing: An Interdisciplinary Journal, 8,* 267–294.

Shankweiler, D., Lundquist, E., Katz, L., Stuebing, K.K., Fletcher, J.M., Brady, S., et al. (1999). Comprehension and decoding: Patterns of association in children with reading difficulties. *Scientific Studies of Reading, 3,* 69–94.

Share, D.L., & Stanovich, K.E. (1995). Cognitive processes in early reading development: Accommodating individual differences into a model of acquisition. *Educational Psychology: Issues in Education, 1,* 1–57.

Shaywitz, S.E. (2003). *Overcoming dyslexia: A new and complete science-based program for reading problems at any level.* New York: Alfred A. Knopf.

Singer, B.D., & Bashir, A.S. (2004). Developmental variations in writing composition skills. In C.A. Stone, E.R. Silliman, B.J. Ehren, & K. Apel (Eds.), *Handbook of lan-*

guage and literacy: Development and disorders (pp. 559–582). New York: Guilford Press.

Snow, C.E. (1990). The development of definitional skill. *Journal of Child Language, 17,* 697–710.

Snow, C.E., Burns, M.S., & Griffin, P. (Eds.). (1998). *Preventing reading difficulties in young children.* Washington, DC: National Academy Press.

Snow, C.E., Griffin, P., & Burns, M.S. (2005). *Knowledge to support the teaching of reading: Preparing teachers for a changing world.* New York: Wiley.

Spear-Swerling, L., & Brucker, P. (2003). Teachers' acquisition of knowledge about English word structure. *Annals of Dyslexia, 53,* 72–103.

Spencer, E.J., Schuele, C.M., Guillot, K.M., & Lee, M.W. (2008). Phonemic awareness skill of speech-language pathologists and other educators. *Language, Speech, and Hearing Services in the Schools, 39,* 512–520.

Sprick, M., Jones, S.V., Dunn, R., & Gunn, B. (2003). *Read Well Kindergarten: Critical foundations in beginning reading.* Colorado: Sopris West.

Stahl, S.A., & Shiel, T.G. (1992). Teaching meaning vocabulary: Productive approaches for poor readers. *Reading and Writing Quarterly: Overcoming Learning Difficulties, 8,* 223–241.

Stolz, J.A., & Feldman, L.B. (1995). The role of orthographic and semantic transparency of the base morpheme in morphological processing. In L.B. Feldman (Ed.), *Morphological aspects of language processing* (pp. 109–130). Mahwah, NJ: Lawrence Erlbaum Associates.

Sweet, R.W. (2004). The big picture: Where we are nationally on the reading front and how we got there. In P. McCardle & V. Chhabra (Eds.), *The voice of evidence in reading research* (pp. 13–44). Baltimore: Paul H. Brookes Publishing Co.

Tangel, D., & Blachman, B. (1995). Effect of phoneme awareness instruction on the invented spelling of first grade children: A one-year follow-up. *Journal of Reading Behavior, 27,* 153–185.

Templeton, S. (1989). Tacit and explicit knowledge of derivational morphology: Foundations for a unified approach to spelling and vocabulary development in the intermediate grades and beyond. *Reading Psychology: An International Quarterly, 10,* 233–253.

Templeton, S., & Bear, D.R. (Eds.). (1992). *Development of orthographic knowledge and the foundations of literacy: A memorial Festschrift for Edmund H. Henderson.* Mahwah, NJ: Lawrence Erlbaum Associates.

Templeton, S., & Scarborough-Franks, L. (1985). The spelling's the thing: Knowledge of derivational morphology in orthography and phonology among older students. *Applied Psycholinguistics, 6,* 371–390.

Torgesen, J.K. (2004). Avoiding the devastating downward spiral: The evidence that early intervention prevents reading failure. *American Educator, 28*(3), 6–9, 12–13, 17–19, 45–47.

Torgesen, J.K., Alexander, A.W., Wagner, R.K., Rashotte, C.A., Voeller, K.K.S., & Conway, T. (2001). Intensive remedial instruction for children with severe reading disabilities: Immediate and long-term outcomes from two instructional approaches. *Journal of Learning Disabilities, 34,* 33–58.

Torgesen, J.T. (2002). The prevention of reading difficulties. *Journal of School Psychology, 40,* 7–26.

Torgesen, J.T. (2005). Remedial interventions for students with dyslexia: National goals and current accomplishments. In S.O. Richardson & J. Gilger (Eds.), *Research-based education and intervention: What we need to know* (pp. 103–123). Baltimore: International Dyslexia Association.

Treiman, R. (1993). *Beginning to spell: A study of first-grade children.* New York: Oxford University Press.

Treiman, R. (1997). Spelling in normal children and dyslexics. In B. Blachman (Ed.), *Foundations of reading acquisition and dyslexia: Implications for early intervention* (pp. 191–218). Mahwah, NJ: Lawrence Erlbaum Associates.

Tyler, A., & Nagy, W. (1989). The acquisition of English derivational morphology. *Journal of Memory and Language, 28,* 649–667.

University of Texas. (n.d.). *Basics of Reed-Kellogg diagrams.* Retrieved August 16, 2009, from http://www.utexas.edu/courses/langling/e360k/handouts/diagrams

Vellutino, F.R., Tunmer, W.E., Jaccard, J.J., & Chen, R. (2007). Components of reading ability: Multivariate evidence for a convergent skills model of reading development. *Scientific Studies of Reading, 11*(1), 3–32.

Venezky, R. (1967). English orthography: Its graphical structure and its relation to sound. *Reading Research Quarterly, 2,* 75–105.

Venezky, R. (1970). *The structure of English orthography.* The Hague, The Netherlands: Mouton.

Walsh, K., Glaser, D., & Dunne-Wilcox, D. (2006). *What education schools aren't teaching about reading and what elementary teachers aren't learning.* Washington, DC: National Council for Teacher Quality.

Wechsler, D. (1992). *Wechsler Individual Achievement Test.* San Antonio, TX: Psychological Corporation.

White, T.G., Power, M.A., & White, S. (1989). Morphological analysis: Implications for teaching and understanding vocabulary growth. *Reading Research Quarterly, 24,* 283–304.

Wolf, M. (2007). *Proust and the squid: The story and science of the reading brain.* New York: HarperCollins.

Wolf, M., & Bowers, P.G. (1999). The double-deficit hypothesis for the developmental dyslexias. *Journal of Educational Psychology, 91,* 415–438.

Wolf, M., Gottwald, S., & Orkin, M. (2009). Serious word play: How multiple linguistic emphases in RAV-O instruction improve multiple reading skills. *Perspectives on Language and Literacy, 35*(4), 21–24.

Woodcock, R.W., & Johnson, M.B. (1989). *Woodcock–Johnson Psychoeducational Battery–Revised.* Allen, TX: DLM.

Wysocki, K., & Jenkins, J.R. (1987). Deriving word meanings through morphological generalization. *Reading Research Quarterly, 22,* 66–81.

Yule, G. (1996). *The study of language* (2nd ed.). Cambridge, England: Cambridge University.

Developmental Spelling Inventories

A qualitative inventory of spelling development is an efficient and valid way of determining at what point children might be in their acquisition of word knowledge. The first versions of this kind of tool were validated by Edmund Henderson and his graduate students at the University of Virginia during the 1980s and 1990s[1]. Two levels of inventory follow, contributed by Dr. Francine Johnston, a coauthor of *Words Their Way*[2]. A few minor changes in Johnston's scoring system have been made for this book.

Directions for Administering the Spelling Inventories

The two tests that follow are designed to assess the orthographic knowledge that elementary school students bring to the tasks of reading and spelling. Students are not to study these words before testing. Doing so would inval-

From WORDS THEIR WAY: WORD STUDY FOR PHONICS, VOCABULARY . . . 2/E by Bear/Invernizzi et al., ©1996. Adapted by permission of Prentice-Hall, Inc., Upper Saddle River, NJ.

idate the purpose of the inventory, which is to find out what students truly know. You can administer this same list of words to measure children's progress three times: in September, January, and May.

These words are ordered in terms of their relative difficulty for children in kindergarten to fifth grade. For this reason you need only to call out the words with features that your children are likely to master during the year. Do call out enough words, however, to get a sense of the range of ability in your class. For most kindergartners you may only need to call out the first five to eight words on the Primary Spelling Inventory. For first graders, call out at least 15 words. For second and third graders, use the entire primary list. Use the entire Elementary Spelling Inventory for fourth and fifth graders and for any third graders who are able to spell more than 20 of the words on the primary list. You should also call out additional words for any kindergartners or first graders who are spelling most of the words correctly.

Testing

Call out the words as you would for any spelling test. Use each word in a sentence to be sure your children know the exact word. Assure your students that this is not for a grade but to help you plan better for their needs. Seat the children to minimize copying, or test the children in small groups (especially in kindergarten and early first grade).

Scoring the Test

Copy an individual score sheet for each child and simply add a point for each correct grapheme or spelling feature of each word. Some of the features are single graphemes that correspond to single phonemes; others are grapheme combinations that spell linguistic units such as onsets, rimes, inflections, or affixes. Add an additional point in the "Correct" column if the entire word is spelled correctly. Note that some words are scored for some features and not others and that the number of possible points varies for each word. For example, in the primary list, you are not asked to look at whether children spell the final consonants correctly in the words *shine* and *blade* or whether the children spell the initial consonant in *talked* correctly.

Assigning Points and Analyzing the Results

Staple each child's spelling test to the individual score sheet. Total the number of points under each feature and across each word. Add the feature and word totals to find the total point score. This number can be compared over time, but the most useful information will be the feature analysis. Look down each feature column to determine the needs of the child. Transfer these numbers to a class composite sheet to get a sense of your group as a whole and to form groups for instruction. Highlight children who are making two or more errors on a particular feature. For example, a child who gets six of seven short vowels correct on the primary list can be considered in pretty good shape, although some review work might be in order. A child who gets only two or three of the seven short vowels, however, needs a lot of work on that feature. Because the total possible number will vary depending on how many words you call out, the criteria for mastery will vary. You can generally think like this: If x is the number of possible correct responses, then a score of x or $x - 1$ indicates good control of the feature, whereas a score of $x - 2$ or more indicates a need for instruction. If a child did not get any points for a feature, it is beyond his or her ability and earlier features need to be addressed first.

ENDNOTES

1. Henderson, 1990; see also Templeton & Bear, 1992.
2. Bear, Invernizzi, Templeton, & Johnston, 1996.

Primary Spelling Inventory—Individual Score Sheet

Child _____ Grade _____ Date _____

Teacher _____ Total points _____

Test words	Initial consonant	Final consonant	Digraph	Blend	Short vowel	Vowel-consonant-e	Vowel team/diphthong	R-controlled vowel	Inflection	Correct? Add 1 point	Word totals
1. fan	f	n			a						
2. pet	p	t			e						
3. dig	d	g			i						
4. mop	m	p			o						
5. rope	r	p				o-consonant-e					
6. wait	w	t					ai				
7. chunk			ch	nk	u						
8. sled				sl	e						
9. stick		-ck		st	i						
10. shine			sh			i-consonant-e					
11. dream				dr			ea				

WORDS THEIR WAY: WORD STUDY FOR PHONICS, VOCABULARY . . . 2/E by Bear/Invernizzi et al., ©1996. Adapted by permission of Prentice-Hall, Inc., Upper Saddle River, NJ.

236

#	Word	Digraph	Blend	a-consonant-e	Vowels	r-controlled	Inflected endings			Total points:
12.	blade		bl	✓						
13.	coach	-ch			oa					
14.	fright		fr		igh					
15.	snowing		sn		ow		-ing			
16.	talked				-a		-ed			
17.	camping		-mp				-ing			
18.	thorn	th				or				
19.	shouted	sh			ou		-ed			
20.	spoil		sp		oi					
21.	growl		gr		ow					
22.	chirp	ch				ir				
23.	clapped		cl				-pped			
24.	tries		tr				-ies			
25.	hiking						-king			
	Feature totals									

WORDS THEIR WAY: WORD STUDY FOR PHONICS, VOCABULARY . . . 2/E by Bear/Invernizzi et al., ©1996. Adapted by permission of Prentice-Hall, Inc., Upper Saddle River, NJ.

Elementary Spelling Inventory—Individual Score Sheet

Child _____ Grade _____

Teacher _____ Date _____

Total points _____

Test words	Short vowel	Blend/digraph	Long vowel pattern	Other vowel	Rule-based variant consonant	Inflection with rule spelling	Syllable juncture	Unaccented syllable	Suffix	Correct? Add 1 point	Word totals
1. speck	e	sp			ck						
2. switch	i	sw			tch						
3. throat			oa								
4. nurse				ur							
5. scrape			a-consonant-e								
6. charge		ch		ar	ge						
7. phone		ph	o-consonant-e								
8. smudge	u	sm			dge						
9. point		nt		oi							
10. squirt		squ		ir							
11. drawing		dr		aw		-ing					

238

12.	trapped	tr				-pped			
13.	waving			ow		-ving			
14.	powerful						-er	-ful	
15.	battle					tt	-tle		
16.	fever					v	-er		
17.	lesson					ss	-on		
18.	pennies					nn	-ies		
19.	fraction							-tion	
20.	sailor					l	-or		
21.	distance					st	-ance		
22.	confusion							-sion	
23.	discovery						dis-	-ery	
24.	resident						si	-dent	
25.	visible							-ible	
Feature totals									

Total points:

Answer Key

Answers appear in italics, with the exception of phonetic symbols.

 ## Brief Survey of Language Knowledge

Phoneme Counting

thrill	*4*	ring	*3*	shook	*3*
does	*3*	fix	*4*	wrinkle	*5*
sawed	*3*	quack	*4*	know	*2*

Syllable Counting

cats	*1*	capital	*3*	shirt	*1*
spoil	*1 or 2*	decidedly	*4*	banana	*3*
recreational	*5*	lawyer	*2*	walked	*1*

Phoneme Matching

1. *sugar*
2. *raid*
3. *nose*
4. *baked*
5. *sink*

Recognition of Sound–Symbol Correspondence

b /e / s / t	f / r / e / sh	s / c / r / a / tch
th / ough	l / au / gh / ed	m / i / dd / le
ch / ir / p	q / u / ai / n / t	

Definitions and Concepts

1. *A vowel sound is an open speech sound that is the nucleus of a syllable.*
2. *A consonant digraph is a two-letter combination corresponding to one unique sound.*
3. *A prefix is a Latin bound morpheme (meaningful part), added before a root, that changes the meaning of the whole word.*
4. *An inflectional morpheme is a grammatical ending added to a verb, adjective, or noun that changes the number, degree, or tense of the word but does not change the meaning or part of speech of the word.*
5. *Phoneme awareness is one (but not the only) necessary skill in learning to read an alphabetic writing system.*
6. *The ability to decode words accurately will not of itself support good reading. In addition to decoding, one needs to read words fluently so that attention can be relegated to comprehension, and one needs to know the meaning of the words and phrases.*

Comprehensive Survey of Language Knowledge

1.

Inflected verb	*slowed*
Compound noun	*sandpaper*
Bound root	*cred (Latin), cyc (Latin, Greek), psych (Greek)*
Derivational suffix	*ful, ible*
Greek combining form	*neuro + psych + ology*

2.

	Syllable	Morphemes
bookworm	2	2
unicorn	3	2
elephant	3	1
believed	2	3

incredible	4	3
finger	2	1
hogs	1	2
telegram	3	2

3. A closed syllable is one that *contains a short vowel and ends in one or more consonants.*

    An open syllable is one that *contains a long vowel sound spelled with one vowel letter that ends the syllable.*

4. How many speech sounds are in the following words?

sigh	2	thrown	4	scratch	5
ice	2	sung	3	poison	5
mix	4	shrink	5	know	2

5. (Both International Phonetic Alphabet and phonic symbols are shown, respectively.)

joyful	/f/	should	/d/	talk	/k/
tinker	/ŋ/ or /ng/	rouge	/ž/ or /zh/	shower	/w/
square	/w/	start	/ɑr/		
protect	/o/	patchwork	/č/ or /ch/		

6. *tele<u>p</u>hone   <u>a</u>ddend<u>a</u>   <u>a</u>long*
    preci<u>ous</u>   imp<u>o</u>siti<u>on</u>   <u>u</u>nless

7. *<u>kn</u>ight   <u>cl</u>imb   <u>wr</u>eck   napkin*
    <u>squ</u>ished   <u>spr</u>ingy   fir<u>st</u>

8. *s<u>ph</u>erical   chur<u>ch</u>   num<u>b</u>*
    <u>sh</u>rink   <u>th</u>ought   whe<u>th</u>er

9. *The spelling ck is used when a /k/ sound follows a stressed, short (lax) vowel.*

10. *e, i, or y following the c*

11. *o, oa, ow, oe, o-consonant-e, ough*

12. *f, ff, gh, ph*

13. *Drop the e if the suffix begins with a vowel; keep the e if the suffix begins with a consonant.*

14. *It might have ph for /f/, ch for /k/, or y for /ĭ/ or /ī/ spelling; it is likely to be constructed from two or more combining forms; and it is likely to be a mythological (myth), a scientific (chlorophyll), or a mathematical (dyscalculia) term.*

Exercise 2.1

ice	_2_	choose	_3_	mix	_4_	soothe	_3_
sigh	_2_	sing	_3_	pitched	_4_	her	_2_
day	_2_	thorn	_3 or 4_	straight	_5_	boy	_2_
aide	_2_	quake	_4_	measure	_4_	shout	_3_

Exercise 2.2

(Both International Phonetic Alphabet and phonic symbols are shown, respectively.)

choose	[z]	pneumonia	[m]	kitchen	[č] or [ch]
writhe	[ð] or [th]	vision	[ž] or [zh]	square	[w]
sink	[ŋ] or [ng]	folk	[k]		

Exercise 2.4

some	[s], [m]	judge	[ǰ], [ǰ]	wide	[w], [d]
knight	[n], [t]	nose	[n], [z]	thing	[θ], [ŋ]
clear	[k], [r]	shoal	[š], [l]	rhyme	[r], [m]
write	[r], [t]	which	[ʍ] or [w], [č]	phone	[f], [n]
once	[w], [s]	choose	[č], [z]	yawn	[y], [n]
thatch	[θ], [č]	comb	[k], [m]	hymn	[h], [m]
guest	[g], [t]	quest	[k], [t]	gem	[ǰ], [m]
gym	[ǰ], [m]	whole	[h], [l]	rouge	[r], [ž]
pave	[p], [v]	there	[ð], [r]	thief	[θ], [f]

Exercise 2.6

put	[pʊt]	putt	[pʌt]	puke	[pjuk]
coin	[kɔjn]	shower	[šæwɚ]	sigh	[saj]
should	[šʊd]	thesis	[θisɪs]	chain	[čen]
sacks	[sæks]	sax	[sæks]	preppy	[prɛpi]
critter	[krɪɾɚ]	ceiling	[silɪŋ]	cymbal	[sɪmbəl]
whether	[ʍɛðɚ] or [wɛðɚ]	question	[kwɛsčən]	measure	[mɛžɚ]

Although the problem of dyslexia is not a condition wherein people see things backward, the symptom of reversals has been overplayed by the press.

Exercise 2.7

a) *All are alveolar consonants.*

b) *All are nasal consonants.*

c) *All are sonorant consonants.*

d) *All are velar consonants.*

e) *All are voiced or voiceless stop consonants.*

f) *All are back rounded vowels.*

Exercise 2.8

a) [u]

b) [ɛ]

c) [ŋ]

d) [θ]

e) [j]

f) [l]

g) [ɔj]

Exercise 2.9

a) *They differ in voicing. Both are interdental fricatives.*

b) *The first is tense; the second is lax. Both are vowels.*

c) *They differ in voicing. Both are affricates.*

d) *They differ in voicing. Both are labiodental fricatives.*

e) *The first is oral; the second is nasal. Both are bilabial stops.*

Exercise 2.10

cheese	[z]	laugh	[f]	enjoy	[ɔj]
attached	[t]	baby	[i]	collage	[ž]
Xerox	[s]	aglow	[o]		
you	[u]	wealth	[θ]		

Exercise 2.11

ðə wɛrld ɪz tu mʌč wɪθ ʌs let ænd sun

gɛtɪŋ ænd spɛndɪŋ wi le west æwɚ pæwɚz

lɪɾl wi si ɪn nečɚ ðæt ɪz æwɚz

wi hæv gɪvən æwɚ hɑrts əwe ə sordɪd bun

ðɪs si ðæt berz hɛr bʊzəm tu ðə mun

ðə wɪndz ðæt wɪl bi hæwlɪŋ æt ɔl æwɚz

ænd ɑr ʌpgæðɚd næw lɑjk slipɪŋ flæwɚz

for ðɪs for ɛvriθɪŋ wi ɑr æwt ʌv tun

ɪt muvz ʌs nɑt

Exercise 2.12

I take it you already know
Of tough *and* bough *and* cough *and* dough.
Some may stumble but not you
On hiccough, thorough, slough, *and* through.
So now you are ready perhaps
To learn of less familiar traps.
Beware of heard, *a dreadful word*
That looks like beard *and sounds like* bird.
And dead? *It's said like* bed, *not* bead;
For goodness sake, don't call it deed.

 Exercise 2.13

a) *WOSUT/wasn't*
b) *CLORER/color*
c) *SGARY/scary*
d) *STASUN/station*
e) *LEDR/letter*
f) *FOWD/food*
g) *INGLISH/English*
h) *SINGIG/singing*

 Exercise 3.1

/m/: glimpse	/n/: dental	/ŋ/: languish
camp	slant	English
ember	prance	anger
simple	ends	inkling

 Exercise 3.2

imitate	(none)	expository	*exposition*
blossom	(none)	argumentative	*argumentation*
about	(none)	orthographic	*orthography*
application	*apply*	competent	*compete*
complexity	*complex*	deleterious	*delete*
narrative	*narrate*	beautiful	*beautician*

Exercise 3.3

kitchen	[kʰɪčən]	steam	[stĩm]
purchase	[pʰɛrčəs]	challenge	[čælənǰ]
tender	[tʰɛ̃ndɚ]	approve	[əpʰruv]
problem	[pʰrɑbləm]	snap	[snæp]
skate	[sket]	threat	[θrɛt]
spirit	[spirət]	solution	[səlušə̃n]

Exercise 3.4

a) *A lax vowel before a velar consonant is raised.*

b) *A /d/ or /t/ before /r/ is affricated.*

c) *The /t/ is pronounced as a tongue flap.*

Exercise 3.5

teach	[čit]	lip	[pʰɪl]	palm	[mɔp]
sigh	[ɑjs]	easy	[izi]	cash	[šæk]
cuts	[stʌk]	judge	[ǰʌǰ]	snitch	[čĩns]
pitch	[čɪp]	speak	[kips]	face	[sef]

Exercise 3.7

tick, chick	5	1.	voicing
seek, sick	4	2.	nasalization
rich, ridge	1	3.	front/back placement
keel, cool	3	4.	tenseness/laxness
whet, when	2	5.	affrication

Exercise 3.8

Aspiration of a voiceless stop consonant occurs when a consonant precedes a vowel or is the first consonant in a beginning blend. Aspiration is a feature that increases the likelihood of a consonant's being identified or perceived within the string of phonemes in a word. When voiceless stop consonants are deaspirated, they are more likely to be misperceived or confused with their voiced equivalents.

Exercise 3.9

Phonology is the system of rules by which we combine, sequence, and produce speech sounds in a language.

Phonetics is the study of the inventory of speech sounds that are used in a phonological system and the production of those sounds.

A *phoneme* is a speech sound in a language system that is distinguished by a set of articulatory features and is used in combination with others to make words. It is the smallest unit of sound that distinguishes one word from another.

An *allophone* is one of two or more variants of a phoneme that is produced by phonological rule or regional/dialect variation.

Exercise 3.10

	Initial	Medial	Final
/k/, /g/	coat, goat	ankle, angle	lock, log
/ǰ/, /č/	jug, chug	ledger, lecher	rich, ridge
/t/, /n/	tape, nape	kettle, kennel	rate, rain
/s/, /š/	sew, show	fasten, fashion	crass, crash
/f/, /v/	fairy, very	rifle, rival	strife, strive
/ŋ/, /n/	n/a	singer, sinner	rung, run

Exercise 3.11

[skɑr]	[rɑks]	[sɑrk]	[sɑkr̩]
[kɑrs]	[ɑskr̩]	[ɑrks]	[ɑksr̩]

They all have complex syllables, with the exception of [sɑkr̩] because /r/ is used as a syllable.

Exercise 3.12

/ž/, /ŋ/

Nasals (/m/, /n/, /ŋ/), glides (/ʍ/, /w/, /j/, /h/), liquids (/l/, /r/), voiced fricatives (/v/, /z/, and /ž/), and affricates (/č/, /ǰ/) are never followed by a consonant before a vowel within a syllable.

Exercise 3.13

a)   sample, chunk, bend
b)   better, little, writer
c)   bead, beet
d)   egg, igloo, ink

Exercise 3.14

a)   These errors show voicing substitution.
b)   These errors show deletion or misplacement of a nasal after a vowel and before consonant.

c)   *These errors show deletion or substitution for liquid /r/.*

Exercise 4.1

Anglo-Saxon	Latin	Greek
ball	orbit	sphere
eye	inspect	ophthalmology
guard	protection	prophylaxis
mother	maternal	matriarch
water	aqueduct	hydrophobia
high	elevation	hyperbole
stormy	tempestuous	catastrophic

Exercise 4.2

Anglo-Saxon (č)	French (š)	Greek (k)
chain	chauffer	school
lunch	chagrin	cholesterol
chalk	chalet	chaos
chapstick	chateau	character
cheek	machine	chemical
chuck	cache	chlorophyll
chestnut		chlorine

Exercise 4.3

Word parts from the same language layer generally combine with one another.

Anglo-Saxon	Latin	Greek
stagecraft	perform	graphic
stagefright	performance	choreograph
stagecoach	deform	choreographed
staged	formal	grapheme
coached	formalize	
	inform	
	information	
	formalism	
	performed	
	informed	
	deformed	
	informal	
	formed	

Exercise 4.4

(sh)irt	debt	(wh)ole	<u>strength</u>	zil(<u>ch</u>)	E(th)ernet
<u>track</u>	illness	<u>squ</u>eeze	Grin(<u>ch</u>)	decoy	psy(ch)ology

 Exercise 4.5

Word	First sound	Second sound	Third sound	Fourth sound	Fifth sound
shriek	sh	r	ie	k	
sow	s	ow			
slew	s	l	ew		
shoe	sh	oe			
batch	b	a	tch		
eight	eigh	t			
neighbor	n	eigh	b	or	
sharp	sh	ar	p		
Jell-o	j	e	ll	o	
tough	t	ou	gh		
through	th	r	ough		
thought	th	ough	t		
drought	d	r	ough	t	
draught	d	r	au	gh	t

Exercise 4.6

cut	kin	whack	quince
camp	kept	check	quack

a)   o, a, u
b)   e, i (and sometimes y)
c)   A short vowel
d)   /k/, /w/

Exercise 4.7

Immediately after a short vowel, use tch *for /č/.*

ch	lch, nch, rch	tch
screech	wrench	blotch
ouch	mulch	scratch
pooch	squelch	fetch
	arch	crutch
	haunch	hatch
	zilch	wretch
		patch

 Exercise 4.8

dge after a short vowel	ge after a long vowel or diphthong	ge after schwa
dodge	wage	village
wedge	gouge	appendage
budge	scrooge	advantage
lodge	siege	steerage
ridge	huge	college
badge	gauge	bandage

a) *No*

b) *To mark its soft sound*

c) *It keeps the vowel in the first syllable from being long or becoming a VCe pattern. It provides extra protection to the short vowel from the influence of letter* e.

 Exercise 4.9

Closed		VCe	Open	Vowel team	Vowel-*r*	Consonant-*le*	Schwa
sent	*lex*	*eme*	*re*	*ail* (2)	*nor*	*gle*	*a*
mid	*im*	*pale*	*hu*	*ea*	*ger*	*ble*	
jun	*com* (2)	*pete*	*mi*	*few*	*mark*	*tle*	
in	*mong*	*bine*	*ta*	*boast*	*er*		
spect	*ful*		*ti*	*hair*	*surd*		
ab (2)	*ment*		*re*				
cess	*cut*						

Exercise 4.10

	Closed		Open
ever	_ev-er_	even	_e-ven_
lemon	_lem-on_	lemur	_le-mur_
wagon	_wag-on_	wager	_wa-ger_
comic	_com-ic_	coma	_co-ma_
polish	_pol-ish_	Polish	_Po-lish_
relish	_rel-ish_	relax	_re-lax_

 Exercise 4.11

beginning	ed
sadness	run
beggar	ed
badly	skip

 Exercise 4.12

If the final syllable is accented, then the consonant is doubled before a suffix beginning with a vowel. If the final syllable is unaccented, then no doubling is required.

 Exercise 4.13

grimy, rudely, grateful, security, shameful, rosy, poking, latest, statement, fared

 Exercise 4.14

studious	*study + ous (changed y to i before a suffix)*
beautiful	*beauty + ful (changed y to i)*
stories	*story + es (changed y to i)*
studying	*study + ing (keep y before ing)*
keyed	*key + ed (ey is a vowel team; the y rule does not apply)*
sillier	*silly + er (change y to i)*
sorriest	*sorry + est (change y to i)*
happiness	*happy + ness (change y to i)*

uglier   *ugly + er (change* y *to* i)

praying   *pray + ing (*ay *is a vowel team; no change)*

buying   *buy + ing (*uy *is a vowel team; no change)*

partying   *party + ing (no change before* ing)

 # Exercise 4.15

Word	Phonetic transcription	Graphemes for phonemes				
		First sound	Second sound	Third sound	Fourth sound	Fifth sound
bread	[brɛd]	b	r	ea	d	
wretch	[rɛč]	wr	e	tch		
chrome	[krõm]	ch	r	o (e)	m	
sling	[slĩŋ]	s	l	i	ng	
single	[sĩŋgl]	s	i	n	g	le
sank	[sæ̃ŋk]	s	a	n	k	
village	[vɪləj]	v	i	ll	a	ge
geared	[gird]	g	ea	r	ed	
create	[kriet]	c	r	e	a (e)	t

 # Exercise 4.16

dumb   fir<u>st</u>   <u>squ</u>awk   <u>shr</u>in<u>k</u>

known   mu<u>skr</u>at   <u>sc</u>otch

Exercise 4.17

<u>wh</u>e<u>th</u>er   <u>sh</u>ep<u>h</u>erd   daughter

<u>ch</u>ur<u>ch</u>   wra<u>ck</u>   <u>ph</u>ysic

Exercise 4.18

Closed	VCe	Open	Vowel team	Vowel-*r*	Consonant-*le*	Other (schwa)
bel		re				
sem					ble	as
cel	brate					e
ex				plor, er		
vant				ser		
cott			boy			
pil, grim						age
bat					tle	
ab, ol, ish						
ox	ide			per		

 Exercise 4.19

/s/	/k/
cereal	caught
receive	pecan
sauce	coagulate
incidence	cuff
civilization	

Rule: *The letter* c *is pronounced* /s/ *when it precedes* e, i, *or* y; *otherwise, it is pronounced* /k/.

Exercise 4.20

If a word ends in a silent e and a suffix with a vowel is added, then drop the e and add the suffix. If the suffix begins with a consonant, then keep the e.

Exercise 4.21

English	bank	ingot	trunk	/ŋ/
errand	band	input	trundle	/n/

Exercise 4.22

All of the pairs have the same vowel sound, even though the vowels are spelled differently.

Exercise 4.23

a) *boatman, deckhand, steamboat, shoemaker, wood-cutter, ploughboy, sundown*

b) *varied, melodious*

c) *mechanics*

d) *intermission*

e) *those, blithe, makes, wife*

f) *ma̲son, be̲longs, ro̲bust, o̲pen*

g) *hear, mea̲sures, beam, ready, leaves, boat, shoe, plough, sewi̲ng, day, night, young, fell̲ows, frie̲ndly, mouths, melodi̲ous*

h) *carpenter̲, cutte̲rs, mother̲, gir̲l, pa̲rty*

i) *Ameri̲ca, mechani̲cs, carpe̲nter, mas̲on (others may also count, depending on regional and personal pronunciations)*

j) *blithe, strong, plank, hand, steam, stands, else, friendly*

Exercise 5.1

earthworm, earthquake (Anglo-Saxon)

extract, export, exportable, report, retract, extractable, retractable (Latin based)

biology, geographic, geology, biographic (Greek based)

Pattern: *Word parts (morphemes) from the same language base combine with one another.*

Exercise 5.2

redcoat: *a British soldier during the American Revolution*

laughing gas: *helium*

looking glass: *mirror*

blackboard: *any surface for writing with chalk in a classroom*

turncoat: *a traitor*

bigwig: *a very important person (VIP)*

rubbernecking: *staring at the scene of an accident*

Exercise 5.3

retro<u>cede</u>: *retreat or move back*

melli<u>flu</u>ous: *flowing sweetly and smoothly*

in<u>cis</u>or: *the part that cuts into; the front teeth*

quad<u>renni</u>um: *the fourth year*

in<u>cred</u>ulity: *state of disbelief*

<u>fact</u>otum: *one who makes or does all; a handyman*

<u>gratu</u>itous: *freely given*

inter<u>locu</u>tion: *speaking between*

pedo<u>mot</u>ive: *vehicle worked by the feet*

non<u>sect</u>arian: *not having to do with the beliefs of a sect or religion*

Exercise 5.4

<u>anti</u>depressant: *against*

<u>con</u>tractual: *with (assimilation of* com*)*

<u>contra</u>dict: *against*

<u>ex</u>pected: *out of*

<u>im</u>balance: *not (assimilation of* in*)*

<u>im</u>press: *into (assimilation of* in*)*

<u>intra</u>mural: *between*

<u>per</u>oxide: *through*

<u>re</u>application: *again*

<u>sub</u>text: *under*

Exercise 5.5

scope: *telescope, periscope, microscope, cystoscope, horoscope*

phon: *telephone, phonology, phonic, phonetic, phonographic, graphophonic*

chrom: *chromatic, chromosome, monochrome, chrome*

cycle: *bicycle, cyclical, recycle, cyclometer, tricycle, cyclone, cylinder*

therm: *thermometer, thermonuclear, isotherm, thermal, hyperthermia*

Exercise 5.6

Word	[d], [t], [əd]	Number of syllables
talked	[t]	1
instituted	[əd]	4
spelled	[d]	1
rebuffed	[t]	2
opened	[d]	2
popped	[t]	1
offended	[əd]	3
exhumed	[d]	2
breathed	[d]	1
approached	[t]	2
enraged	[d]	2
prevented	[əd]	3
surpassed	[t]	2

Base words ending in a voiced consonant or vowel add a voiced past tense marker, [d]. Base words ending in a voiceless consonant add the voiceless past tense [t]. Base words ending in [t] or [d] require addition of the syllable [əd].

 # Exercise 5.7

preside	*v*	president	*n*
legislate	*v*	legislature	*n*
compete	*v*	competition	*n*
invent	*v*	inventor	*n*
sign	*n or v*	signify	*v*
peril	*n*	perilous	*a*
disturb	*v*	disturbance	*n*
active	*a*	activity	*n*
type	*n or v*	typify	*v*
face	*n or v*	facial	*a*

 # Exercise 5.8

decide	*verb*	adjective	*decisive*
successive	*adjective*	noun	*success*
extent	*noun*	verb	*extend*

depend	_verb_	adjective	_dependable_
occur	_verb_	noun	_occurrence_
teach	_verb_	noun	_teacher_
pretense	_noun_	verb	_pretend_
revise	_verb_	noun	_revision_
prevent	_verb_	adverb	_preventatively_

Exercise 5.9

inducement<u>s</u>	high<u>er</u>	sing<u>ing</u>	unhappi<u>est</u>
legaliz<u>ing</u>	disentangl<u>ed</u>	tardi<u>est</u>	misunder<u>stood</u>
production<u>s</u>	factor<u>s</u>	sho<u>ed</u>	<u>lost</u>

Note: Inflections occur after derivational suffixes. Irregular past tense words carry the inflection into a change in base word form.

Exercise 5.10

1. reference   _(refer)_
    precision   _preci(se)_
    dramatic   _(drama)_
    theatrical   _thea(ter)_
    possession   _posse(ss)_
    originality   _(origin)_
    ridiculous   _(ridicule)_
    sociology   _(soci)ety_
    political   _(politic)_
    ritual   _(rite)_

2. wide, width   _4_
    differ, difference   _1_
    sun, sunny   _2_
    athlete, athletic   _4_
    personal, personality   _3_
    propel, propeller   _2_
    combine, combination   _4_
    idiot, idiotic   _3_
    usual, usually   _1_
    extend, extension   _4_
    ration, rational   _1_
    define, definition   _4_
    assist, assistance   _1_

Exercise 5.11

watch-dog	tele-market-ing	con-sist-ent
mistletoe	odo-meter	in-ject-ion
pip(e)-ed	pre-vari-cate	bio-de-grad-able
dodg(e)-er-s	il-leg-al	tower

Exercise 5.12

sympathizer	*One who sympathizes, noun*
butter	*(er is not a morpheme), noun*
loftier	*More lofty, adjective*
father	*(er is not a morpheme), noun*
preacher	*One who preaches, noun*
higher	*More high, adjective*
hirer	*One who hires, noun*
water	*(er is not a morpheme), noun*
infer	*(fer is the morpheme), verb*

Exercise 5.13

inspire, inspiration, inspired
incredible, credible, discredited
nonsectarian, insect, intersected, intersection
prevaricate, invariable
interrupted, disruption, interruptible, disrupted
Nonwords: *intervaricate, dispirable, preruption*

Exercise 5.14

Each person's answers to this exercise may vary, but most people agree that joy/join, amnesty/amniotic, catch/ketchup, and cap/capture are unrelated pairs.

Exercise 5.15

mis + spell	stimul + ate	in + sane + ly
sens + (i)ble	a(d) + tach + ed	forget(t) + able
in + oper + able	beaut(y) + ful + ly	con + tinu + ity
psych + ology	ex + cite + ment	dis + miss
pre + fer + (r)ing	in + spir(e) + (a)tion	re + com + mend
morph + em(e) + ic	pac + ify	tele + vis + ion

Exercise 5.16

psychic, psychology, psychodynamic, neuropsychological, psychiatrist, psychiatric, psychometric, neuropsychiatry, parapsychology, psycho, psychotic, psychopath, psychotherapy, psychosis, psychobabble, psychoanalysis, psychedelic, psyche, psychosomatic, psychogenic, psychoneurosis

Exercise 5.17

	Syllables	Morphemes
competition	*com-pet-i-tion*	*com-pet(e)-(i)tion*
precision	*pre-ci-sion*	*pre-cis(e)-ion*
scaling	*sca-ling*	*scal(e)-ing*
tractor	*trac-tor*	*tract-or*
invasive	*in-va-sive*	*in-vas-ive*
gentle	*gen-tle*	*gent-le*

Exercise 5.18

hammer, delight, battery, bison, cattle, ceiling, infant, dollop

Exercise 5.19

Possibilities include exorbaceous, pretractation, subneurometrics, unfractable, and discredurious.

Exercise 5.20

compitition	<u>competition</u>	*compete*
persperation	<u>perspiration</u>	*perspire*
<u>physician</u>	physision	*physical*
restiration	<u>restoration</u>	*restore*
<u>pleasure</u>	plesure	*please*
<u>resign</u>	resine	*resignation*
publisity	<u>publicity</u>	*public*
electrisity	<u>electricity</u>	*electric*
demacratic	<u>democratic</u>	*democracy*
<u>president</u>	presedent	*preside*
comprable	<u>comparable</u>	*compare*
<u>history</u>	histry	*historical*
janiter	<u>janitor</u>	*janitorial*

managor	<u>manager</u>	*managerial*
majer	<u>major</u>	*majority*
<u>industry</u>	indistry	*industrial*

Exercise 5.21

incredible *(5)*

credits *(3)*

accredit *(1)*

cred *(4)*

creditor *(2)*

Exercise 5.22

Messy: *The word* messy *has two syllables; there is a base word and an adjective suffix; the base word follows the* f, l, s *doubling rule (the /s/ is spelled with a doubled* s *because it is a one-syllable word with a short vowel).*

Incredulous: *The word* incredulous *has four syllables; it has a prefix, root, and suffix; the root is* cred *(to believe); accent falls on the root; the* d *in* cred *is affricated (pronounced like* [ǰ]*) because of the glide in the following* u [ju]*.*

Solemn: *The* n *is silent; in a related word form, the* n *is pronounced (*solemnity*); stress is on the first syllable, which is closed even though there is only one consonant between the two syllables.*

Exercise 6.1

Me and Harry went on a trip together.

An object pronoun, me, *is used where there should be a subject pronoun,* I.

I don't have no more gum to share.

The double negative is ungrammatical; any *is required instead of* no.

If you breathe deep, you will be able to hold your breath longer.

The adverb form is deeply.

Justina did real good on her examinations.

The adverb well *should be used instead of the adjective,* good.

My friend was stressing over all she had to do before vacation.

Stress *is a noun; its use as a verb is new or generational.*

Due to overbooking, Bart was not able to get on the flight.

The introductory clause does not modify the noun, Bart; *we could say,* Bart's inability to get on the flight was due to overbooking.

Can I take my dog with me in the car, Mom?

May I used to be the convention when permission was asked; this distinction is probably lost in current American English dialects.

Do you have enough to go around?

To most, this sentence is probably grammatical. A century ago, the convention was to say, Have you enough?

Molly slept the baby all night.

The verb to sleep *cannot be followed by a direct object.*

Exercise 6.2

in written material	*PP*	consider the options	*VP*	of a dialect	*PP*
joined the opposition	*VP*	played quietly	*VP*	many students	*NP*
with profound regret	*PP*	a spectacular sunset	*NP*	is a has been	*VP*
was waiting	*VP*	body weight	*NP*	beside the stream	*PP*

Exercise 6.3

while the baby slept	*DC*
seeing is believing	*IC*
all the pretty horses	*P*
unrelenting school pressures	*P*
Mary spent her fortune	*IC*
over the hill	*P*
who voted in the affirmative	*DC*
wrapped corn is baking	*IC*
which he helped accomplish	*DC*
until the play was done	*DC*
into thin air	*P*
although the evidence accumulates	*DC*
pound dogs need homes	*IC*

Exercise 6.4

Typical insights are that we automatically try to group words into phrases, we locate the main verb and main subject, and we resolve ambiguities by trying words in different syntactic roles.

Exercise 6.5

Set 1

The determined team won the league championship game in overtime.

The determined team, which was playing for the league championship, won in overtime.

Set 2

Immediately after the plane crash, the Coast Guard pessimistically undertook a mission to search for debris and survivors.

Operations: *These operations required constructing prepositional phrases, inserting adjectives to modify nouns, and joining nouns in a prepositional phrase.*

 Exercise 6.6

Before the impeachment trial, journalists in Washington alleged that the president had lied.

Many screaming fans in the stadium swooned when the rock band came on stage.

Hawaii calls again, she thought, remembering the beaches, waterfalls, and volcanoes that she saw on her last trip there.

 Exercise 6.7

As schools of herring encircled the drawler, the young mate accidently hooked a feeding dolphin, releasing it promptly to the sea.

 Exercise 6.8

'Twas brillig *(adj.)* and the slithy *(adj.)* toves *(n)* did gyre *(v)* and gimble *(v)* in the wabe *(n)*.
Subject: toves; *predicate:* did gyre and gimble

All mimsy *(adj.)* were *(v)* the borogoves *(n)* and the mome *(adj.)* raths *(n)* outgrabe *(adj.)*.
Subject: borogoves *and* mome raths; *predicate:* were

 Exercise 6.9

In both the present tense and past tense of the verb to be *in nonstandard dialect, the changes from standard represent a regularization of an irregular form. The speaker is using the same form for all voices. Regularization of irregular forms is a logical adaptation of a language pattern.*

Exercise 6.10

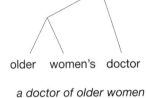

negative   film   developer

*a film developer who has a
negative attitude*

negative   film   developer

*someone who develops
film negatives*

older   women's   doctor

a doctor of older women

older   women's   doctor

*an older doctor whose
patients are women*

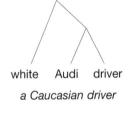

English   language   translator

a translator of English

English   language   translator

a translator from England

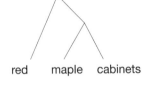

white   Audi   driver

a Caucasian driver

white   Audi   driver

a driver of a white Audi

red   maple   cabinets

cabinets painted red

red   maple   cabinets

cabinets made from red maple

Exercise 6.11

a) *Create an independent clause for this adverbial clause to modify.*

b) *Omit the indefinite pronoun* it, *and use* I was alone *as the independent or
main clause.*

c) *Identify the subject noun* (things), *the relative clause* (that are frightening), *and the main verb and object in the first independent clause* (can scare you). *Identify the second independent clause* (you will not know what happened to you). *Decide whether to make a compound with* so *as the conjunction or keep the sentences separate.*

d) *The sentence needs a subject. The word* bad *modifies the verb and needs an* ly. *If the scary monster* is *the subject, then change from the passive to active voice and identify an object.*

e) *This sentence needs a predicate. Tell what the game was or was doing.*

Exercise 7.1

Gut: *A part of the body including the stomach and intestines; the mid-section of the body. A large gut predicts higher risk for heart disease.*

Family: *A group of similar or related people or things, such as parents and children residing in a household. The traditional "nuclear family" of two parents and two children constitutes only about one-quarter of households in the United States.*

Princess: *The daughter of a king or queen or the wife of a prince. A princess usually lives a life of luxury and privilege.*

Impeach: *Accuse and prosecute an elected official on charges of wrongdoing against the state. Used rarely by the U.S. Congress against a sitting President.*

Powder: *A type of snow that is soft, fluffy, and sought after by skiers. Powder skiing is exhilarating.*

Exercise 7.2

TREES

Softwood	Hardwood	Products	Parts	Tools
pine	*maple*	*paper*	*bark*	*axe*
spruce	*oak*	*rope*	*trunk*	*chainsaw*
	birch	*paneling*	*root*	*skidder*
	mahogany	*mulch*	*needle*	*truck*
		beams	*branch*	
		kindling	*leaf*	
		guitar		

Exercise 7.3

1. *All of these are wild African animals that are also found in zoos.*
2. *All of these are blood relatives of family.*
3. *All of these are manmade sources of light.*

4. *All of these are ways to style hair.*

5. *All of these are grains.*

 # Exercise 7.4

	trees	processed	grows	large	burns	rots	breathes
wood	–	+	–	–	+	+	–
timber	+	–	+	+	+	+	+

 # Exercise 7.5

elated   *overjoyed, delighted, happy, indifferent, sad, forlorn*   depressed

scalding   *boiling, hot, warm, tepid, cool, cold, frosty, frigid*   freezing

expensive   *outrageous, costly, dear, affordable, a bargain*   cheap

 # Exercise 7.6

light, heavy   _g_   introvert, extrovert   _g_

left, right   _c_   terrestrial, celestial   _c_

pretty, ugly   _g_   present, absent   _c_

awake, asleep _c_   empty, full   _g_

open, shut   _c_   indoors, outdoors   _c_

buy, sell   _c_   civilized, barbaric   _g_

 # Exercise 7.8

lying over and over: *dissembling repeatedly*

a curious fantasy: *an odd flight of imagination*

stuff and nonsense: *bric-a-brac*

guests at the execution: *invited onlookers at the planned killing*

ignore the petty details: *overlook the unimportant bits*

blazing away brightly: *burning luminously*

mind the master's words: *obey the chief's orders*

these melancholy little sighs: *these forlorn expirations*

Exercise 7.9

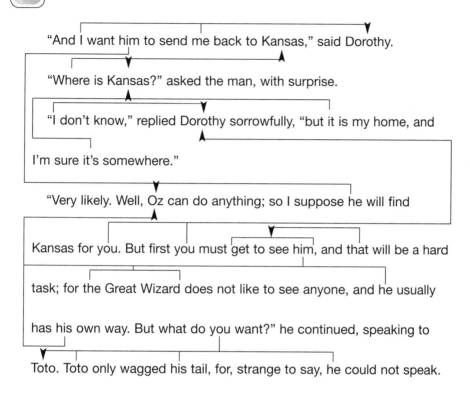

"And I want him to send me back to Kansas," said Dorothy.

"Where is Kansas?" asked the man, with surprise.

"I don't know," replied Dorothy sorrowfully, "but it is my home, and

I'm sure it's somewhere."

"Very likely. Well, Oz can do anything; so I suppose he will find

Kansas for you. But first you must get to see him, and that will be a hard

task; for the Great Wizard does not like to see anyone, and he usually

has his own way. But what do you want?" he continued, speaking to

Toto. Toto only wagged his tail, for, strange to say, he could not speak.

Exercise 7.10

mark my words: *I'll be right about the future*

hit me up: *asked me for*

tread on his toes: *invaded his territory or took his prerogative*

blow the whistle: *stop, tell the authorities about wrongdoing*

leave her high and dry: *abandon*

bite your tongue: *restrain your verbal impulses*

'til the cows come home: *forever*

get out of my hair: *leave me alone*

line your pockets: *obtain money or goods*

Exercise 7.11

Invertebrates

Species	Body parts	Homes
mosquitoes	wings	web
locusts	abdomen	nest
cockroaches	antennae	soil
flies	legs	cocoon
ants	head	burrow
grasshoppers	thorax	

Phases	Locomotion	Food
sac	hop	blood
egg	crawl	microbes
larva	creep	algae
pupa		leaves
adult		

Exercise 7.12

An advantage is that context shows the connotative and pragmatic uses of a word; a disadvantage is that several exposures to examples may be necessary before the meaning is clear.

Exercise 7.13

a)   *They are all females (family members versus professions).*

b)   *They are all domesticated animals (male versus female).*

c)   *They are all nouns (solid versus liquid).*

d)   *They are all nouns (concrete versus abstract).*

e)   *They are all people (family members versus professions).*

f)   *They are all family members (vertical versus lateral relatives).*

Exercise 7.14

dead/alive	*complementary*
hot/cold	*gradable*
above/below	*complementary*
married/single	*complementary*
bland/spicy	*gradable*
hostile/welcoming	*gradable*

hideous/gorgeous	_gradable_
straight/curved	_complementary_
introvert/extrovert	_gradable_
winner/loser	_complementary_

Scale: *furious, angry, irritated, irked, indifferent, pleased, delighted, thrilled*

Exercise 7.15

	cup	glass	mug	bowl
handle	+	−	+	−
ceramic	+	−	+	+
round	+	+	+	+
tall	−	+	−	−
holds hot liquid	+	−	+	+
holds cold liquid	+	+	−	+
paper	+	−	−	−
transparent	−	+	−	−

Exercise 7.16

*A **web** is a matrix of threads that spiders spin to catch insects for food.*

*A **tornado** is a violent wind storm that spins in a circular pattern and has a calm "eye" in the middle.*

*A **poem** is language arranged in a pattern that is designed to evoke images and emotions.*

Exercise 7.17

Walk: *first gate on horseback; a stroll; a path for walking; 4 balls in baseball*

Mouth: *origin of a river; opening to a cave; orifice for eating; imitate articulation of words*

Star: *the top performer; top billing in a film or play; celestial body; geometric shape*

Book: *bound reading material; secure reservations; register at police station following arrest*

Exercise 7.18

Large, magnificent, royal, luxurious, spacious, ostentatious, ornate; sometimes used pejoratively for excessively large and/or tasteless homes built to show off wealth

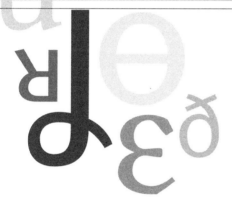

Glossary

adjective phrase Phrase that modifies or describes a noun.

adverbial phrase Phrase that modifies or tells more about the verb.

affix A morpheme or meaningful part of a word attached before or after a root or base word to modify its meaning; a category that includes prefixes and suffixes.

affricate Consonant phoneme articulated as a stop before a fricative, such as /č/ or /ǰ/.

agent Thematic role of the noun in a sentence whose referent performs the action of the verb (*The girl threw the ball*).

allophone A predictable phonetic variant of a phoneme, such as nasalized vowels.

allophonic variation Systematic variability in production of phonemes; the fact that speech sounds "heard" as the same phoneme differ slightly in articulation depending on where they occur in a word, for example the aspirated and unaspirated forms [pʰ] and [p].

alphabetic Pertaining to a writing system that uses a symbol for each speech sound of the language.

alphabetic principle   The idea or concept that letters and letter combinations represent phonemes in an orthography.

alveolar   Consonant spoken with the tip of the tongue on the ridge behind the upper teeth, such as /t/.

anaphora   Referential linking between pairs of words within or between sentences; the process of replacing a longer word or phrase with a shorter one, as with the use of a pronoun for a noun or a noun phrase.

Anglo-Saxon   Old English, the base language for Modern English.

antonyms   Words considered to represent opposite meanings.

articles   Determiners; words in a grammatical class of noun modifiers that are not adjectives, such as *the, a, an.*

aspiration   A puff of breath that accompanies voiceless stop consonants in initial position.

assimilated prefix   A prefix changed from its abstract form so that it matches the initial sound of the root to which it is attached, such as *at* in *attach* (*ad* + *tach* = *attach*).

assimilation   Process by which the phonetic features of one phoneme influence or are spread to a neighboring phoneme; assimilation results in phonemes becoming similar.

automaticity   Fluent performance without the conscious deployment of attention.

auxiliary verbs   Helping verbs that co-occur with a main verb to denote tense, aspect, or modality (*I will have been gone*).

back vowels   Vowels formed in the back of the mouth, such as /o/ or /u/.

base word   A free morpheme, usually of Anglo-Saxon origin, to which affixes can be added.

bilabial   Consonant formed with the lips together, such as /b/.

blend   A consonant sequence before or after a vowel within a syllable, such as *cl, br,* or *st*; the written language equivalent of *consonant cluster.*

bound morpheme   A morpheme, usually of Latin origin in English, that cannot stand alone but is used to form a family of words with related meanings. A bound root (such as *fer*) has meaning only in combination with a prefix and/or a suffix.

central linguistic processing   The mental activity of language encoding, comprehension, and recall that occurs independently of speech or hearing.

clause   A group of words that contains both a subject and a predicate.

closed syllable   In orthography, a syllable with a short vowel followed by one or more consonants.

coarticulated   Spoken together so that separate segments are not easily detected.

coda   The part of a syllable that comes after the nucleus or peak.

combining form   A morpheme that occurs only in combination with other forms but may combine in various ways with other morphemes to create compounds or derivatives; many Greek-derived morphemes are combining forms.

complementary antonyms   Opposites that do not overlap; the negation of one is the meaning of the other (*male–female*).

complementary distribution The relationship between two or more allophones such that each occurs in phonetic environments where the other(s) never do.

complex sentence A sentence with at least one dependent clause attached to or subordinated within the main, independent clause.

complex syllables Syllables that contain one or more consonant clusters.

compound predicates Verb phrases with more than one main verb.

compound sentence Sentence in which two or more independent clauses have been joined by a coordinating conjunction.

compound subjects Clause with more than one head noun in the subject.

comprehension monitoring The mental act of knowing when one does and does not understand what one is reading.

confrontation naming Timed tests of labeling a series of pictures.

conjunctions Words such as *and*, *but*, and *or* that perform the grammatical function of joining sentences, phrases, words, or clauses.

connotative meaning The affective and experiential associations conjured up by a word.

considerate text Text written in such a way that takes into account the needs of the reader for structure, clarity, completeness, redundancy, and other clues to meaning.

consolidated phase A stage of reading development in which students are developing automatic, accurate recognition of graphemes, syllables, and morphemes, and are reading with fluency.

consonant A phoneme that is not a vowel and is formed with obstruction of the flow of air with the teeth, lips, or tongue; also called a *closed sound* in some instructional programs; English has 40 or more consonants.

consonant blend In syllable structure, two or three adjacent consonant graphemes before or after a vowel.

consonant cluster Adjacent consonants within a syllable, before or after a vowel sound; oral language equivalent of the term *consonant blend*.

consonant digraph Written letter combination that corresponds to one speech sound but is not represented by either letter alone, such as *th* or *ph*.

content words Nouns, verbs, adjectives, and adverbs; words that carry most of the meaning in a sentence.

continuant Speech sound that can be spoken uninterrupted until the speaker runs out of breath (/m/, /s/, /v/).

co-referent Noun phrases that refer to the same entity.

correlative conjunctions Pairs of words used together to join similar elements.

countable nouns Nouns that can be enumerated.

decodable text Text in which a large proportion of words (approximately 70%–80%) comprise sound–symbol relationships that have already been taught; used to provide practice with specific decoding skills and to form a bridge between learning phonics and applying phonics in independent reading of text.

decoding   Ability to translate a word from print to speech, usually by employing knowledge of sound–symbol correspondences; also, the act of deciphering a new word by sounding it out.

deixis   Reference that relies entirely on context, as in *here* and *there*.

denotative meaning   Dictionary meaning; what a word refers to.

dependent clause   A clause that cannot stand alone and must be attached to an independent clause.

derivational complexity   The number and type of changes in a derived word that is built from a base word.

derivational morpheme   Morphemes, added to roots or bases to form new words, that may or may not change the grammatical category of a word.

descriptive grammar   A linguist's description of what speakers unconsciously learn about the rules of their language.

digraph   A two-letter combination that spells a single speech sound.

diphthongs   Vowels that have a glide and may feel as though they have two parts, especially the vowels /æw/ as in *house* and /ɔj/ as in *oil*; some linguistics texts also classify all tense vowels as diphthongs.

direct object   Noun that is the object of the verb.

discourse   Linguistic units larger than the single sentence.

distinguishing features   Phonetic properties of phonemes that account for their contrast with other phonemes.

doubles   Doubled *f, l, s,* or *z* in one-syllable words.

early alphabetic   A stage of reading development in which the alphabetic principle is first understood.

encode   When speech information is translated into mental representations.

entailment   A logical relationship between two sentences such that the truth or falsehood of the first sentence necessarily implies the truth or falsehood of the second sentence.

euphony   Ease of pronunciation.

expository text   Text that reports factual information and the relationships among ideas.

five essential components   Reference to the components of effective reading programs as identified by the National Reading Panel of 2000: phoneme awareness, phonics, fluency, vocabulary, and comprehension.

floss rule   The *f, l, s* letter doubling pattern.

free morpheme   A morpheme that can stand alone in word formation.

fricatives   A class of speech sounds articulated with a hiss or friction.

front vowel   Vowel spoken with the tongue positioned in the front of the mouth.

function word   Belonging to the grammatical classes of words that are not content words, including conjunctions, articles, pronouns, prepositions, and auxiliaries; these are closed categories to which new words are seldom added.

generalization   The act of applying a linguistic rule or pattern to a new word, phrase, or sentence; also, a pattern in the spelling system that generalizes to a substantial family of words.

generative In a grammar, the quality of rule structure that allows an infinite number of specific, novel expressions.

gerunds Nouns created from verbs.

glide A consonant phoneme that glides immediately into a vowel; also called *semivowel*.

glottal stop When the vocal air stream is stopped completely by closing the opening between the vocal cords (the *glottis*).

goal The thematic role of the noun phrase toward whose referent the action of the verb is directed (*The actor strode toward <u>the open stage</u>*).

gradable antonyms Opposites having a relationship in which more of one is less than the other; the relationship exists on a continuum on which degrees of a quality can be specified (*brilliant–dull*).

grammatical category Traditionally called a *part of speech*; members of a category can be used only in certain specified ways within the structure of a sentence.

grapheme A letter or letter combination that spells a single phoneme; in English, a grapheme may be one, two, three, or four letters, such as *e, ei, igh,* or *eigh*.

head noun Main noun in a phrase.

hierarchical structure The arrangement of groupings and subgroupings of phrases within a sentence.

hieroglyphics Egyptian picture writing.

high Vowel sounds formed by placing the tongue close to the roof of the mouth.

homorganic nasal rule Rule that a consonant that follows a nasal consonant will be produced in the same place of articulation as the nasal (*co<u>nt</u>act*).

ideographic writing system Writing system that uses stylized characters to denote whole concepts or words directly.

idiom An expression whose meaning may be unrelated to the meaning of its parts.

independent clause A group of words with a subject and predicate that can stand alone as a complete sentence.

inflectional morpheme A bound morpheme that combines with base words to indicate tense, number, mood, person, or gender (*peach<u>es</u>, walk<u>ing</u>*); contrasts with *derivational morpheme*.

instrument The thematic role of a noun phrase that refers to the means by which an action is performed.

interdental Consonant sound spoken with the tongue between the teeth.

intonation Pitch level of the voice; contour.

labials Consonant sounds articulated with the lips; includes bilabials and labiodentals.

labiodental Consonant sound articulated with the lower lip and upper teeth.

later alphabetic The stage of reading development characterized by full phonemic awareness and reasonable, complete mappings of phonemes to graphemes.

Latin The language of Ancient Rome which has heavily influenced English.

lax Short vowels produced with little tension in the vocal cords; contrasts with *tense*.

lexical semantics   The study of meanings of words and their relationships.

lexicon   The mental dictionary of a speaker; the part of linguistic memory that contains knowledge of words.

linguistic context   The context provided by the language in which a word is embedded.

liquid   Speech sound in which air is obstructed but not enough to cause friction.

location   The thematic role of the noun phrase whose referent is the place where the action of the verb occurs.

logographic   A stage of reading development characterized by lack of awareness that letters represent speech sounds.

long   Term used by educators to denote a vowel that is spoken with tension in the vocal cords and that is often pronounced with relatively longer duration than lax vowels.

long-term memory (LTM)   The aspect of memory that stores words, images, or ideas for future retrieval.

low   Referring to the position of the tongue away from the roof of the mouth.

manner of articulation   How a sound is made, or the production of airflow through the mouth.

marked   Referring to the member of a gradable antonym pair that is not used in formulating questions of degree (*low* is the marked member of *low*/*high*; for example, one asks, "How *high* is the deck?").

metalinguistic   Pertaining to an acquired awareness of language structure and function that allows one to reflect on and consciously manipulate the language.

metaphor   An implied or indirectly stated comparison between an idea and an unusual referent.

mid   Spoken with the tongue midway between the roof of the mouth (high) and its lowest position away from the roof of the mouth.

minimal pair   A pair of words that contrast only in one phoneme.

morpheme   The smallest meaningful unit of language.

morphology   The study of meaningful units of language and how they are combined in word formation.

morphophonemic   Pertaining to rules or aspects of language that specify the pronunciation of morphemes; pertaining to a writing system that spells meaningful units (morphemes) instead of surface phonetic details in speech; a characteristic of English orthography.

multisyllabic   Having more than one syllable.

naming   Verbal retrieval that involves extracting a word from the mental dictionary.

narrative text   Text, usually with the structure of a story, that tells about sequences of fictional or real events and is often contrasted with expository text.

nasal (stop)   Sound spoken with the air stream directed through the nasal cavity.

nasalization   *See* Vowel nasalization.

natural grammatical knowledge   Understanding of grammar learned from exposure to language and requires little formal instruction.

neutral (derivational) suffix   A suffix that does not change the base form or root to which it is added.

noncountable nouns   Nouns that cannot be enumerated.

nonneutral (derivational) suffix   A suffix that changes the pronunciation and/or spelling of the base word or root to which it is added.

nonsystematic   Pertaining to variation in speech that is not predicted by rule, that is incidental or regional or individual.

noun phrase (NP)   The syntactic category of expressions containing some form of noun and capable of functioning as the subject or object in a sentence.

object   The noun phrase that follows a verb that depicts action performed on or to something (Tom held _the red pencil_).

obstruents   Consonants that are produced with an obstruction of the air stream, including stops, fricatives, and affricates; contrasts with _sonorants_.

onset   The part of a syllable before the vowel; some syllables do not have onsets.

opaque orthography   Writing system in which the relationship between sound and symbol is somewhat obscure, irregular, or influenced by morpheme structure; also called a _deep orthography._

open syllable   In orthography, a syllable with a long vowel at the end, spelled with one vowel letter.

orthography   A writing system.

palatal   Spoken with the tongue against the roof of the mouth behind the alveolar ridge.

paraphrase   A restatement of a phrase or sentence that uses different words to express the same idea.

partially productive   A characteristic of morphemes that can be used for word formation only to a limited extent.

participle   A word formed from a verb that can function as part of a verb phrase.

peak   The part of the syllable, usually the vowel, that carries the most vocal energy; also called the _nucleus._

phone   A phonetic realization of a phoneme; the speech sound that is actually produced in spoken words.

phoneme   A speech sound that combines with others in a language system to make words.

phoneme awareness   The conscious awareness that words are made up of segments of our own speech that are represented with letters in an alphabetic orthography; also called _phonemic awareness._

phoneme blending   The act of assembling single speech sounds into a whole word.

phoneme deletion   The act of leaving out a sound in a word in order to make a new word.

phoneme discrimination   The ability to distinguish words that differ only in one phoneme.

phoneme identification   The act of showing, by pointing to a picture, object, or symbol, which speech sound is in the beginning, middle, or end of a word.

phoneme segmentation   The act of separating a word into its component speech sounds.

phoneme–grapheme mapping   The act of associating phonemes with graphemes.

phonemic awareness   *See* Phoneme awareness.

phonetic alphabet   An alphabet in which each speech sound has its own unique symbol.

phonetic variation   Variability in the way speakers of a language articulate the phonemes.

phonetics   The study of linguistic speech sounds and how they are produced and perceived.

phonics   The study of the relationships between letters and the sounds they represent; also used to describe reading instruction that teaches sound–symbol correspondences, such as "the phonics approach" or "phonic reading."

phonological awareness   Metalinguistic awareness of all levels of the speech sound system, including word boundaries, stress patterns, syllables, onset–rime units, and phonemes; a more encompassing term than *phoneme awareness*.

phonological processing   Perception, interpretation, recall, and production of language at the level of the speech sound system, including functions such as pronouncing words, remembering names and lists, identifying words and syllables, giving rhymes, detecting syllable stress, and segmenting and blending phonemes.

phonological representation   Speech-based codes in memory that embody the pronunciation of the word.

phonological retrieval   Retrieval of the phonological form of a word from long-term memory; refers to the mental act of formulating and pronouncing the word.

phonological rules   A level of language structure; rules that embody what speakers know about the speech sounds in their language.

phonological working memory (PWM)   Temporary storage of speech codes in memory that allows meanings of language to be extracted and stored in longer term memory.

phonology   The rule system within a language by which phonemes are sequenced and uttered to make words; also, the study of this rule system.

phrasal grammatical category   A constituent of a tree diagram depicting sentence structure that is potentially larger than one word.

phrase   A part of a sentence that is potentially larger than one word and that serves a grammatical function as a unit.

pictograms   Visual or graphic symbols that directly depict their own meaning, such as the *no smoking* symbol common in hotels and restaurants.

pitch   The tonal level of a vocal or nonvocal sound, determined by its sound frequencies.

place of articulation   Where sound is made, or the position of the lips, teeth, and tongue in the front, middle, or back of the mouth when producing a sound.

polysemous   Having multiple meanings.

pragmatics   The system of rules and conventions for using language and related gestures in social contexts; the study of that rule system.

prealphabetic   A stage of reading development characterized by lack of awareness that letters represent speech sounds.

predicate   One of two main constituents of a sentence, containing the verb.

prefix   A morpheme that precedes a root or base word and that contributes to or modifies the meaning of a word; a common linguistic unit in Latin-based words.

prepositional phrase (PP)   natural grouping of words in which a noun phrase is introduced by a preposition.

prepositions   A class of function words that occur first in a prepositional phrase.

prereading   Pertaining to the stage of reading development before children understand the alphabetic principle.

prescriptive grammar   The attempts of grammarians to define, legislate, or dictate proper use of language in a culture.

priming effect   Phenomenon where using or hearing familiar words mentally activates all of the words a person has learned within that semantic network.

pronouns   A class of function words that are used as substitutes for nouns or noun phrases.

rapid automatic naming (RAN)   The task of naming a repeating sequence of objects, colors, numbers, or letters under timed conditions; also known as *rapid serial naming*.

***r*-controlled**   Pertaining to a vowel immediately followed by the consonant /r/, such that its pronunciation is affected or even dominated by the /r/.

reading fluency   Speed of reading; also, the ability to read text with sufficient speed to support comprehension.

reference   The association of one entity in a noun phrase with another.

referent   The entity referred to by a noun phrase.

relational antonyms   Antonyms that describe a relationship between two people, such as *husband/wife, parent/child*.

retrieval   The mental process of recalling words, such as the names of objects, pictures, or ideas.

rime   A linguistic term for the part of a syllable that includes the vowel and what follows it; different from the language play activity of *rhyming*.

root   A morpheme, usually of Latin origin in English, that cannot stand alone but that is used to form a family of words with related meanings.

schwa   A nondistinct vowel found in unstressed syllables in English.

semantic class   A group of words that are treated as members of a category.

semantic feature analysis   Formal identification of the features that distinguish one object or idea from another.

semantic features   A symbol system of pluses and minuses used to denote abstract qualities of noun meaning.

semantic field   A group of words connected by meaning associations, such as all of the words that denote the quality of height.

semantic properties   The component features of the meaning of a word.

semantics   The study of word and phrase meanings.

semivowel   Another term for a consonant glide that has vowel-like qualities.

sentential semantics   The study of sentence meaning.

short   Used by educators to denote a lax vowel.

sight words   Words that are known as wholes, do not have to be sounded out to be recognized quickly, and are often taught and learned as "exception," "outlaw," or "nonphonetic" words.

simple sentence   A sentence composed of a single noun phrase and a single verb phrase.

simple syllables   Syllables that have no consonant blends or clusters.

situational context   The context for comprehending language that is provided by the person who is speaking, the person who is listening, the objects or experiences that are being referred to, and other background information.

sonorants   Speech sounds that are spoken with resonance and continuancy, including vowels, glides, liquids, and nasals; contrasts with *obstruents*.

speech discrimination   Ability to distinguish words that differ only in one phoneme.

speech perception   Ability to distinguish between words that sound almost alike (e.g., *dusk/dust; fill/fail*) and recognize any word that has been spoken.

speech production   Expressive language skill that includes articulating or pronouncing speech sounds and speech–sound sequences.

stop   Consonant speech sound that is articulated with a stop of the air stream.

stressed   Accented syllable articulated with greater loudness, duration, or pitch.

subject   The grammatical role of a noun phrase that appears directly below the *S* in a phrase structure diagram, one of two necessary parts of a sentence.

subordinate category   A category that is subsumed by another or included within a superordinate category.

suffix   A morpheme, added to a root or base word, that often changes the word's part of speech and that modifies its meaning.

suffix addition rules   In orthography, rules for adding suffixes to words ending in single consonants, silent *e*, or *y*.

superordinate category   A category that subsumes others; the main or umbrella category under which others are included.

suppletive   A verb form to which rules for adding inflections do not apply, such as *went, gone*, or *lay*.

suprasegmental   Prosodic features such as tone, utterance length, and stress.

surface   The visible or audible linguistic expression that may be the result of transformations applied to a deep or hidden linguistic form.

syllabary   A writing system designed to represent syllable units with single symbols.

syllabic   A phonetic feature present in the sounds that constitute the nucleus of syllables, including vowels, liquids, and nasals.

syllabic consonant   Consonant that becomes the nucleus of a syllable; liquid and nasal consonants may be syllabic.

syllable   Unit of pronunciation that is organized around a vowel; it may or may not have consonants before or after the vowel.

syllable boundary   Division between adjacent syllables, which is not always the same in speech as in print.

syllable division rules   Principles for analyzing multisyllabic words to determine the likely sound of the vowel in each syllable.

syllable juncture   The break between syllables within a word.

synonym   A word that means the same or almost the same thing as another.

syntactic categories   Groupings of words, phrases, or clauses that play the same role or fill the same slot within a sentence structure.

syntax   The rule system governing sentence formation; the study of sentence structure.

system   A group of interrelated elements forming a complex whole; the functional relationship of those elements.

systematic   Methodical; carried out using step-by-step procedures determined by the nature of the system being used or taught.

tense   Linguistic term for a long vowel, spoken with tension in the vocal cords.

thematic role   A semantic property of a verb that determines what noun and prepositional phrases must accompany that verb in a sentence.

theme   The thematic role of the noun phrase whose referent undergoes the action of a verb.

transformation   An operation that converts the constituents of a sentence structure into a different sentence structure by adding, deleting, or rearranging those constituents.

transitive property   The property of verbs that must be followed by a direct object.

transparent orthography   A writing system in which there is a direct, consistent relationship between sound and symbol; also called a *shallow orthography*.

trigraphs   Three-letter spellings that stand for one consonant sound.

truth conditions   The circumstances that must be known to determine whether a sentence is true.

underlying   The aspects of linguistic rule systems that are invisible or that lie below the surface of an utterance.

universals   Properties that are found in all human languages.

unsegmented   Pertaining to a word that has not been broken down into its constituent syllables, onsets and rimes, or phonemes.

unstressed   Unaccented syllable.

unvoiced   Spoken with no vocal resonance; also called *voiceless*.

velar   Speech sound articulated with the tongue on the ridge behind the teeth.

velum   Soft palate of the mouth.

verb phrase (VP)   The syntactic category of a phrase that contains the verb and that can function as the predicate of a sentence.

voiced   A speech sound articulated with vibrating vocal cords.

voiceless   *See* Unvoiced.

vowel   An open phoneme that is the nucleus of every syllable and is classified by tongue position and height, such as high/low or front/mid/back; English has 15 vowel phonemes.

vowel lengthening   When the duration of articulation of a vowel before a voiced consonant is longer than it would be before a voiceless consonant; also called *elongation.*

vowel nasalization   When a vowel sound is directed through the nose because it is articulated immediately before a nasal consonant.

vowel raising   As a result of coarticulation, the tongue is raised and a vowel is articulated like a vowel that is higher in the mouth.

vowel team   A vowel grapheme or spelling that uses two or more letters for a single speech sound.

vowel-consonant-*e* (VCe) syllable   A syllable with a long vowel sound spelled with a vowel-consonant-silent *e* pattern.

Index

Page numbers followed by *f* or *t* indicate figures or tables, respectively.